# Migration and the Ukraine Crisis

## A Two-Country Perspective

EDITED BY

AGNIESZKA PIKULICKA-WILCZEWSKA & GRETA UEHLING

**E-INTERNATIONAL RELATIONS PUBLISHING**

E-International Relations
www.E-IR.info
Bristol, England
2017

ISBN 978-1-910814-27-7 (paperback)
ISBN 978-1-910814-28-4 (e-book)

This book is published under a Creative Commons CC BY-NC 4.0 license. You are free to:

- **Share** – copy and redistribute the material in any medium or format
- **Adapt** – remix, transform, and build upon the material

Under the following terms:

- **Attribution** – You must give appropriate credit, provide a link to the license, and indicate if changes were made. You may do so in any reasonable manner, but not in any way that suggests the licensor endorses you or your use.
- **Non-Commercial** – You may not use the material for commercial purposes.

Any of the above conditions can be waived if you get permission. Please contact info@e-ir.info for any such enquiries, including for licensing and translation requests.

Other than the terms noted above, there are no restrictions placed on the use and dissemination of this book for student learning materials / scholarly use.

Production: Michael Tang
Cover Image: aaron007

A catalogue record for this book is available from the British Library

**E-IR Edited Collections**

Series Editors: Stephen McGlinchey, Marianna Karakoulaki and Agnieszka Pikulicka-Wilczewska

Editorial assistance: Mariam Ali, Konstantina Bandutova, Naomi McMillen, Nicholas Saffari & Patricia Salas Sanchez

E-IR's Edited Collections are open access scholarly books presented in a format that preferences brevity and accessibility while retaining academic conventions. Each book is available in print and e-book, and is published under a Creative Commons CC BY-NC 4.0 license. As E-International Relations is committed to open access in the fullest sense, free electronic versions of all of our books, including this one, are available on the E-International Relations website.

Find out more at: http://www.e-ir.info/publications

**About the E-International Relations website**

E-International Relations (www.E-IR.info) is the world's leading open access website for students and scholars of international politics, reaching over 3 million unique readers. E-IR's daily publications feature expert articles, blogs, reviews and interviews – as well as student learning resources. The website is run by a registered non-profit organisation based in Bristol, England and staffed with an all-volunteer team of students and scholars.

## Abstract

Since the Russian annexation of Crimea in 2014 and the beginning of the war in Donbas, Eastern Europe has been facing a migration crisis. Several million Ukrainians are internally displaced or have fled the country and now face an uncertain future. At the same time, Western-imposed sanctions and the creation of the Eurasian Economic Union have affected Russia's migration policies. These largely ignored processes have a potential to change the social landscape of the region for many years to come. The aim of this collection is to shed light on the forgotten migrant crisis at the European Union's doorstep and make sense of the various migration processes in and out of Ukraine and Russia.

## Editors

**Agnieszka Pikulicka-Wilczewska** is an Editor-at-large and Editorial Board Member of E-International Relations, and an editor with New Eastern Europe. She was a co-editor (with Richard Sakwa) of *Ukraine and Russia: People, Politics, Propaganda and Perspectives* (E-International Relations, 2015).

**Greta Uehling** teaches at the Program on International and Comparative Studies at the University of Michigan in Ann Arbor, where she is also an Associate Faculty Member with the Center for Russian and East European Studies. Currently, she has a Fulbright grant to study internal displacement within Ukraine and is hosted by the Taras Shevchenko National University in Kyiv. Her first book, *Beyond Memory: The Deportation and Return of the Crimean Tatars* (2004), is based on ethnographic fieldwork in former Soviet areas.

## Contributors

**Tania Bulakh** is a PhD student in Socio-Cultural Anthropology at Indiana University Bloomington (USA) with a minor in Russian and East European Studies. Her research interests include post-socialist transformations, displacement, citizenship, state and power. She also worked as a senior project manager for an international PR agency and as a journalist for several Ukrainian publications.

**Mikhail Denisenko** is a Deputy Director at the Institute of Demography, National Research University – Higher School of Economics (NRU-HSE, Russia). For over ten years he worked as a professor and researcher at the Population Studies Centre at Lomonosov Moscow State University. Between 1998 and 2000 he worked at the Population Division of the Department of Economic and Social Affairs (DESA) of the United Nations Secretariat. He has participated in various research projects including 'Replacement migration' (UN Population Division, 2000), 'Population analysis and projection for the Russian Federation' (the World Bank, 2008), 'Mortality in Central Asia' (National Institute of Child Health and Human Development, USA, 2007-2012), 'Migration and remittances in Central Asia and South Caucasia' (UN ESCAP, 2010), 'Population development and prospects of Kyrgyzstan' (UNFPA, 2011-2012), and 'Population Development in the post-Soviet states' (Russian Humanitarian Science Foundation, 2015-2016).

**Joanna Fomina** is an Assistant Professor at the Institute of Philosophy and Sociology of the Polish Academy of Sciences. In 2007-2008 she worked and conducted research as a Marie Curie fellow at the University of Bradford. She has taken part in a number of research projects including 'The Perception of Poles in Ukraine and Ukrainians in Poland' (Institute of Public Affairs, Warsaw 2013 and 2010); 'Bilingualism, Identity and Media' (University of Helsinki, 2008-2011); 'Gendered Citizenship in Multicultural Europe' (University of Bergen, 2007-2011); 'The Image of Polish Migrants in the British Press' (Institute of Public Affairs, 2006). In 2010-2013 she also coordinated the Europe without Barriers international coalition of NGOs working towards the EU visa liberalisation for the Eastern Partnership countries. She authored and co-authored two book publications: *Immigration and Diversity in Europe: Lessons from British Multiculturalism* (VDM Verlag Dr. Müller, 2010) and *Lived Diversities: Space and Identities in the Multi-Ethnic City* (Policy Press, 2010), and a number of articles in peer-reviewed journals and research reports.

**Michael Gentile** is Professor of Human Geography at the Department of Sociology and Human Geography, University of Oslo. He has conducted research in different countries of the former Soviet Union and has published extensively on various aspects of these countries' urban social geographies. His recent work has touched upon residential segregation, gentrification, geopolitical identities, labour migration, and socialist-era housing allocation practice, with his latest publications figuring in the *Annals of the Association of American Geographers*, *Post-Soviet Affairs*, *Urban Geography* and in the *International Journal of Urban and Regional Research*. Until very recently, his research field base was in the Ukrainian city of Luhansk, which is one of the epicentres of the ongoing Donbas conflict.

**Kateryna Ivashchenko-Stadnik** is a Research Fellow at the Department of Methodology and Methods of Social Research at the Institute of Sociology of the National Academy of Sciences – an institutional partner of the European Social Survey in Ukraine. She previously worked as a Social Policy Advisor for the United Nations Development Programme (Ukraine) and as a cultural curator (Arthouse Traffic, SOTA Cinema Group). She has extensive experience in cross-national studies and has acted as a Ukrainian country expert within a number of international research schemes with a focus on social change, migration and mobility. Her recent publications include: 'The Impact of the Current Military Conflict on Migration and Mobility in Ukraine' (Robert Schuman Centre for Advanced Studies & Journal of Social Science Research Network) and 'Ukraine one year on: the challenge of preventing a new migration crisis in central Europe' (Migration Policy Centre Blog).

**Marina A. Kingsbury** is Adjunct Professor of Political Science at Alabama A&M University. She earned her PhD in Political Science from the University of New Mexico in 2015. She specialises in Comparative Politics with an emphasis on comparative social welfare policy and International Relations. Her main research interests are xenophobia in post-communist European countries, radical right politics and its influence on public policies, and Russian domestic and foreign policy. She has recently participated in a collaborative project aimed at investigating the problems of migrant integration in Russia which was funded by the Eurasia Foundation's US-Russia Social Expertise Exchange Program. Her most recent project focuses on issues of integration of migrant families with children at the point of access to education.

**Irina Kuznetsova** is a sociologist and social geographer. She works at the School of Geography, Earth and Environmental Studies at the University of Birmingham, United Kingdom. She previously worked as a Director of the EU Centre and the Institute for Comparative Studies of Modernity at the Kazan Federal University, Russia. She has conducted and participated in various applied and academic studies founded by regional bodies in Russia, the

European Commission, the Open Society Institute, MacArthur Foundation and the Russian Foundation for Humanities. Her recent projects include 'Asylum seekers from Eastern Ukraine in Russia: identities, policies and discourse in the context of forced migration from the Ukraine conflict' (British Academy, 2016-2017) and 'The everyday lives of Central Asian migrants in Moscow and Kazan in the context of Russia's Migration 2025 Concept: from legislation to practice' (Open Society Foundation, with John Round).

**Viacheslav Morozov** is Professor of EU-Russia Studies at the University of Tartu. He works on issues related to Russian national identity and foreign policy. His book *Russia and the Others: Identity and Boundaries of a Political Community* (Moscow: NLO Books, 2009) introduces neo-Gramscian theory of hegemony to Russian identity studies. His more recent research aims to reveal how Russia's political and social development has been conditioned by the country's position in the international system. This approach has been laid out in his most recent monograph *Russia's Postcolonial Identity: A Subaltern Empire in a Eurocentric World* (Palgrave, 2015), while the comparative dimension has been explored, inter alia, in the edited volume *Decentring the West: The Idea of Democracy and the Struggle for Hegemony* (Ashgate, 2013) and in 'Indigeneity and subaltern subjectivity in decolonial discourses: a comparative study of Bolivia and Russia' (*Journal of International Relations and Development,* co-authored with Elena Pavlova, forthcoming). Morozov is a member of the Program on New Approaches to Research and Security in Eurasia (PONARS Eurasia) based at the George Washington University. Between 2007 and 2010, he was a member of the Executive Council of the Central and East European International Studies Association (CEEISA).

**Vladimir Mukomel** is a Doctor of Sociology and a PhD candidate in Economics. He is the Head of Division of the Institute of Sociology, Russian Academy of Sciences, and the Director of the Center for Ethno-political and Regional Studies (NGO). His research interests include migration studies and migration policy, national minorities, ethnic policy as well as ethno-demographic and socio-economic consequences of conflicts. Mukomel's most recent projects include 'Socio-economic and socio-cultural factors in inter-ethnic tensions and conflicts' (Russian Science Foundation, 2015-2017), 'Interethnic accord as a resource in the consolidation of Russian society: regional variations' (Russian Science Foundation, 2014-2016), 'Diaspora – Partner in the Development of Tajikistan' (International Organization for Migration – IOM, 2014), 'Analysis of the peculiarities of the mutual adaptation and integration potential of the Russian youth and young migrants from Central Asia and Transcaucasia' (Russian Foundation for Humanities, 2013-2014), 'Analysis of the adaptation and integration of the '1.5 generation' migrants from Central Asia and Transcaucasia in Russian cities' (Russian Foundation for Humanities, 2011-2012) and 'Moldovans in the Russian

Federation: socio-economic profile and policy challenges' (IOM, 2011-2012).

**Olga Oleinikova** is a post-doctoral Research Fellow and Director of Ukraine Democracy Initiative at the University of Sydney. As Research Fellow, she works with the Sydney Democracy Network and is involved in a project on Diaspora and Democracy and on Governance and Anti-Corruption Reform in Ukraine. Both projects focus on the challenges, performance and prospects for democracy in Ukraine. As Director of Ukraine Democracy Initiative, she runs a research web-platform and global network of academics, politicians, civil activists and policy makers focused on the development of Ukrainian democracy. Oleinikova has a PhD in Sociology and Social Policy from the University of Sydney.

**Caress Schenk** is an Assistant Professor of Political Science and International Relations at Nazarbayev University, teaching on topics related to comparative politics, national identity, immigration control, and Eurasian politics and public policy. Her current projects include an analysis of federal vs. regional-level management of migration in Russia, comparative work on migration and rights in the countries of the former Soviet Union, and a new project on labour migration within the framework of the Eurasian Economic Union. These projects have been funded by the American Councils for International Education, the Fulbright Scholar Program and Nazarbayev University. Schenk's work has been published in *Demokratizatisya*, *Europe-Asia Studies*, *Nationalities Papers* and *Russia Beyond the Headlines* and she has also worked on INGO contract projects related to government and civil society responses to migration, human trafficking, and labour slavery in Russia, Kazakhstan, and Ukraine.

# Contents

INTRODUCTION
Agnieszka Pikulicka-Wilczewska     1

## PART ONE - UKRAINE

1. GEOPOLITICAL FAULT-LINE CITIES
   Michael Gentile     6

2. THE SOCIAL CHALLENGE OF INTERNAL DISPLACEMENT IN UKRAINE: THE HOST COMMUNITY'S PERSPECTIVE
   Kateryna Ivashchenko-Stadnik     25

3. 'STRANGERS AMONG OURS': STATE AND CIVIL RESPONSES TO THE PHENOMENON OF INTERNAL DISPLACEMENT IN UKRAINE
   Tania Bulakh     49

4. A HYBRID DEPORTATION: INTERNALLY DISPLACED FROM CRIMEA IN UKRAINE
   Greta Uehling     62

5. ECONOMIC MIGRATION OF UKRAINIANS TO THE EUROPEAN UNION: A VIEW FROM POLAND
   Joanna Fomina     78

6. MOVING OUT OF 'THEIR' PLACES: 1991–2016 MIGRATION OF UKRAINIANS TO AUSTRALIA
   Olga Oleinikova     90

## PART TWO - RUSSIA

7. MIGRATION OF UKRAINIANS TO RUSSIA IN 2014–2015. DISCOURSES AND PERCEPTIONS OF THE LOCAL POPULATION
   Vladimir Mukomel     105

8. RUSSIAN SOCIETY AND THE CONFLICT IN UKRAINE: MASSES, ELITES AND NATIONAL IDENTITY
   Viacheslav Morozov     116

9. MIGRATION TO RUSSIA AND THE CURRENT ECONOMIC CRISIS
   Mikhail Denisenko                                                    129

10. DANGEROUS AND UNWANTED: POLICY AND EVERYDAY DISCOURSES
    OF MIGRANTS IN RUSSIA
    Irina Kuznetsova                                                    149

11. LABOUR MIGRATION IN THE EURASIAN ECONOMIC UNION
    Caress Schenk                                                       164

12. BEYOND ATTITUDES: RUSSIAN XENOPHOBIA AS A POLITICAL
    LEGITIMATION TOOL
    Marina A. Kingsbury                                                 178

CONCLUSION
Greta Uehling                                                           196

NOTE ON INDEXING                                                        204

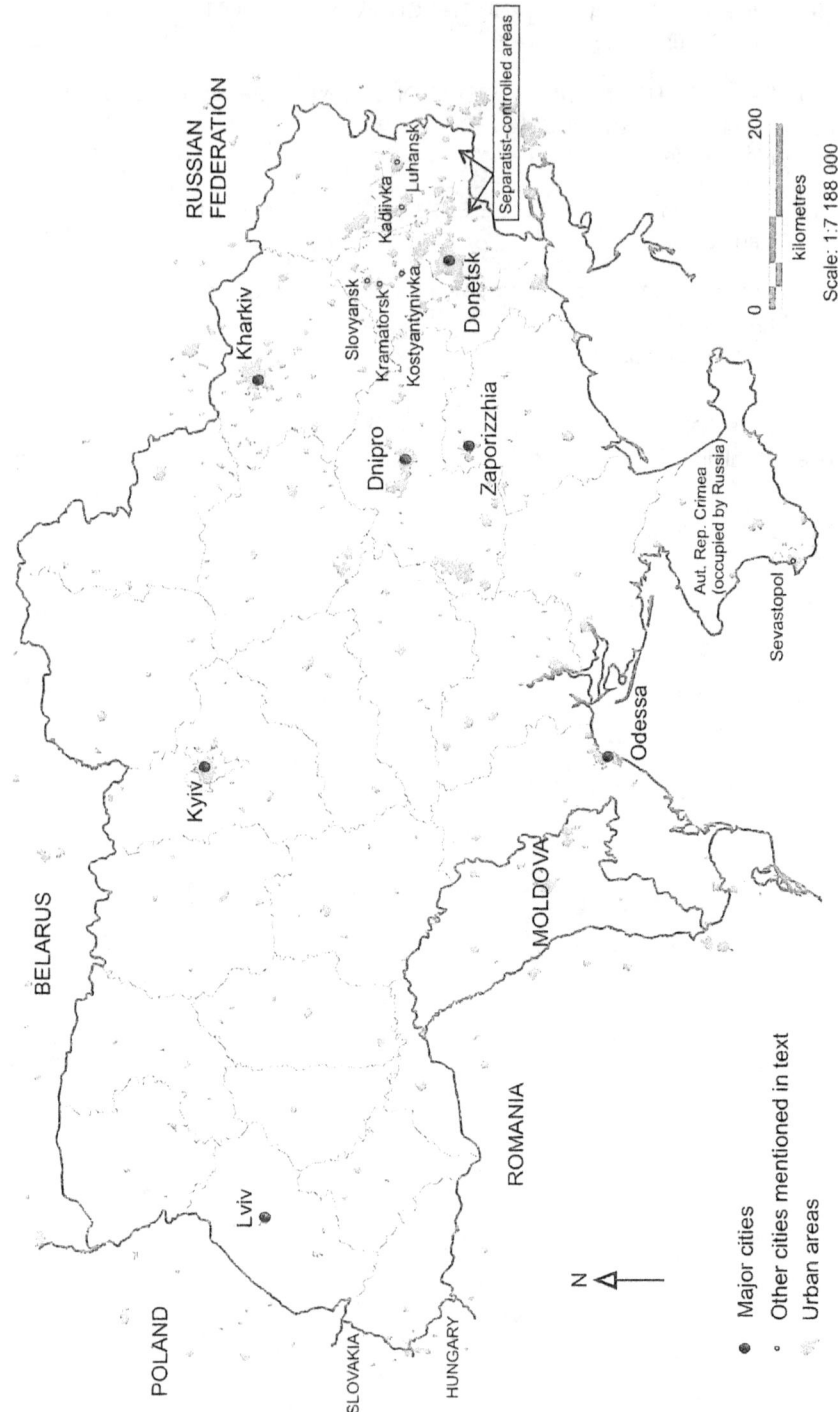

# Introduction

AGNIESZKA PIKULICKA-WILCZEWSKA

In 2015, when the European Union was facing a rapid inflow of migrants from the Middle East and Africa, which culminated in what is often referred to as 'the migration crisis', its Eastern neighbour was undergoing its own mass reshuffling of the population. With the fifth largest number of internally displaced persons (IDPs) in the world, reaching nearly 1.8 million[1], Ukraine has found it arduous to deal with the immense and long-term consequences of the war in its eastern region of Donbas.

The rapid inflow of people from the east and south of Ukraine to other regions has not only seen an ad-hoc and poorly elaborated governmental response, but also led to a number of problems related to the integration of newcomers, unemployment, as well as prejudice, xenophobia and distrust towards the Other. However, it has also seen an unprecedented mobilisation of civil society in support of the displaced, reflected in a variety of selfless acts of human kindness.

But the effects of the Ukraine crisis in terms of migration have been tremendous not only within Ukraine. Over the course of the conflict, the number of Ukrainian citizens in Russia has increased by 0.9 million, reaching 2.6 million in March 2015. Many of the asylum seekers have been confronted with unwelcoming attitudes, distrust and fear. Moreover, the economic crisis, which began in Russia as a result of the western-imposed sanctions, and the subsequent creation of the Eurasian Economic Union, have further affected Russia's policy towards migrants and migration into the country. Therefore, it can be argued that the indirect consequences of the Ukraine crisis for migration have been much wider and far-fetched than it may seem at first glance.

The aim of this collection is to shed light on the forgotten migrant crisis at the

---

[1] According to Ukraine's Ministry of Social Policy, 1,785,740 internally displaced persons were registered as of 6 June 2016.

European Union's doorstep and make sense of the various migration processes in and out of Ukraine and Russia, which have been taking place at the time of the war in Donbas. Given the scarcity of research on the various aspects of the topic, the book by no means exhausts it, but seeks to provide an overview of the existing scholarship and a point of reference for future studies.

The book is divided into two sections. The first section deals with migration processes that have taken place within Ukraine or have involved Ukrainian citizens' migration out of the country, excluding Russia. The second section discusses how the situation has developed within Russia, the country's response to the rapid inflow of migrants from Ukraine, its changing migration policies and their effect on migrants, as well as other processes related to the phenomenon over the course of the Ukraine crisis.

**Ukraine**

In the opening chapter, Michael Gentile introduces the concept of geopolitical fault-line cities – places with a high potential for the spread of conflict, where contested and remote-controlled narratives come together polarising the population. Ukraine's fault-line cities, Gentile argues, are of pivotal importance for the European integration project and the global geopolitical order. The truths presented by the information spaces of both sides of the war in Donbas widen the gap between the opposing factions and activate the fault-line between them.

Second, Kateryna Ivashchenko-Stadnik analyses the attitudes of the host community towards the newcomers. As the survey data demonstrate, after the two years of conflict, the IDPs are still perceived as semi-fellows and semi-citizens, limited in their access to social life. The reframing of such attitudes, Ivashchenko-Stadnik argues, is crucial to avoid IDPs' long-term exclusion.

In the third chapter, Tania Bulakh discusses the changes in the social response to the internally displaced persons in Ukraine, in particular to those from the Donbas region. She argues that while, initially, all migrants were largely accepted by the wider population, over the past year regional belonging has become a marker of social stigmatisation. People from Donbas, Bulakh argues, have been portrayed less favourably than those who fled Crimea, which has translated into everyday discrimination.

In the following chapter, the co-editor of the collection, Greta Uehling, presents the results of her two-year-long research on the experiences of the internally displaced persons from Crimea. She concludes that one of the effects of displacement has been the development of a new civic identity within Ukraine. Moreover, there is a widespread feeling of being abandoned and betrayed by the government among the displaced, Uehling argues, and the main task ahead is to remove the barriers standing in the way of IDP integration.

Further, Joanna Fomina analyses several aspects of economic migration from Ukraine to Poland, the most popular destination for Ukrainians, in the context of the military conflict in Donbas. While the war has increased migration flows into the country, especially among young men, Fomina argues that the motives of migrants have remained mostly economic. However, despite the primary goal being financial, the conflict has seen an unprecedented mobilisation of Polish-based Ukrainians as well as greater institutionalisation of Ukrainian civil society in the country.

In the last piece of the section, Olga Oleinikova analyses the structural variables that have shaped Ukrainian migration to Australia and lays out three profiles of Ukrainian migrants based on the period of migration, from 1991 to 2016. She argues that the post-Euromaidan events impacted life trajectories of Ukrainian citizens which has translated into the increase in the number of asylum applications submitted in Australia and a shift towards survival-based migration.

**Russia**

The second section begins with a chapter by Vladimir Mukomel discussing the migration of Ukrainians to Russia following the war in Donbas. It also presents the dominant attitudes towards Ukrainians in the country, including asylum seekers, in the country. Mukomel argues that the recent geopolitical changes have had a negative impact on Russians' attitude towards migrants from Ukraine. The shift in public opinion, he asserts, can lead to serious social problems if the tensions between refugees and local population, resulting from migrants' low integration level, continue.

In the following chapter, Viacheslav Morozov analyses how the Russian society reacted to the conflict in Ukraine. He argues that while it is true that President Putin has enjoyed wide support from the population, the phenomenon cannot be attributed to propaganda only, but has strong roots in nationalism, national identity and the fear of Western expansionism.

Further, Mikhail Denisenko seeks to address the question of how the volume and structure of migration flows into Russia have changed since the beginning of the recession – a result of the fall in oil prices and the imposition of Western sanctions. He also discusses how the crisis has affected the level of remittances received by the countries of the Commonwealth of Independent States (CIS). He concludes that the current crisis has contributed to the fall in the inflow of migrant workers to Russia as well as the decrease in remittances sent to CIS countries.

Further, Irina Kuznetsova analyses the formation process of the myth of a 'dangerous migrant' in relation to nationals of CIS countries through politics and media discourse. She also looks at the impact of the recent migration legislation restrictions on migrants. While the Russian state and society have made a lot of effort to support refugees from Eastern Ukraine by creating special employment conditions for the group, foreigners with non-Slavic appearance often fall victim to racist attacks. Moreover, due to their frequent participation in the informal economy, migrants often face issues related to access to health care and work safety.

Subsequently, Caress Schenk looks at the gap between the obligations put forward in the Eurasian Economic Union (EEU) treaty and the existing domestic immigration laws and procedures in Russia and Kazakhstan. In the highly politicised aftermath of the Ukraine crisis, Schenk argues, migration can be seen as a vital issue of sovereignty and states might not like a supranational organisation to regulate it. Therefore, if new members are being attracted to EEU membership due to the promise of an open labour market, the reality of migrant experience on the ground is likely to be disappointing.

Finally, in the last chapter, Marina A. Kingsbury explains how complex historical, political and social events shape the patterns of xenophobia and how it is used as a political legitimation tool by the Kremlin. By demonising migrants, Kingsbury argues, the government re-directed public dissatisfaction to the visible and powerless migrant. However, as the Russian economy suffered from the sanctions imposed by the West in response to the conflict in Ukraine, the immigrants were no longer the prime enemy of the state and animosity shifted towards the external enemy: the United States and the European Union.

In conclusion, Greta Uehling summarises the arguments of the authors and discusses what new approaches and questions they have presented. She also analyses the policy relevance of individual contributions.

Part One

# UKRAINE

# 1

# Geopolitical Fault-Line Cities

MICHAEL GENTILE

## Introduction

On 22 June 2016, people across most of the former Soviet Union were united in their remembrance of the beginning of the Great Patriotic War (GPW)[2]. This temporary appearance of unity comes against a background of political and ideological divisions largely centred on the question of how to interpret the Soviet past and its problematic legacies. Having experienced decades of suppression of historical facts, such as the Molotov-Ribbentrop pact's secret protocol,[3] the Ukrainian population, like that of the entire Soviet Union, was confronted with a wide range of uncomfortable or unexpected new truths about the violent and coercive nature of Soviet power. In the western regions of contemporary Ukraine, which had been invaded by the USSR in 1939, these truths were largely known already. Elsewhere in the country, where the original invader was Nazi Germany, they were harder to believe and accept (Zhurzhenko 2007, Portnov 2011, Osipian 2015), and consensus on the country's post-totalitarian politics of memory did not emerge because independent Ukraine started off as a society divided into three very different political factions (Shevel 2011, 148-149). In the absence of a concerted, sustained, consequent and decisive effort on behalf of the central authority in Kyiv to de-Sovietise the country's historical memory (as was done in most of

---

[2] The Great Patriotic War (GPW) is the Soviet and later Russian name for the Second World War. However, unlike the Second World War, the GPW only started when Nazi Germany invaded the Soviet Union in June 1941. The Soviet propaganda machine effectively silenced or misrepresented most of what happened before this date, including the Soviet occupation of parts of Poland and of the Baltics, as well as the war on Finland (see Portnov 2011 for an insightful discussion on the official memory of the GPW in Ukraine and Belarus since 1991).

[3] The Molotov-Ribbentrop pact was a non-aggression pact signed by Germany and the Soviet Union in August 1939. It included a secret protocol that agreed upon and specified the areas and extent of the countries' respective spheres of influence.

Central Europe and in the Baltic states, see Czepczyński and Sooväli-Sepping 2016), this context enabled the preservation and development of powerful alternative narratives manufactured during the years of the Soviet monopoly on historical truth, and inventively revised in Russia under Vladimir Putin. The most powerful of them all surrounds the GPW, which, as Zhurzhenko (2007, 4) notes, is the 'founding myth of the new Russia'.

Geopolitical fault-line cities are places where such contested remote-controlled narratives come together in space, trumping local issues of greater day-to-day relevance, and polarising the population on issues that differ substantially from the matters that typically split the residents of classic divided cities such as Belfast or Johannesburg. Inspired by the author's extensive experience of fieldwork in the Donbas until late 2013, and by observations made during subsequent shorter visits to Kharkiv and Odessa, this chapter aims at opening up a theoretical discussion on the conditions and challenges present in such cities. It proceeds with a general discussion of the idea of the fault-line within geopolitical discourse, followed by a more focused section on fault-line cities, which discusses three separate, but related, issues: (1) the overlapping of contradictory information spaces, (2) the meaning of border and frontline location, and (3) memory, identity politics and political confrontation.

**Fault-line and Borderland Narratives**

The idea of the fault-line evokes powerful imageries and associations, and is well established in geopolitical discourse. Nevertheless, a quick Google Ngram viewer search indicates that the term's usage outside of the field of plate tectonics is relatively recent. In combination with 'geopolitical', the concept appeared around 1970, but it did not take off until the early 1990s, paradoxically at a time when the end of the Cold War should have made it sound somewhat obsolete. It peaked in the late 1990s, and then stabilised at a somewhat lower level since the 9/11 terrorist attacks. Meanwhile, the less frequently used but more recently introduced 'civilisational fault-line' surged twice: first, following the publication of Samuel Huntington's (1993) notorious Clash of Civilizations thesis, and then again after 9/11, when many observers interpreted the attacks as evidence in support of it.

Since the 9/11 terrorist attacks, Huntington's (1993, 1996) outline of the future of planetary international relations – one in which seven or eight civilizations will be confronting each other and in which the primary division will be between the West and the Rest – has been widely revisited, revalued and re-critiqued. The argument, as it goes, is that the death of the ideological battleground of the Cold War, elsewhere known as 'the end of history'

(Fukuyama 1989), re-activates humanity's traditional conflict tendencies, most notably those stemming from the cultural incompatibilities between civilisations. Some countries, including Russia and Ukraine, must face the difficult task of hosting and managing one or more boundaries between different civilizations, and are therefore seen as 'torn' countries. On this basis, Huntington suggested that Ukraine could split along civilizational lines at some point in the future (see Bassin 2007, 361). While this may sound superficially prophetic given the recent Russian annexation of Crimea and the establishment of two Soviet-nostalgic 'People's Republics', these developments clearly lack the ethnic, religious or cultural underpinnings that would characterize a civilisational fault-line conflict.

Because geopolitical preferences and allegiances may be more susceptible to manipulation than ethnic, national and religious identities, they are arguably easier to mobilise too (O'Loughlin *et al.* 2006, Gentile 2015, Wilson 2016), particularly when societies reach critical junctures or transitional moments, during which the competition for hegemony between opposing geopolitical narratives intensifies (Mamadouh and Dijkink 2006, 358). However, a power that intends to rely on geopolitically rooted identities will have to come to terms with the fact that the pendulum may swing back rapidly, which was nicely illustrated by the rapid rise and fall of the geopolitical conception of Novorossiya (Laruelle 2015, O'Loughlin *et al.* 2016). Hence, stable identity-building work may require crafting or grafting stickier forms of identification – national, religious, cultural, or whatever – onto the geopolitical identity framework. This is where the early 1990s' separatist movement in Crimea failed (Dawson 1997).

With an appropriate treatment by political technology, and corroborated by the onset of armed conflict, geopolitical identities can rapidly morph into more resistant, if artificial, national or regional identities. The Donbas offers a case in point: long lacking any clear sense of national identity, the least blurred aspect uniting its population was its fervent opposition to the imagined Atlantic geopolitical Other, epitomised globally by NATO (Kubicek 2000, Barkanov 2015, Gentile 2015) and locally by the 'Fascist-Banderite' myth projected upon western Ukraine (Osipian 2015). Yet, such opposition is not sufficient to explain the current hostilities. For the outbreak of war to materialise, vapid geopolitical differences demanded heavy exaggeration and to some extent re-framing as civilisational differences (see Laruelle 2015, Jekaterynczuk 2016), and direct military involvement from Moscow was indispensable. In Huntington's words, this would have implied a transition from a fluid and predominantly 'which side are you on?' based identity towards an identity centred on the more inelastic 'what are you?' (see Huntington 1993, 27). Finally, without the support of the local elites – the klepto-kakistocrats (incompetent thieves) of the Party of Regions and their oligarch associates – this shift would have been far less likely (Zhurzhenko 2014, Kuzio 2015, Osipian 2015, Portnov 2015, Wilson 2016).

By contrast, beyond the occupied territories of the Donbas and Crimea, the Russian aggression has strongly contributed to the formation and consolidation of Ukrainian national identity in those regions where it was traditionally considered weak, i.e. across the south and east of the country (Härtel 2016, Kulyk 2016). However, this does not appear to have altered the Ukrainian population's positive view of the Russian ethnic Other significantly (Barrington 2002, Armandon 2013, Onuch 2015), nor has ethnicity or language status been politicised in mainstream politics (the incendiary rhetoric of the far right parties Svoboda and Pravyi Sektor enjoy scant popular support). This is not the kind of context that would favour the development of inter-ethnic hostilities, let alone the outbreak of war: for this to happen, foreign (Russian) intervention would appear to be indispensable. Yet, such an intervention would have to exploit actually existing divisions, and because cultural, ethno-national or linguistic divisions have little to offer in this sense, geopolitical orientations are the only viable alternative.

**Fault-line Cities**

Fault-line cities are cities located where two or more ethno-cultural ('civilisational'), ethno-national, economic or geopolitical realms intersect or overlap, and where this condition may, under certain circumstances, express itself through heightened conflict, violence or outright warfare. Some fault-line cities are therefore characterised as contested, polarised and/or divided – often literally so, by walls, fences, gates, and exclusionary turfs, as in Nicosia or Jerusalem – but far from all fault-line cities are contested and not all contested cities are on fault-lines.

For the emergence of conflict, the politicisation of local differences is essential (Dawson 1997, Anderson 2008, Silver 2010). However, the recent Russian land grab of the Autonomous Republic of Crimea and of Sevastopol, as well as the conflict in the Donbas, come against a local background of moderate and shrinking tensions *within* these regions, despite the heightened tensions stemming from Russia's mounting geopolitical assertiveness on the international arena (Dawson 1997, Armandon 2013). This has prompted an increase in research on seemingly peaceful, or at least pacified, fault-line regions, including northern Kazakhstan (Diener 2015) and Estonia (Trimbach and O'Lear 2015), where inter-ethnic divisions are increasingly subordinate to geopolitics.

Like much of contemporary urban theory, the literature on contested or divided cities is skewed towards a limited set of paradigmatic cities, towards a handful of iconic sites characterised by deeply rooted ethno-national, religious and political conflict (Allegra et al. 2012). These cities – places such as Beirut or Sarajevo – are indeed typically located on the geographical margins of Huntington's civilisations, yet they exist amidst scores of peaceful civilisational fault-line cities (Anderson 2008, 20). Interestingly, while noting that divided cities are usually found at the edge of (former) empires, and that conflict is particularly likely to emerge when the empire reaches its endgame, Anderson nevertheless understands divisions in the light of assumed ethno-national(ist) causes, even when these overlap with regional or global geopolitical interests. Following this – largely implicit – logic, conflict in civilisational or ethno-national fault-line cities may be instrumentalised by distant geopolitical agents, but it remains primarily embedded in the local ethno-national rift. Thus, this line of thought suggests that ethno-national divisions are the key issue, and that, given the right circumstances, these may be used by remote powers to forward their own interests. Indeed, this was the case in Estonia during the 1990s (Merritt 2000).

Yet, there exist cities that are located on the interfaces of different global-scaled geopolitical spheres of interest, cities where ethno-national divisions are either absent or subordinate to the power of clashing geopolitical imaginaries, and in which potent but irreconcilable historical and geopolitical narratives and discourses overlap, dividing the population into opposing factions. Essentially, these are geopolitical fault-line cities, cities whose inhabitants may use the same language, but not the same vocabulary, in their approach to contentious issues such as historical memory, foreign policy preferences and geopolitical alignment. In a geopolitical fault-line city, membership in NATO is more likely to lead to hard feelings than the decision to divert funds from schools towards the construction of an underfunded ring road. Moreover, whereas residential segregation (by religion, ethnicity, wealth, etc.) is one of the most salient features in most divided/contested cities (Allegra et al. 2012), this is not the case in geopolitical fault-line cities: there are no NATO-supporter ghettos, other than where NATO support correlates with other population characteristics.

Geopolitical fault-line cities are also cities where the production and consumption of geopolitical meaning are exceptionally multi-sited (cf. Fregonese 2009), cities in which multiple, opposing, sometimes abruptly emerging, and frequently ephemeral geopolitical narratives of both local and non-local origin come into conversation with different parts of local society and with the built environment. When the salience of the overlapping geopolitical narratives suddenly increases, e.g. as a result of significant external impulses or during critical junctures (as was the case during and after the Euromaidan revolution in Ukraine), the probability of violent conflict increases. Yet, the roots of such conflict, as well as its prospective solutions, are rather to be sought outside of the city than within it. In this sense, the geopolitical fault-line city is an empty canvas upon which struggles on matters that are of little concern to the daily running of city life are projected, meaning that there is ultimately little to fight about. And because there is little to fight about, the dynamics of conflict in geopolitical fault-line cities are far more volatile than in ethno-nationally divided cities, where conflict tends to evolve more predictably and in relation to universal concerns such as ethno-politics, security, policing and discrimination (Calame and Charlesworth 2009, 7).

**Information Fault-lines in the City**

A crucial aspect characterising geopolitical fault-line cities is their exposure to overlapping, but contradictory, spaces of information which, in today's globalised media landscape, does not necessarily command a border(land) physical location. Moreover, while global geopolitical imaginaries may well be coloured by religious or ethno-national differences, they orbit around a core of vague concepts such as polarity (uni-, bi-, multi-) and global status, democracy (or not), military power, and political ideology. Cultural differences may become part of the equation too, but unlike the case along Huntington's civilisational fault-lines, rather than being 'not only real [but] basic' (Huntington 1993, 25), they may be very artificial. The recent Kremlin-supported talk of a civilisational rift between a value-conservative Russia and the allegedly decadent West is a case in point (see Hutchings and Szostek 2015).

The collapse of the Iron Curtain and the rise of the internet took place almost simultaneously. If the previous global order was one of insulated regional spaces of information, only at times broken by e.g. *samizdat* publications or Radio Free Europe/Radio Liberty broadcasts within the Soviet sphere, the circulation of information since 1991 has been almost boundless, despite some authoritarian governments' unrelenting efforts to contain it. People's ability to assimilate this information, however, has changed far less, depending on foreign language skills and on the heavily socialising legacy of the informational past. One may thus expect the population of geopolitical fault-line cities to be divided on prominent issues by age, education, socio-economic status and language skills; indeed, my own research in Luhansk, which was conducted during the months preceding the Euromaidan, suggested that this was the case in relation to both NATO and, especially, EU support (Gentile 2015), squaring in with findings from earlier research conducted in Ukraine on this and on other related topics (Katchanovski 2006, Munro 2007, Armandon 2013).[1] Moreover, Charnysh (2013, 7) noted that

---

[1] It should be noted that the diversity in popular opinions on geopolitical matters is

Ukrainians and Russians increasingly consume different media, causing a polarisation of opinions on political matters, and similar observations have been made by Koort (2014) in relation to Estonia and its Russian minority, and by Birka (2016) for Latvia. The major difference between Ukraine and Estonia, in this respect, is the fact that almost the entire population of Ukraine is a potential consumer of Russian-language media products, whereas this certainly is not the case in Estonia. Following the Russian news broadcasts in Narva is less of a matter of choice than in Kyiv, where Russian nevertheless remains widely spoken among its residents, Ukrainian and Russian alike.

**The Meaning of Border and/or Military Frontline Location**

Geopolitical fault-line cities are frequently located in proximity of borders between states with differing geopolitical interests or ambitions, irrespective of the degree of confrontation between them. Most cities in eastern Ukraine belong to this group, including prominent metropolises such as Kharkiv, Donetsk and Dnipro.[2] The borderland location has several implications. First, close proximity to the border is likely to increase the quantity and quality of cross-border economic, social, cultural, and even kinship ties. Second, it entails an enhanced exposure to the informational spaces of the neighbouring country, especially in the absence of a significant language barrier. Consequentially, third, it implies relatively weak connections to the national centre of power, unless the borderland fault-line city *is* the centre of power. Instead, stronger cross-border connections may be expected, including

---

not a characteristic that is limited to geopolitical fault-line cities. During the early 2000s, when the Russian media landscape was not quite as unidirectional as it is today, popular views and imaginations of Russia's role in the international arena were far more diverse than they are today (O'Loughlin *et al.* 2005). However, more recently, and especially since about 2012, popular views on foreign policy have converged; e.g. the annexation ('re-unification') of Crimea and the country's policy towards Ukraine (however contradictory) enjoy widespread support (Morozov, this collection).

[2] Other borderland geopolitical fault-line cities include Daugavpils (Latvia), Narva (Estonia) and Chișinău (Moldova). While it may be tempting to interpret these cities as ethno-nationally divided and straddling a 'civilisational fault-line' – for example a 'Slavic/Finno-Ugrian fault-line' (Anderson 2008, 9) running across Estonia – inter-ethnic tensions are in fact negligible in these cities, despite the recent rise of a more distinct form of Russian-speaker identity in the region (Cheskin 2015, 16, see also Birka 2016). Like in Ukraine, tensions run stronger in relation to foreign policy preferences and geopolitical alignment. Until relatively recently, formal citizenship was also a major grievance among Russian speakers in these cities, but the problem has been greatly reduced over recent years, not least because 'non-citizen' status has its perks in the form of visa-free travel from Lisbon all the way to Vladivostok (Selga 2016). At the same time, however, the relative attractiveness of non-citizenship may exacerbate some of the geopolitical fault-line characteristics of the cities where non-citizens are most numerous.

enhanced migration flows, particularly in the presence of large real wage differentials. Fourth, residents of borderland fault-line cities are prone to identity hybridity or blurring, creating a sense of relative detachment from the core and strengthening the sense of a unique local or regional identity (cf. Trimbach and O'Lear 2015 for northeast Estonia, Zhurzhenko 2011 for Kharkiv, Pirie 1996 and Kubicek 2000 for the Donbas).

Today all cities in eastern Ukraine are geopolitical fault-line cities, and many are located near the country's external borders. Moreover, many are dangerously close to the military frontline, adding an additional layer of complications. The most evident complications stem from what it means to be located near a military frontline in the first place. First, this means that there is a real and constant threat of invasion, yet the perceptions of this threat are far from uniform, as are the feelings towards the potential invader. Second, this context may embolden the faultline-frontline cities' 'risk entrepreneurs', actors who may seek opportunities to cooperate with the potentially invading state's authorities for personal, economic or political gain. Third, being perceived as high-risk sites means that such cities inevitably deflect investment, contributing to increased economic hardship and dependency on external support. Finally, there are the flows of internally displaced persons (IDPs) and refugees generated by the conflict. Such flows are usually initially directed towards safe areas within short distances from the areas of armed conflict, confronting the local authorities with an immediate requirement to provide shelter, while simultaneously increasing housing demand and the burden on public services such as healthcare and schooling.

Because it is common for IDPs and refugees to experience social, economic and psychological distress, it is crucial for frontline-faultline cities to work for their correct and rapid integration. Moreover, in the Donbas there are cities that have experienced temporary Russian proxy occupation by the 'People's Republics', cities such as Slovyansk or Kostyantynivka, which are now net IDP/refugee-importers after having been net exporters during the four months of 'people's occupation'. Former IDPs who have had to spend time elsewhere in Ukraine have now returned to cities where they must re-encounter neighbours who had chosen to escape to Russia. Presumably, these two groups of returnees have been exposed to very different conditions and narratives, and this may have influenced their national/ethnic/civic self-identification in potentially conflictual ways. Geopolitical faultline-frontline cities must thus also contend with the task of mending the relations between groups with opposing experiences of the war, particularly among IDPs and returnees, but also among those who chose not to leave. Also, recent research on the twin faultline-frontline cities of Slovyansk and Kramatorsk suggests that opinions tend to be divided between those who have been directly victimised by the conflict and those who have not, with the former tending to exhibit a stronger pro-West position than the latter (Coupé and Obrizan 2016).

**Memory, Identity Politics and Political Confrontation**

Geopolitical fault-line cities are sites of heightened political confrontation, places where irreconcilable narratives tensely coexist, and where fundamental aspects of historical memory collide. With the partial and anachronistic exception of Belarus, Moscow's role as ideological *axis mundi* was rapidly disposed of throughout Central and Eastern Europe (CEE), prompting a return to narratives centred on the historical homeland and the search for a new role within the Western world, signifying a Return to Europe (Czepczyński and Sooväli-Sepping 2016). Concordantly, identity politics in CEE heavily relies on the othering of the alien ideology of Communism (Light and Young 2010, 946), which, like a zombie, re-surfaces time and time again to scare off any attempt at challenging the main tenets of the new (neoliberal) order (Chelcea and Druța 2016, see also Etkind 2009). During the 1990s, both Russia and Ukraine followed this path, albeit with hesitation, but neither country ever succeeded in making a clean break with its past (Burant 1995, Pipes 1997). In Moscow, the voices of the Soviet hardliners backed by the security services and by the military were never fully suppressed; Kyiv, for its part, struggled with regional differences in political support 'so acute that more polarisation would be difficult to imagine' (Kubicek 2000, 290).

While the ideology of Communism may have suffered a fatal blow around 1990, from which it was never to recover, it is still notable that 'the 'subjects' of post-socialist transformation will retain a memory of the past which, in its inevitably incomplete and remoulded shape, continues to influence evaluations of the present' (Hörschelmann 2002, 63). In other words, while Communism may well be dead, memories of the Communist past are not, but these memories are fragmented, open to manipulation and, above all, highly contested. In Ukraine, and to some extent in Russia and Kazakhstan, one such crucial element of historical memory refers to the Holodomor – the mass famine orchestrated by Joseph Stalin in 1932–1933 – which has come to epitomise the tensions existing between pro-Russia/pro-Soviet and pro-Ukrainian factions in Kharkiv. At the centre of this process is the status of the Holodomor as genocide aimed specifically at Ukrainians (as decreed by law under President Yushchenko), or as a tragedy victimising all, irrespective of ethnicity. In practice, the local elites handled the matter by looking for some kind of compromise, e.g. in relation to the location and characteristics of new monuments commemorating the victims of the Holodomor, yet this compromise only confirmed Kharkiv's hybrid borderland identity status, rather than promoting the city's new status as Ukrainian (Zhurzhenko 2011, 608).

Therefore, Zhurzhenko (2011, 619) concludes, '[...] the new memory regime is contested, renegotiated, and modified at the local level, resulting in decentralisation and fragmentation of the official narrative of the Holodomor as genocide'.

Thus, in geopolitical fault-line cities, like in ethno-nationally divided cities, 'truth has to be negotiated' (Brand 2009, 49), and memory politics are rife. However, as Zhurzhenko (2007) explains, 'memory politics [in Ukraine] is less about the communist past than about the future political and economic hegemony on the European continent, [...] it is always the *geopolitics of memory*' (original emphasis). Hence, the monument commemorating the 21 Luhansk natives that fell victim to the Ukrainian Insurgent Army (OUN-UPA), which was uncovered in Luhansk as late as in 2010, is far more eye-catching than the stone raised two years earlier in remembrance of the thousands of local victims of the Holodomor.

While the Holodomor is one of the major *enjeux* in the geopolitics of memory – both within Ukraine and beyond its borders – it is by far not the only one. Geopolitical fault-line cities such as Kharkiv or Luhansk persistently experience conflict over antagonistic symbols, and while Soviet and Soviet-inspired monuments and street-names dominate their cityscapes (or at least, they did until the implementation of the recent laws on de-communisation[3]), they offer resistance to the dominant anti-Soviet counter-narrative stemming from Kyiv. The political controversies and polarised opinions surrounding the ubiquitous Lenin statues in eastern Ukraine are ultimately about 'empty signifiers' (Zhurzhenko 2014 and 2015), symbols that have come to represent something that is separate from the person/thing they represent. Except for a small number of true Communist believers, Lenin has become more a symbol of resistance against nationalist Kyiv-Ukraine, rather than of the very ideology he championed (Zhurzhenko 2015). Thus, unlike in ethno-nationally divided cities, where tailored myths are artificially projected onto specific sites and into the overall aesthetics of the city (Bakshi 2014, 189), geopolitical fault-line cities experience a more thorough decoupling between place and meaning. In

---

[3] The decommunisation laws entered into force in May 2015. They require the effacement of all communist symbols, monuments and toponyms present on Ukrainian soil, with the exception of those commemorating the Soviet victory over Nazi Germany in the Second World War. A recent high profile city renaming is that of former Dnipropetrovsk, now Dnipro. Initially thought to be controversial, evidence suggests that the laws have not been met with much resistance on ideological grounds (Shevel 2016). Importantly, the renaming of cities has not left the occupied territories untouched: for example, the city of Stakhanov in Luhansk *oblast'* was recently returned its old name Kadiivka, but this is not reflected in the city's current official website (Stahanov.info, accessed 27 July 2016), as the self-proclaimed Luhansk People's Republic does not intend to implement the Ukrainian decommunisation laws.

other words, there is more ambiguity in the air, there is a multitude of narratives and counter-narratives, but also plenty of symbolic capital up for grabs by local elites and political entrepreneurs (cf. Forest and Johnson 2002). In Kharkiv, the Party of Regions ultimately consigned interpretations of history that were alternative to those dominating in the city to discursive and visual marginality and insignificance, and the attention was shifted towards smaller monuments (Zhurzhenko 2015). However, as Bakshi (2014, 208) notes, conflict and disruption alter the bond between place and memory at its core. Accordingly, following the Euromaidan and the subsequent wave of successful and unsuccessful attempts at establishing 'people's republics' (notable failed attempts took place Kharkiv and Odessa) and Anti-Maidan movements throughout southeast Ukraine, tensions run higher than ever, and small explosions and bomb threats have ostensibly supplanted the battle of signs and symbols that had been characterising Kharkiv. Conflict has now reached the grassroots, with the population having become extremely polarised in regard to the city's largely unreformed landscape of signs and symbols – empty signifiers that have been activated as a result of the intensification of the discourses surrounding them (Zhurzhenko 2015).

In June 2015, when I last visited Kharkiv, the city's walls were virtually free from any graffiti in favour of or against the Ukrainian state, the Security Service (SBU), Putin, NATO, the EU, or the 'Kharkov People's Republic'[4]. Likewise, unlike in Kyiv, where the colours of the Ukrainian flag are ubiquitous, the celebration of Ukrainian Kharkiv was at best timid. Almost complete semiotic silence enveloped the city's public spaces, yet, behind the facades, in the inner courtyards, and away from the bustling life of the city centre, the walls still revealed the fading voices of the most active period of conflict between separatists and supporters of Ukrainian unity. The local administration, it seems, had silenced the elephant in the living room.[5] Meanwhile, Lenin's right boot was all that was left on the pedestal located in the middle of Freedom Square. Swimming with the tide, Hennadyi Kernes, the city's scandalous mayor, has opportunistically announced that the entire area will be given a European appearance in the future (Radio Svoboda 2015). Ironically, this was not long after he declared that he would have defended the Lenin monument at any cost (Bershidsky 2014). In Kharkiv, like elsewhere in CEE, both Europe and Lenin may well be empty signifiers, but they remain each other's antonyms.

---

[4]  The Kharkov People's Republic was an early attempt at establishing separatist rule in the city in March-April 2014. Unlike similar efforts in the Donbas, it did not succeed. 'Kharkov' is the Russian-language version of Kharkiv.

[5]  Interestingly, the authorities in Odessa appear to have adopted a lightly more *laissez faire* strategy. Unlike in Kharkiv, as of October 2015, Odessa's walls offered a visual archive of the tense atmosphere that prevailed in the city following the Euromaidan and, especially, after the 2 May 2014 Trade Unions Building fire.

## Conclusion

This chapter cautiously theorised the geopolitical fault-line city, attempting to extract it as a useful concept from the heterogeneous club of cities that are spoken of as divided, contested, polarised or dual. Any comprehensive analysis of geopolitical fault-line cities – or of any city for that matter – would necessitate deep engagement, possibly including ethnographic fieldwork, with the characteristics and sources of the conflicts taking place in them (cf. Allegra et al. 2012), revealing complex entanglements of local, national and transnational identities with a diverse set of geopolitical commitments. For this reason, as Véron (2016) sensibly suggests in relation to the closely related literature on divided cities, it is important to listen to the multiple voices present in the city, not just to the hegemonic storylines that tend to essentialise, and perhaps even contribute to, the sources of conflict (see also Nagle 2016). Yet, key dissonances between views on historical memory, foreign policy, geopolitical alignment and geopolitical identity are among the most important sources of conflict in geopolitical fault-line cities; locally, these dissonances translate into heated battles over 'empty signifiers' such as the many Lenins and Dzerzhinskiys scattered across south-eastern Ukraine that still stand vigilant against the imminent threat of a 'Fascist-Banderite invasion'. In this sense, conflict in geopolitical fault-line cities is truly 'glocal'. Ukraine's geopolitical fault-line cities are for the global geopolitical order what the voters of Ohio are for the United States presidential elections: their swinging status, and their future socio-political trajectories and alignment are of pivotal importance, not only to the regions and countries within which they are located, but also for the entire European integration project (and conversely, for the corresponding Eurasian project led by Vladimir Putin).

A crucial aspect distinguishing the geopolitical fault-line city from other divided cities relates to the potential for the spread of conflict. If conflict in classic fault-line cities tends to remain localised – because it mostly relates to localised concrete concerns held by opposing groups – conflict in geopolitical fault-line cities tends to be very abstract and, therefore, easier to manipulate and export. Therefore, the Donbas war and the furtive Russian annexation of Crimea have revamped the confrontational attitudes present between parts of the Russian-speaking community and the non-Russian majority elsewhere, especially in Latvia, projecting cities such as Riga and Daugavpils into the frontlines of the current geopolitical struggle over the minds and allegiances of their populations. Yet Riga and Daugavpils are fundamentally different: while Daugavpils is an almost entirely Russian-speaking borderland city, Riga is a multi-lingual geopolitical fault-line *capital* where a growing geopolitical identity schism (Birka 2016) overlaps with the unsettling characteristics of classic divided cities, particularly ethnic residential segregation. This may exacerbate the potential for conflict in this city.

Summing up, contested memories and conflicting identities come together in geopolitical fault-line cities, diverting the population's attention from issues concerning the more mundane aspects of urban life. Geopolitical imaginaries and controversies over empty signifiers hijack and polarise the political debate and population alike. Because the disputed issues are only partially rooted in the local conditions, the situation in geopolitical fault-line cities is potentially more volatile, and the unfolding of conflict less predictable. Until two or three years ago, Odessa, Dnipro, Kharkiv and Donetsk were generally assumed to be similar in terms of the political orientations and geopolitical preferences of their residents. Previously underestimated differences between these cities and, above all, physical distance from the Russian Federation, have rapidly tilted the balance in favour of the one or of the other side. However, in the meantime, the widening gap between the truths portrayed within the Russian and non-Russian informational spaces activates the fault-line between opposing factions in these cities. New earthquakes cannot be excluded.

## References

Allegra, M., Casaglia, A. and Rokem, J. "The Political Geographies of Urban Polarization: A Critical Review of Research on Divided Cities," *Geography Compass* 6, no. 9 (2012): 560-574.

Anderson, J. *"From Empires to Ethno-National Conflicts: A Framework for Studying 'Divided Cities' in 'Contested States' – Part I,"* (electronic document available from www.conflictincities.org/workingpapers.html) Belfast: Queen's University Belfast (2008).

Armandon, E. "Popular Assessments of Ukraine's Relations with Russia and the European Union under Yanukovych," *Demokratizatsiya: The Journal of Post-Soviet Democratization* 21, no.2 (2013): 289-308.

Bakshi, A. "Urban Form and Memory Discourses: Spatial Practices in Contested Cities," *Journal of Urban Design* 19, no.2 (2014): 189-210.

Barkanov, B. "Crisis in Ukraine: Clash of Civilization or Geopolitics?" in *Power, Politics and Confrontation in Eurasia – Foreign Policy in a Contested Region,* edited by M. Sussex and R. E. Kanet (London: Palgrave Macmillan, 2015), 210-239.

Barrington, L. "Views of the 'Ethnic Other' in Ukraine," *Nationalism and Ethnic Politics* 8, no.2 (2002): 83-96.

Bassin, M. "Civilisations and their Discontents: Political Geography and Geopolitics in the Huntington Thesis," *Geopolitics* 12, no.3 (2007): 351-374.

Bershidsky, L. "Toppling Lenin 20 Years Too Late," *Bloomberg View*, September 29, 2014, accessed June 30, 2016, https://www.bloomberg.com/view/articles/2014-09-29/toppling-lenin-20-years-too-late.

Birka, I. "Expressed Attachment to Russia and Social Integration: The Case of Young Russian Speakers in Latvia, 2004-2010," *Journal of Baltic Studies* 47, no.2 (2016): 219-238.

Brand, R. "Urban Artifacts and Social Practices in a Contested City," *Journal of Urban Technology* 16, no.2-3 (2009): 35-60.

Burant, S. "Foreign Policy and National Identity: A Comparison of Ukraine and Belarus," *Europe-Asia Studies* 47, no.7 (1995): 1125-1144.

Calame, J. and E. Charlesworth, *Divided Cities: Belfast, Beirut, Jerusalem, Mostar and Nicosia* (Philadelphia: University of Pennsylvania Press, 2009).

Charnysh, V. "Analysis of Current Events: Identity Mobilization in Hybrid Regimes: Language in Ukrainian Politics," *Nationalities Papers* 41, no.1 (2013): 1-14.

Chelcea, L. and O. Druţa, *"Zombie Socialism: Post-socialism from Post- to Ghost*, (unpublished manuscript supplied by authors), submitted 2016.

Cheskin, A. "Identity and Integration of Russian Speakers in the Baltic States: A Framework for Analysis," *Ethnopolitics* 14, no.1 (2015): 72-93.

Coupé, T. and M. Obrizan, "Violence and Political Outcomes in Ukraine – Evidence from Sloviansk and Kramatorsk," *Journal of Comparative Economics* 44, no.1 (2016): 201-212.

Czepczyński, M. and H. Sooväli-Sepping, "From Sacrum to Profanum: Reinterpretation of Communist Places of Power in Baltic Cities," *Journal of Baltic Studies* 47, no.2 (2016): 239-255.

Dawson, J. "Ethnicity, Ideology and Geopolitics in Crimea," *Communist and Post-Communist Studies* 30, no.4 (1997): 427-444.

Diener, A. "Assessing Potential Russian Irredentism and Separatism in Kazakhstan's Northern Oblasts," *Eurasian Geography and Economics* 56, no.5 (2015): 469-492.

Etkind, A. "Post-Soviet Hauntology: Cultural Memory of the Soviet Terror," *Constellations* 16, no.1 (2009): 182-200.

Forest, B. and J. Johnson, "Unravelling the Threads of History: Soviet-era Monuments and Post-Soviet National Identity in Moscow," *Annals of the Association of American Geographers* 92, no.3 (2002): 524-547.

Fregonese, S. "The Urbicide of Beirut? Geopolitics and the Built Environment in the Lebanese Civil War (1975-1976)," *Political Geography* 28 (2009): 309-318.

Fukuyama, F. "The End of History?" *The National Interest* 16 (Summer 1989): 3-18.

Gentile, M. "West-Oriented in the East-Oriented Donbas: A Political Stratigraphy of Geopolitical Identity in Luhansk, Ukraine," *Post-Soviet Affairs* 31, no.3 (2015): 201-223.

Härtel, A. "Where Putin's Russia Ends: 'Novorossija' and the Development of National Consciousness in Ukraine," *International Reports of the Konrad-Adenauer-Stiftung* 2 (2016): 107-125.

Hörschelmann, K. "History After the End: Post-socialist Difference in a (Post) Modern World," *Transactions of the Institute of British Geographers* 27, no.1 (2002): 52-66.

Huntington, S. "The Clash of Civilizations?" *Foreign Affairs* 72, no.3 (1993): 22-49.

Huntington, S. "The West: Unique, Not Universal," *Foreign Affairs* 75, no.6 (1996): 28-46.

Hutchings, S. and Szostek, J. "Dominant Narratives in Russian Political and Media Discourse During the Ukraine Crisis', in *Ukraine and Russia: People, Politics, Propaganda and Perspectives* edited by A. Pikulicka-Wilczewska and R. Sakwa (Bristol: E-International Relations Publishing, 2015), pp. 173-194.

Jekaterynczuk, A. "The Religious Factor of the Russo-Ukrainian War: Selected Aspects," *Naukovi zapiski natsional'noho universitetu 'Ostroz'ka Akademiya', seriya 'Kul'turologiya'* 17 (2016): 251-267.

Katchanovski, I. "Regional Political Divisions in Ukraine in 1991-2006," *Nationalities Papers* 34, no.5 (2006): 507-532.

Koort, K. "The Russians of Estonia - Twenty Years After," *World Affairs* (July/August 2014).

Kubicek, P. "Regional Polarization in Ukraine: Public Opinion, Voting and Legislative Behavior," *Europe-Asia Studies* 52, no.2 (2000): 273-294.

Kulyk, V. "National Identity in Ukraine: Impact of Euromaidan and the War," *Europe-Asia Studies* 68, no.4 (2016): 588-608.

Kuzio, T. "Rise and Fall of the Party of Regions Political Machine," *Problems of Post-Communism* 62, no.3 (2015): 174-186.

Laruelle, M. "The Three Colors of Novorossiya, or the Russian Nationalist Mythmaking of the Ukrainian Crisis," *Post-Soviet Affairs* 32, no.1 (2015): 55-74.

Mamadouh, V. and G. Dijkink, "Geopolitics, International Relations and Political Geography: The Politics of Geopolitical Discourse," *Geopolitics* 11, no.3 (2006): 349-366.

Merritt, M. "A Geopolitics of Identity: Drawing the Line Between Russia and Estonia," *Nationalities Papers* 28, no.2 (2000): 243-262.

Morozov, V. "Russian Society and the Conflict in Ukraine: Masses, Elites and National Identity," in *Migration and the Ukraine Crisis: A Two-Country Perspective* edited by A. Pikulicka-Wilczewska and G. Uehling (Bristol: E-International Relations, 2017).

Munro, N. "Which Way Does Ukraine Face? Popular Orientations Toward Russia and Western Europe," *Problems of Post-Communism* 54, no.6 (2007): 43-58.

Nagle, J. "Ghosts, Memory and the Right to the Divided City: Resisting Amnesia in Beirut City Centre," *Antipode* (2016), pre-published online, DOI: 10.1111/anti.12263.

O'Loughlin, J., G. Ó Tuathail and V. Kolossov, "Russian Geopolitical Culture and Public Opinion: The Masks of Proteus Revisited," *Transactions of the Institute of British Geographers* 30, no.3 (2005): 322-335.

O'Loughlin, J., G. Ó Tuathail and V. Kolossov, "The Geopolitical Orientations of Ordinary Russians: A Public Opinion Analysis," *Eurasian Geography and Economics* 47, no.2 (2006): 129-152.

O'Loughlin, J., G. Ó Tuathail and V. Kolossov, "The Rise and Fall of 'Novorossiya': Examining Support for a Separatist Geopolitical Imaginary in Southeast Ukraine," *Post-Soviet Affairs* (2016), pre-published online, DOI: 10.1080/1060586X.2016.1146452.

Onuch, O. "Brothers Grimm or Brothers Karamazov: The Myth and the Reality of how Russians and Ukrainians View the Other," in *Ukraine and Russia: People, Politics, Propaganda and Perspectives* edited by A. Pikulicka-Wilczewska and R. Sakwa (Bristol: E-International Relations Publishing, 2015), pp. 35-56.

Osipian, A. "Historical Myths, Enemy Images, and Regional Identity in the Donbas Insurgency," *Journal of Soviet and Post-Soviet Politics and Society* 1, no.1 (2015): 109-140.

Pipes, R. "Is Russia Still an Enemy?" *Foreign Affairs* 76, no.5 (1997): 65-78.

Pirie, P. "National Identity and Politics in Southern and Eastern Ukraine," *Europe-Asia Studies* 48, no.7 (1996): 1079-1104.

Portnov, A. "Post-Soviet Ukraine and Belarus Dealing with 'The Great Patriotic War'" in *20 Years after the Collapse of Communism. Expectations, Achievements, and Disillusions of 1989* edited by N. Hayoz, L. Jesień and D. Koleva (Bern: Peter Lang, 2011), 369-381.

Portnov, A. "Post-Maidan Europe and the New Ukrainian Studies," *Slavic Review* 74, no.4 (2015): 723-731.

Radio Svoboda "*Kernes: Pam'yatnik Leninu v Kharkovi ne vidnovliuvatimut'* [Kernes: Lenin monument in Kharkiv not to be restored]," last modified November 20, 2015, http://www.radiosvoboda.org/a/news/27377463.html.

Selga, E. "Latvia's Citizenship Law – A Chink in Latvian Armor," Foreign Policy Research Institute *Baltic Bulletin* 2 (2016), accessed June 28, 2016, http://www.fpri.org/docs/selga_latvia_citizenship.pdf.

Shevel, O. "The Politics of Memory in a Divided Society: A Comparison of Post-Franco Spain and Post-Soviet Ukraine," *Slavic Review* 70, no.1 (2011): 137-164.

Shevel, O. "Decommunization in Post-Euromaidan Ukraine: Law and Practice," PONARS *Eurasia Policy Memo* (January 2016).

Silver, H. "Divided Cities in the Middle East," *City & Community* 9, no.4 (2010): 345-357.

Trimbach, D. and S. O'Lear "Russians in Estonia: Is Narva the Next Crimea?" *Eurasian Geography and Economics* 56, no.5 (2015): 493-504.

Wilson, A. "The Donbas Conflict in 2014: Explaining Civil Conflict Perhaps, but Not Civil War," *Europe-Asia Studies* 68, no.4 (2016): 631-652.

Véron, O. "Contesting the Divided City: Arts of Resistance in Skopje," *Antipode* (2016) pre-published online, DOI: 10.1111/anti.12269.

Young, C. and D. Light, "Place, National Identity and Post-Socialist Transformations: An Introduction," *Political Geography* 20, no.8 (2001): 941-955.

Zhurzhenko, T. "The Geopolitics of Memory," *Eurozine*, May 10, 2007, www.eurozine.com.

Zhurzhenko, T. "Capital of Despair' – Holodomor Memory and Political Conflicts in Kharkiv After the Orange Revolution," *East European Politics and Societies* 25, no.3 (2011): 597-639.

Zhurzhenko, T. "From Borderlands to Bloodlands," *Eurozine*, 19 September 2014, www.eurozine.com.

Zhurzhenko, T. "Memory Wars in Post-Soviet Kharkiv [English translation of 'Erinnerungskonflikte. Gedenkpolitik im postsowjetischen Charkiv']," *Osteuropa* 4 (2015): 153-171.

# 2

# The Social Challenge of Internal Displacement in Ukraine: The Host Community's Perspective

KATERYNA IVASHCHENKO-STADNIK

> *Unknown saints arrived in the city.*
> *They used stones for saying prayers and carpets for spending the nights.*
> *How to reach God now, when the coverage isn't good enough?*
> *Just draw crosses on the houses you need.*
>
> *You anyway won't be happy there, where no one expected you to come.*
> *Exile always turns to one's silent lips[6].*
>
> Serhiy Zhadan, The Templars (2016)

**The Phenomenon of IDPs in Ukraine: Gone with the War?**

With Russia's annexation of Crimea and Russian-backed offensive in Donbas, the forced destabilisation of Ukraine, one of Europe's largest countries, has had devastating security consequences, both internationally

---

[6] (Ukr.) В місті з'явилися невідомі святі,
молились камінню й спали на килимах.
Який зв'язок із Господом при такому покритті?
Малюй хрести на потрібних тобі домах.
...ви все одно не зможете бути щасливими там, де вас ніхто не чекав.
Вигнання завжди обертається тишею на вустах.
Sergyi Zhadan (born in 1974 in Starobelsk, Luhansk region) is a famous Ukrainian poet and civil activist who writes extensively on the issues related to the population in Ukraine's east — before, during and after the conflict. *The Templars*, his latest poem, is devoted to the undeclared war and raises the question of reconciliation, love and hope.

and domestically. According to the UN estimates the potential pool of those who have been affected by the conflict and need humanitarian assistance can be as high as five million individuals, as of October 2015 (USAID, 2016). Having, thus far, a relatively stable migration history, Ukraine has seen an unprecedented exodus of civilians from the conflict-affected territories. Unlike internally displaced persons (IDPs) who can remain unregistered, the estimations on the number of people seeking asylum or other forms of stay abroad are more reliable due to the rather strict cross-border regulations (although, there is no way to verify how many of those left Ukraine as a result of the conflict).

As of August 2015, the number of Ukrainians seeking asylum in neighboring countries was 388,800, other forms of stay — 732,000 (UNHCR, 2015). As Eurostat reports, for the last 12 months (as of the first quarter of 2016) the number of Ukrainians seeking asylum in the European Union reached 19,000 individuals (with a tendency to decrease). It should be noted that most asylum-seekers from Ukraine are refused refugee status because a life-threatening situation is present only in some parts of the country (EUROSTAT, 2016). Most displaced move internally: as of June 2016, 1,783,900 IDPs from Crimea and Donbas have been officially registered (in August 2015 the figure was 1,438,000) (Ministry of Social Policy of Ukraine, 2016). However, experts estimate that the real number of uprooted within Ukraine, including those who do not apply for registration, is considerably higher.

Accuracy aside, one can estimate that no less than four per cent of Ukraine's 42.5 million citizens have been internally displaced due to conflict (something the country had never experienced before[1]). If one takes a global look, in 2015 Ukraine found itself among the five countries in the world with the highest number of IDPs associated with conflict and violence (after Yemen, Syria, Iraq and Nigeria) and ranks first in Europe (GRID 2016). As Ukraine has had little experience of dealing with IDPs, experts argue that it should follow the United Nations principles as regards forced displacement and, specifically, the standards developed during conflicts in the former socialist countries such as Azerbaijan, Georgia, Moldova and Yugoslavia. Still, each individual case creates a unique cluster of problems and each requires sensible policies that can facilitate better strategies.

Contemporary literature on displacement pays a growing attention to the

---

[1] As a Soviet Republic, Ukraine experienced a mass displacement in 1986, when the Chornobyl nuclear accident resulted in the displacement of the affected population (including 116,000 inhabitants from 188 settlements). See Meynatyan S. (2014) Nuclear disasters and displacement *Forced Migration Review*, No.45, February 2014. Available at: http://www.fmreview.org/sites/fmr/files/FMRdownloads/en/crisis/meybatyan.pdf

social dimension of the forced movement, in particular to its conflict-driven patterns. Caused by the 'inability to return readily and freely' to their homes (Brettel 2015, 148-153), it complicates the trauma of one's 'conflict-induced eviction' from the habitual environment, a sudden 'break-up of families, loss of belonging, status and identity' (Rajput 2013, 4-6), something that profoundly distinguishes IDPs from the local population. The arrival of the displaced people into host communities involves a complex intergroup dynamics, often marked by prejudice, stereotyping, discrimination, and power relations (Bradley 2015, Rajput 2015). Experts argue that under poor socioeconomic conditions as well as deteriorating political and security situation, IDPs can fall victim of the host community's intolerance (Haider 2014) which might lead to further clashes (Bohnet et al. 2013, Shlapentokh at al. 2016).

An analysis of contemporary conflicts shows that in a state-sponsored war, civilians living in the enemy camp, even if they are not engaged in hostilities, are conceived by the other side as 'failed citizens' (Diken & Laustsen 2005), as 'neither a friend nor a foe' (Korostelina and Cherkaoui 2012). As previous findings on the contemporary conflicts have shown, when the strategic goal of the targeted violence is to destroy a community's or territory's integrity, intergroup conflicts cannot be described as clear instances of ethnic, religious or other differences (Spini et al. 2014). In that respect, Ukraine constitutes a typical, but at the same time a profoundly difficult, case of displacement.

First, not only the public perception of the displacement's root causes provokes considerable public discontent, but officially, too, the external aggression has not been acknowledged in Ukraine (Batrin 2015). The misleading term 'civil war in Ukraine' widely used by the top Russian officials and, occasionally, by the international community (including the UN high representatives, politicians and foreign observers) infiltrates public discourse through the media channels in a harmful way. The term hybrid war, a different way of defining the conflict in Ukraine that parts of the local and international community use, makes it even more complicated to the wide public[2]. From the host society's perspective, as long as the war remains undeclared but Russian weapons and paramilitary forces are used against Ukraine in the east of the country, the role of the local population in Donbas, be it active or passive, will be perceived as hostile. Although the Ukrainian society in different regions shares ambiguous views of the war, the majority still perceive it as an external aggression with a considerable role of the locals

---

[2] The rather new concept was formed at the end of the Cold War with reference to multi-faceted conflicts consisting of conventional war tactics through both paramilitary and military detachments, cyberwar activities and widely used mass communication channels. See: Hybrid war and the conflict between Russia and Ukraine, *Science Daily*, 3 October 2016. Available at: https://www.sciencedaily.com/releases/2016/10/161003092438.htm

financed and coordinated by the Russian Federation (Ukrainian society 2015, 627-630). With a mass military call-up for the country's conflict in Donbas, local people's escape from the conflict zone often provokes moral stigma. In a sense, they are seen as both victims and perpetrators[3].

Second, Ukraine's IDPs by and large are not a socially, ethnically, religiously or ideologically homogeneous group. They reflect the country's cultural diversity, represent different social strata and have different political views (from a fundamentally pro-Soviet to radically pro-European). In addition, some of the registered displaced persons have not been resettled: they applied for IDP status to claim their social welfare payments in Ukraine (specifically pensions and childcare subsidies), but have been either unable to rent accommodation or unwilling to abandon their dwellings in the occupied territories. As a result, they move back and forth with no endeavour to integrate into a new community. Before a more rigid system of control over payments was launched, many of the 'shuttling IDPs' used their ambivalent status of being-here-and-there to receive double social payments both from the Ukrainian state and from the Donbas self-proclaimed republics[4]. Others have not registered at all (a pattern widespread among the young employed, reluctant to waste time on exhaustive bureaucratic procedures), but were eager to use the opportunity of settling in other parts of Ukraine for good with no will to return, even if the conflict is over.

The phenomenon of 'hybrid IDPs' (having an official status but not being displaced or being displaced without gaining an official status) can be viewed as a consequence of the complexity of the Ukraine crisis and is worth analysing in further studies. What is important for us, is the fact that, without questioning the main role of the Russian authorities in unleashing and maintaining the conflict, the Ukrainian central and regional elites (a firm alloy of oligarchs and people in power) have done everything they could to keep the legal contours of the conflict within the safe margins in order to secure their businesses and status (Pietsukh 2016). Not surprisingly therefore, the public perception of the war and its spinoffs, including the displaced

---

[3] The database created by the National Museum of War and History of Ukraine shows war casualties across the regions. As of 1 March 2016, 2860 Ukrainian soldiers died in Donbas, with four regions recording the highest numbers of deaths (Dnipro — 359, Lviv — 180, Zhytomyr — 177 and Volyn — 150). Although Ukrainian soldiers from Donbas have also taken part in the anti-terrorist operation (Donetsk has lost 79 and Luhansk 48 lives), it is commonly understood that the majority of young men from the occupied territories avoid mass conscription.

[4] Formally, one is not eligible to any social payments from the Ukrainian state if they reside in the occupied territories. However, as my informal talks with the Donbas informants prove, a considerable number of people paid bribes to get their social payments from Ukraine without leaving their place of residence in the occupied area.

population from the east hit by the conflict, remains hybrid too (Samayeva 2016), and we shall see how this is reflected in the survey data.

Although considerably diverse as a group (registered and unregistered, economically active and inactive, pro-Ukrainian, rationally neutral and covertly anti-Ukrainian), IDPs are united in their will to secure their status and gain credibility (Baron and Gatrell 2004, 5). Given the IDPs' uneven distribution across the regions, with the largest concentration in Kyiv, the surrounding Kyiv area and the neighbouring eastern regions (the peaceful parts of Donbas under Ukraine's control as well as Kharkov and Dnipropetrovsk regions), internal displacement can be seen as a process of tremendous change for those who have been 'on the move' or resettled and an unparalleled challenge for those who remain rooted in the host communities.

**New NIMBIES[5]: Are IDPs a Problem to Host Neighborhoods?**

In social analyses of migration processes, three perspectives usually capture the primary interest of researchers: people who move, people who stay behind and people who form host communities (Collier 2013, 22-24). This paper seeks to analyse the last group, to which less attention is usually paid. As the uprooted come to new places to become part of the host landscape, the consequences of this inflowing largely depend on how they are related to by the locals. As my conversations with NGO activists demonstrate, the IDPs, scattered across the country, are limited in exercising their rights to political participation[6] and have problems with raising their collective voice at the top-level domains through the available agencies[7]. In addition, having a

---

[5] Acronym for 'Not in My Back Yard' which is used to label an attitude of individuals who oppose a given project in their neighborhood but not somewhere else (see: Aeschbacher 2006). It is used in literature about facility siting. See: http://www.uns.ethz.ch/pub/publications/pdf/1518.pdf. It also refers to the attitudes of host community who might advocate in favour of a given idea, but oppose implementing it in a way that would affect their lives or require any contribution on their part.

[6] In particular, limitations refer to voting rights as Ukraine's electoral regulations link it to the place of residence.

[7] In the first year of the conflict, the cooperation between NGOs helping IDPs and the Ukrainian state was rather formal and often lacked common sense. Ukrainian authorities 'require a lot but are not ready to offer help' (at the beginning of the conflict, they did not keep record of IDPs and referred to NGOs to get the data; then they used these statistics at their websites with no references to the NGOs). 'The President should admit that they have difficulties with defining the ATO zone and controlling the surrounding area. It is rather clear that they are unable to solve lots of problems any time soon, and more cooperation with other agents is needed', one activist said. 'The responsible ministries do not even admit the existing problems. It seems as if we lived in parallel worlds, so it is very hard to cooperate with them when they are not

dependent status (IDPs from Donbas and Crimea are seen by respondents as the least influential agents in the national social pyramid[8]) (Ukrainian society 2015, 620), they remain subordinated to the public (set by the state) and private (formed by host individuals, groups, networks) regulations. Ukrainian public institutions seem to be designed to sustain the basic displacement management: since the active mechanisms to process IDP applications have been elaborated, it is difficult but still possible to get the payable social package[9] from the state. The available resources are enough to prevent mass IDPs' street begging, yet they are insufficient to stop deprivation among the most vulnerable groups and facilitate a good start for those who are able to become self-sufficient. To survive, move on and, possibly, help those who stayed behind (a common situation of many IDPs who have elderly relatives or other dependants unable to resettle), IDPs need more support from the host community. In order to get access to more resources, they need credibility to be accepted by the locals. In that respect, host communities cannot be underestimated as potentially powerful agents of change in IDPs' new lives. Are they ready for such a role?

It should be noted that internal migration (including intra- and inter-regional circular movements) has been traditionally prevalent over external movements both in the Soviet Ukraine and during the period of independence. In the last decade internal migration amounted to 96 per cent of all movements (about 60 per cent of those were intra-regional movements related to seasonal or long-term labour migration from rural areas and small towns to cities where wages have been traditionally higher than the national average) (Pribytkova 2009, 58-59). Before the crisis — as the freedom of movement was constitutionally guaranteed, and as *propiska*, a rigid scheme

---

straightforward. The main weakness of state authorities is that they do not speak out'. My interview with Aleksandra Dvoretskaya, a human right activist of the VOSTOK-SOS, (one of the most active NGOs advocating for IDPs' rights), 14 November 2014. Although the situation has been slowly changing, many of the drawbacks are still in place.

[8] As the data from 2015 demonstrate, oligarchs are considered the most influential group in the Ukrainian society (by 44.6 per cent of the respondents). They are followed by workers (34.6 per cent), businessmen (33.3), leaders of political parties (27.2), peasants and military men (25.4-25.2). Migrants, including Ukrainian diaspora (9.2), Ukrainian labour migrants (7.5) and foreigners of non-Ukrainian origin (6.4) are among the bottom five groups in terms of influence (together with pensioners - 5.7 and IDPs - 3.4).

[9] Ukraine's IDPs monthly allowance is 441 UAH (nearly 18 USD based on July 2016 exchange rate) for those able to work and 882 UAH (nearly 36 USD) for disabled. The minimum wage in Ukraine is defined as follows: 1450 UAH (59 USD) for those able to work and 1130 UAH (46 USD) for disabled. Regardless of the official income data, the costs of living in Ukraine remain high. See: http://www.numbeo.com/cost-of-living/country_result.jsp?country=Ukraine

of state control over migration, was replaced by a more flexible notification system for registering a place of residence — voluntary movement to a location within the country that promises better jobs, education, environment or housing opportunities was considered to be common (between 20 and 30 per cent of respondents in national surveys report on working outside of their permanent place of residence) (Ukrainian society 2015, 573; Social Impact 2012, 9).

Overall, a person who moved into a given location in order to improve her standards of living was considered 'one of us' (national of the same country), usually making the social space more competitive and bringing little or no risks of destabilisation to the host community. With the forced movements in place, the issue of registration has been brought to focus again: now it is not only controlled by the state but also watched by the host community in a range of situations related to housing, employment, social care, etc. (Mikheeva, Sereda 2015, 29-33). In the public discourse, a displaced person is usually seen as a representative of a victimised group with a descending social mobility associated with lost status, who demonstrates desperate patterns of behaviour and brings high risk of instability to the host neighbourhood[10]. At the same time, in the society struggling with a multi-faceted crisis, those who demonstrate different, successful, social patterns, might cause distrust and provoke discontent, too[11] (CRIMEA SOS 2015).

The data of the recent survey indicate that mass forced displacement has become an established troublesome spot on the social landscape:

---

[10] Arsen Avakov, Ukraine's Interior Minister, argued in September 2016 that the inflow of IDPs to Kyiv (800,000 according to the Ministry's estimations) has been one of the key factors which contributed to the rise in crime (together with three other factors, such as the current economic crisis, continuing war in the East and painful police reform). See: http://nv.ua/ukr/ukraine/events/avakov-nazvav-tri-kljuchovi-prichini-rostu-kriminogennosti-v-ukrajini-227444.html. The IDPs are often depicted in the media as passive recipients of assistance and a cause of price increases, unemployment and lack of social protection services. As CRIMEA SOS's report stated in 2015, criminal news is usually reported with a focus on the place of residence of suspects or victims. See: *Relationships between host communities and IDPs in Ukraine. Overcoming the negative effects of stigma* (2015), CRIMEA SOS, UNHRC, Embassy of Canada in Ukraine. Available at: http://krymsos.com/files/5/9/59137aa-----------------------------------
---eng.pdf

[11] For example, in big Ukrainian cities luxury cars with Donetsk and Luhansk plates are usually referred to by the locals as a typical example of aggressive and rude driving behavior. As the CRIMEA SOS's report suggested, 'the deterioration of the political situation, aggravation of the economic crisis along with reduction/non-allocation of additional resources for IDPs, escalation of armed conflict, increase of IDP population, and degradation of living standards due to the ongoing armed conflict' might have reinforced the negative stereotypes about IDPs.

respondents see the influx of IDPs and other newcomers as a growing fear (with the highest number of such responses in Kyiv — 27 per cent, and the lowest in non-occupied parts of Donetsk and Luhansk regions — three per cent in 2015[12]). Still, facing other pressing issues such as rising prices, unemployment, non-payment of salaries and pensions and external aggression against Ukraine (Ukrainian Society 2015, 564), host populations outside of the capital do not rank IDPs in the top ten fears (see Table 1).

**Table 1: In your view, what do people fear most of all nowadays?**

(all regions, by percentage)

|  | 1992 | 2004 | 2015 | 2016 |
|---|---|---|---|---|
| Rise in prices | 66.4 | 75.2 | 75.4 | 81.1 |
| Unemployment | 60.3 | 67.9 | 70.3 | 72.6 |
| Non-payment of salaries, pensions, etc. | n/a | 56.5 | 68.5 | 61.1 |
| External aggression against Ukraine | 14.2 | 10.5 | 51.8 | 42.8 |
| Rise in crime | 68.0 | 54.9 | 41.3 | 51.4 |
| Famine | 50.3 | 45.5 | 39.0 | 38.8 |
| Shutdown of enterprises | 13.2 | 35.3 | 38.7 | 37.8 |
| Disintegration of the Ukrainian state | 17.2 | 10.8 | 29.3 | 32.5 |
| Street riots | 21.2 | 16.1 | 26.2 | 28.1 |
| Lack of heating in the house | 17.2 | 30.7 | 25.6 | 29.4 |
| Life-threatening infections (tuberculosis, HIV, etc.) | n/a | 43.0 | 19.6 | 23.7 |
| Establishment of a dictatorship in Ukraine | 11.6 | 10.2 | 17.4 | 20.3 |
| Flow of refugees, IDPs and other newcomers | n/a | 7.4 | 15.1 | 20.4 |
| Consequences of the Chornobyl disaster | 46.5 | 24.9 | 12.2 | 11.9 |
| Return to the old system associated with the era of stagnation | 13.2 | 5.2 | 13.1 | 10.9 |
| Interethnic conflicts | 48.9 | 12.8 | 7.8 | 24.9 |
| Interreligious conflicts | n/a | 6.4 | 7.8 | 11.2 |

Source: Українське суспільство 1992-2012. Стан та динаміка змін. Соціологічний моніторинг. (під ред. Ворони В., Шульги М.) Київ: Інститут соціології НАНУ, 2012. [Ukrainian Society: 1992-2012: current status and dynamics of change. Monitoring study] [in Ukrainian] and unpublished data of the 2016 Institute of Sociology's survey.

---

[12] The distribution of answers changes over time with a tendency to become more balanced; in 2016 in Donbas 13.3 per cent of respondents thought that people fear the influx of newcomers, in Kyiv — 21.4.

The unprecedented intensity and mass character of the forced movement in Ukraine explains a high level of personal awareness about the problem among the host population: more than half of respondents in Luhansk and Donetsk regions and more than one fifth in Kyiv have IDPs among people they know, including relatives and friends (see Table 2). However, it does not directly influence the level of personal involvement in supporting the displaced: in 2015 overall less than eight per cent of respondents acknowledged voluntarily helping the IDPs (compare that to 28.3 who helped the Ukrainian army) (Ukrainian society 2015, 640-641). Most claimed that they are either unable to help (from 11.5 per cent in Kyiv to 22.9 in Donetsk and Luhansk) or think that it is the state that should be responsible for such assistance (from 12.8 per cent in the west to 33.7 in Donbas).

The ambivalent response of the host community is also illustrated by the views on state policies towards the disputed territories, those who stayed behind and those who moved. In spring and summer of 2015 nearly a third of respondents found it difficult to decide what Ukraine should do in relation to the parts of Donbas currently out of its control; 38 per cent thought that Ukraine should wait until the economic situation in Donbas further deteriorates and recovers in Ukraine to restore the integrity of the state; 18.9 per cent would have supported a military action to return the lost territories; and 12.4 per cent said that Ukraine should abandon Donbas as a ballast hindering the country's development (Ukrainian society 2015, 631). Only one third supported the idea of Ukraine's financial support for the territories outside of its control because citizens of Ukraine live there; 32 per cent were in favour of the self-proclaimed bodies taking care of the own budgets; 19 per cent — in favour of Russia taking care of Donbas. Finally, nearly 18 per cent found it difficult to answer what the state policy towards the IDPs should be, 5.2 per cent were against any state support for the displaced; 34.2 were in favor of the regular social support for the IDPs from the state; 21.9 per cent thought the state should reimburse them their lost property; and 46.2 per cent argued that certain amendments should be made to national laws to enable IDPs' entrepreneurship and further integration into their new environment[13] (Ukrainian society 2015, 631).

---

[13] That was a multiple-option question in the questionnaire.

**Table 2: Having IDPs from Donbas and Crimea among family members, friends or other people you know personally (if DO HAVE, where they are now)**

(selected regions, by percentage)

|  | Non-occupied parts of Donbas | East | Kyiv | West | All Ukraine |
|---|---|---|---|---|---|
| Stay in the same place/region where I live | 21.7 | 12.5 | 12.2 | 11.8 | 11.5 |
| Stay in a different region (other than where I live) | 32.5 | 14.3 | 5.8 | 11.7 | 12.9 |
| Stay in Russia | 38.6 | 10.8 | 6.5 | 3.2 | 9.5 |
| Stay abroad | 4.2 | 3.4 | 5.1 | 2.9 | 3.5 |
| Don't have IDPs among people I know | 37.3 | 57.7 | 66.9 | 66.4 | 64.9 |
| No response | 9.0 | 8.6 | 9.4 | 11.2 | 7.8 |
| Voluntary helping the IDPs | 13.9 | 9.8 | 15.1 | 2.4 | 7.9 |

Source: Іващенко К., Стегній О. (2015) Між близькістю та відчуженням: ставлення населення України до вимушених переселенців з Криму та Донбасу (проблеми, тенденції та рекомендації) Українське суспільство: моніторинг соціальних змін (під ред. Ворони В., Шульги М.). Київ: Інститут соціології НАНУ, с.295. [*Between closeness and alienation: the attitudes of the Ukraine's population towards IDPs from Crimea and Donbas: problems, tendencies and policy recommendation*] [in Ukrainian].

A reference to the NIMBY ('Not in My Back Yard') concept seems applicable here as long as the Ukrainian society finds itself in the trap of ambiguous loyalties. Traditionally, people tolerate newcomers of the same culture and ethnicity (Panina 2005, Pribytkova 2006). Nowadays, when, in light of its ambitions to join the European Union, Ukraine has to adhere to the European standards of tolerance, this attitude is also widely supported by the mainstream. Yet, during the conflict and hardship, the society has not avoided radicalisation and often loose neutrality, particularly when the stakes are high. Independence, reforms and growth do not necessarily require one shared national language, ethnicity and undisputed attitudes to the country's historical past (Hrytsak 2016, Milakovsky 2016), but common values and shared goals seem indispensable to move ahead. Whatever side of the ideological divide one is on, all levels of interaction — **private** (communicating with family, friends, neighbours), **professional** (co-working) and **civil** (co-existing as citizens) inevitably entail the issues of trust and mutual responsibility. Sometimes, working together and living nearby IDPs in one's own neighbourhood *now* might be a more challenging task than advocating for the vague, as yet, imaginary plan of Donbas' reintegration into

Ukraine *after the war*[14].

**Alienation vs Cooperation**

Although a recent study by the United Nations Refugee Agency (UNHCR) shows that after the two years of conflict more than 80 per cent of respondents declared to be positive or neutral towards IDPs (UNHCR, 2016), placing the research focus on the displaced itself indicates a high public concern over the issue. Media and NGOs' reports indicate a growing anxiety over social marginalisation of this group in Ukraine and make it emblematic as a potential threat to the established community's tolerance in relation to the displaced from the east, particularly, as the conflict in Donbas escalates (CRIMEA SOS 2015). The lack of appropriate approaches leads to the situation which is described by experts in terms of causes and consequences: being triggered by conflicts, they can 'directly or indirectly be involved in the conflict diffusion process' (Bohnet et al. 2013). We will see if playing on these fears resonates with the data.

In this study, using a modification of the Emory Bogardus Social Distance scale which measures secure interpretations of the varying degrees and grades of feeling that exist in a range of social situations (Bogardus 1925, 299), further work has been carried out on adjusting and updating questionnaire tools to compare 'levels of acceptance' defined by the host population in relation to different migration-based groups in the three general domains of social relations: private, professional, and civil[15]. It is suggested that 'the practice of allowing or permitting' others, which is possible only if one is in a position to allow or disallow, reflects toleration (Raphael 1988, 139) and helps to understand how far one group of people think to differ from another group 'in their intentions, powers and values' (Rummel 1975).

The core of primary data on which this paper is based was obtained from the representative national survey of Ukrainian society (N = 1802 aged 18 and above) conducted by the Institute of Sociology (Kyiv, Ukraine). The fieldwork was conducted in July 2015 in all regions of the country

---

[14] See Vice-Minister for Occupied Territories' comment on Ukraine's plan to Reintegrate Donbas (24 July 2016). Available at: http://podrobnosti.ua/2122350-tuka-objasnil-razlichija-mezhdu-interesami-kieva-i-kremlja.html. What if Donbas is ours tomorrow? *Novoje vremia*, 9 February 2016. Available at: http://nv.ua/ukr/project/Donbas-nash.html

[15] For more details on the research methodology, see: Ivashchenko-Stadnik K. (2016) *Too close or too far: contemporary challenges and opportunities of the 'Near Diasporas' from a country of origin perspective (warning on migrants-stayers nexus)*, Wien, ERSTE Foundation Working Paper Series (forthcoming).

(excluding the annexed Crimea and occupied parts of Donbas). The randomly selected respondents were asked to complete self-administered questionnaires, which, among other thematic sections covering a broad range of topics related to socio-economic and political issues, included an ad-hoc set of questions on attitudes towards IDPs.

*Private Level: Neighbours versus Friends*

Forced migration is usually a rapid movement that puts at risk personal ties and networks. Once the established connections are left behind, one has to engage with other people. For most IDPs the initial level of being introduced to the host environment is often connected with a purely formal (vertical, rigid, based on collectivity, and fixed by agreements such as the available IDPs-related legislation) process of applying to state institutions for necessary documents to confirm their displaced status (required in order to receive basic social benefits). In rare cases, state agencies are able to provide adequate assistance in finding jobs and making housing arrangements. Nevertheless, the majority of IDPs use the informal (horizontal, less rigid, either based on personality or narrow groups, not based on contracts) social networks to get fundamental needs met. It is the host population that is in a position to decide if a newcomer can be accepted as a member of the informal local network, and if one's engagement is successful. As the economist Paul Collier acutely notes, 'in a modern economy well-being is greatly enhanced by mutual regard' that is 'something stronger than mutual respect (fulfilled by keeping a respectful distance from others' in the "Don't dis me" society)'; mutual respect is 'akin to sympathy or being fellow-feeling' (Collier 2013, 61). Sympathy is also connected to loyalty and solidarity with those fellow members who are less fortunate (Collier 2013, 62).

The data obtained in 2015 show that the degrees of closest possible acceptance of the displaced people are different across the two groups: the IDPs from Crimea are generally a little more welcome than those from Donbas (although in most cases the difference remains fairly within the margin of sampling error, it is still stable on all levels, from private to civil). The data present interesting observations across regions: the difference in attitudes of the respondents from the east and the respondents from the non-occupied Donbas is much bigger than if we take east-west or east-Kyiv perspectives[16]. It is revealed that on the private level accepting IDPs as 'neighbours' would be the most comfortable option for a majority of the respondents in all regions. The figure indicates that private level acceptance for the displaced drops when it requires 'fellow-feelings' (family members,

---

[16] As other recent data confirm, east-Kyiv-west form a new line of the national identity in Ukraine.

friends) — see Figure 1. This tendency is also confirmed by the qualitative data collected by other researchers: the IDPs, in particular those from Donbas, are often perceived by the locals in the majority of Ukraine's host regions as bearers of different (non-fellow) values, that is why they usually prefer 'not to speak up in public' as it might reveal their 'otherness' (Mikheeva, Sereda 2015, 26-27).

**Figure 1: Views on accepting IDPs on the private level by percentage across regions**

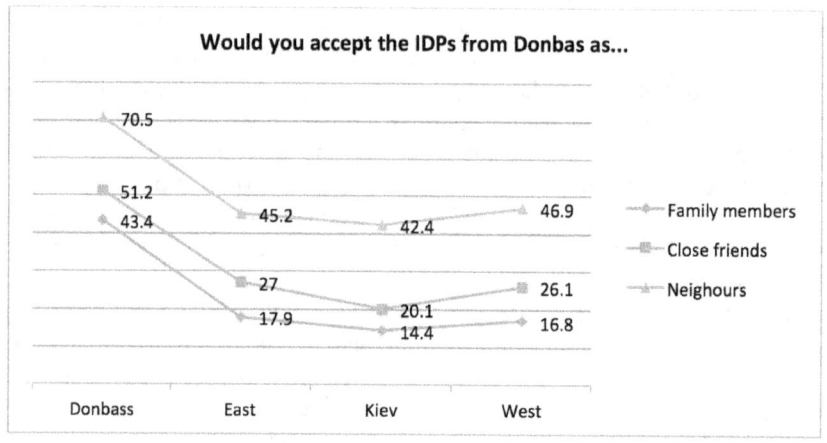

* Donbas here and onwards in the tables includes only territories under Ukraine's control.

*Professional level: co-workers versus 'employer-employee'*

There is statistical evidence that the flow of newcomers might have different economic effects on host communities. One of the possible scenarios in low-income countries like Ukraine is that the wages of lower skill workers drop, the pressure on housing increases and the number of dependants per person of working age rises (Collier 2013, 111-117, 123). Indeed, the recent International Organisation for Migration's report confirms such trends and points out that the influx of IDPs into regional communities has been a strain on local budgets and local social infrastructure (IOM 2016). However, the focused study of IDPs proves that only 11 per cent of them are people of retirement age and people with special needs, while 35 per cent are children. The remaining majority are people of working age. At the same time, the IOM survey series on IDPs integration reveals that only slightly more than a half of those employed before displacement managed to find a job at a new place (IOM 2016).

The real statistics are made of thousands of individual stories of succeeding and falling behind in the Ukrainian chaotic, rarely competitive and often non-competitive (largely based on networks and personal connections) labour market. Apart from the confused rules and requirements on the part of employers, another important factor of low employment rate among the IDPs is the lack of motivation for re-entering labour marker in the new place: less than one-tenth of the surveyed registered displaced persons reported their need for employment (Kharchenko, Panioto 2015). The main reason is usually a manifested intention to return (eight per cent among the surveyed Crimean IDPs, nearly 50 per cent among the Donetsk IDPs and nearly 40 per cent among the Luhansk IDPs confirmed in 2015 their plans to go back home). Still, a majority of the displaced either have no clear visions of their future or have decided that the return is not possible at all (IOM 2015, 12). Obviously, they need more integration to the local labour market and should look for network connections with the host population.

The figure below demonstrates the models of 'office hierarchy' the respondents representing the host community would assign to IDPs: most would choose co-workers rather than 'employer-employee' type of relationships. The levels of acceptance are almost identical for the displaced from Donbas and Crimea and follow similar models in all regions, except for a slightly higher acceptance in favour of IDPs in a supervisory role in Donbas and, surprisingly, in the west (considering a particularly low level of real employment rate among IDPs in the western region in 2014-2015 – see *Migration during crisis*, 2015. The latter might reflect some encouraging tolerance for IDPs to enter the local labour market)[17]. However, a generally modest acceptance of the IDPs as potential employees in all regions not only reflects many problems related to the widespread prejudices about the displaced as unreliable workers (ready to quit any time, particularly if hot conflict in their location is over), heavy-industry-oriented type of labour force (which is partly true) etc., but also indicates that the national labour market is in trouble (a growing gap between the number of people looking for a job and the number of vacancies, low wages, unstable career of local workers in unstable economy).

---

[17] Such subjective reinforcement, together with the effective local policies, seems to have produced some results. Recent reports of 2016 argue that IDPs resettled in the west, although not very numerous as compared to the east, are increasingly proactive in seeking employment (the number of those who have applied to the employment service is significantly higher than in the east of Ukraine, as of June 2016) (Smal 2016).

**Figure 2: Views on accepting IDPs on the professional level by percentage across region**

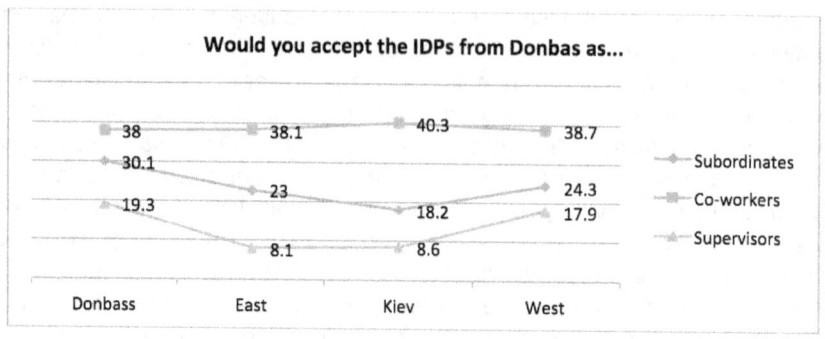

*Civil Level: Semi-citizens with a Limited Access to the Top?*

The economic and humanitarian consequences of displacement usually draw the biggest attention of experts who study IDPs. However, as successful institutions and inclusive practices are crucial for economic and social well-being, the political/civic concerns should not be ignored. Displacement should be seen not only as a burden to the local budgets, but also as a factor that generates pressure for better governance and reforms (Collier 2013, 180). Different domains of citizenship refer to the rights of an individual to participate in civil, political, socio-economic and cultural spaces (Hébert, Sears 2001). Our study focused on the two key domains: political – involving the right to vote and to possess political power, and economic – implying the access to benefits.

The post-Euromaidan Ukraine remains a country hobbled by ill political practices which are often mistakenly explained as post-Soviet legacies. Corruption, the lack of transparency, low competitiveness and a high degree of nepotism in the national decision-making at all levels are rigorously preserved by the Ukrainian crisis-driven elite (often raised after the Soviet period), as strongholds of their power positions. Whether the current crisis in Crimea and Donbas is the local citizens' fault, or the central and local elite proved unable or unwilling to protect Ukraine's territorial integrity and sovereignty, remain the big questions for further discussions and, hopefully, impartial investigations. Whatever the answer is, the issues of inclusive citizenship, both for the displaced and the host communities, are crucial for Ukraine's future development.

The figure below shows what the host community views as acceptable empowerment of IDPs in terms of their participation in public bodies (including participation in local and central authorities). In all regions, the lower the level of power, the higher the acceptance — see Figure 3.1. Although the displaced as potential people in charge of local bodies would be seen more favourably in Donbas than in the rest of the regions, the subjective demand for IDPs' participation in local and central authorities is low everywhere. It should be mentioned that people from the Donetsk and Luhansk regions dominated the most influential spheres of the national economy and public administration for more than a decade before the crisis and often triggered disappointment, anger and fatigue in the local debates (Leshchenko 2015; Forostyna 2015; Kudelia and Kuzio 2015). Lots of the Yanukovich clan's remnants still hold power positions. Thus, the references to IDPs' urgent needs occasionally made in public by the high-rank representatives of the troublesome regions are not enough to encourage inclusive citizenship of the displaced. The data illustrate a strikingly low level of acceptance of IDPs as fully-fledged citizens with voting rights in all regions. The challenge is underestimated: unable to vote (as Ukraine's electoral regulations link the exercise of electoral rights to the place of residence), IDPs are denied a voice in the key decisions that directly affect the country's life and, indirectly, influence scenarios for their future.

Yet, in public's view, restrictions on voting rights are compensated by some limited allowances in the economic sphere: 12 per cent in Kyiv and 15 per cent in the west would accept tax exemptions for IDPs from Donbas (although the figure is modest, it is almost twice as high as that for labour migrants, regardless of their unprecedented role in the national economy[18]) — see Figure 3.2. The data meaningfully speak of the different approach towards the IDPs as potential holders of power positions across the regions: with the lower per cent of allowing answers in the east, known since the conflict for its strong pro-Ukrainian attitudes[19], and the highest in the Ukraine-controlled Donbas. For all regions, IDPs are more likely to be accepted in positions which allow little space for possibly discomforting narratives, views, and decisions. Allowing someone as a co-participant in the political process requires trust which is rather impossible 'without a clear understanding of the political motivations involved', therefore exchange of views 'are crucial for establishing durable solutions' (Lischer 2007, 144).

---

[18] According to the National Bank of Ukraine in 2014 the remittances sent from abroad made up 6.5 billion USD which constituted nearly five per cent of Ukraine's GDP.
[19] See Zhurzhenko T. (2015). Ukraine's Eastern Borderlands: The end of ambiguity? / *What does Ukraine think?* (edited by Andrew Wilson). European Council of Foreign Relations, 46. Available at: http://www.ecfr.eu/page/-/WHAT_DOES_UKRAINE_THINK_pdf.pdf (Accessed 10 October 2016). As Zhurzhenko points out, 'the Ukrainian east reflects a new pro-Ukrainian consensus among local elites, business, and civil society, one that has emerged in response to the serious threat of internal destabilisation and Russian invasion'.

**Figure 3.1: Views on accepting IDPs on the political level by percentage across regions**

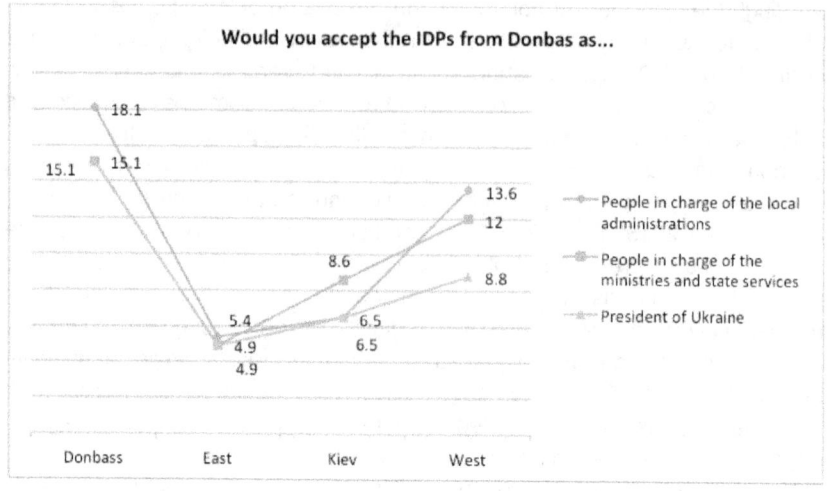

**Figure 3.2: Views on accepting IDPs on the civil and economic levels by percentage across regions**

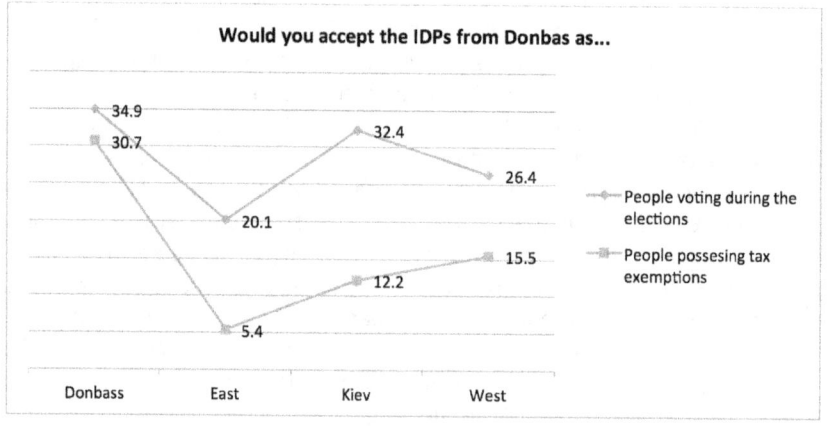

Speaking of the factors that influence the level of tolerance, data show that age does not have a significant impact on one's acceptance of IDPs, contrary to education, which appears to be an important factor (the higher the level of education, the higher the level of tolerance). The regional factor is the most significant of all the socio-demographic categories (on the private level, the highest tolerance towards the IDPs from Donbas is observed in the Ukraine-held border territories of the Donetsk and Luhansk regions, and towards the IDPs from Crimea — in Donetsk, Luhansk and the south). Moreover, respondents from small cities and villages are more welcoming towards the IDPs on all levels (presumably, that owes to the less competitive environment in small urban and rural areas). Type of employment has some influence on the acceptance on the professional level (small entrepreneurs are likely to accept IDPs as employees, and workers of state-owned enterprises are willing see IDPs as co-workers). Importantly, the effect of language on the acceptance of IDPs is low across all regions.

**Conclusion: Reframing the Challenge of Internal Displacement**

We have seen that the problem of internal displacement in Ukraine cannot be explained in pure numbers (due to under-registration) and should not be understood in terms of a simplistic model of positive-negative attitudes towards the IDPs in host communities (owing to the complicated political context beyond the forced movement in Ukraine). As the conflict is not over, it remains unclear how far it will go and whether the eventual return of the majority of the displaced is even possible. In any of the feasible scenarios, keeping the IDPs on the margins of society will not serve the host communities' interests.

Although the surveys' data indicate that only roughly one-fifth of the respondents have negative views of IDPs from Donbas and Crimea and would not accept them in any of the positions on private, professional and civil levels, the remaining vast positive spectrum should not be misinterpreted as unconditionally welcoming attitudes. It stands as an open question whether neutral or positive perception of the IDPs, manifested during the survey, can provide a firm ground for a friendly interaction in real life (equally, negative views, if not contextualised, might or might not lead to real hostilities). Still, attitudes might predetermine the reality. As social practice proves, intolerance in relation to newcomers is spontaneous (Mukomel 2014), particularly if they remain badly integrated (Mikheeva, Sereda 2015). Even if the IDPs are of the same ethnic origin as the host community, as in the case of Ukraine, possible 'strained relations, frustration and indifference' (OSCE 2016) towards them call upon a discussion on their status and future role in the host environment.

The issue of mutual respect between the host and the uprooted groups involves not only trust and sympathy but also equal distribution of civil rights and duties. As the data demonstrate, after the two years of conflict the IDPs are still perceived by large part of the host community as semi-fellows and semi-citizens limited in their access to society's life. Reframing such attitudes is indispensable to avoid camp-type recognition of the IDPs. If not accepted as equals, they will not be able to contribute to the competitiveness and facilitate positive changes. The host community and the displaced need to understand each other in the new post-Euromaidan reality. The lack of possibilities for future inclusive development in one state seems to be the biggest challenge for both.

**References**

Aeschbacher, M. "Not in My Backyard," Swiss Federal Institute of Technology, 2006, http://www.uns.ethz.ch/pub/publications/pdf/1518.pdf

Avakov, A. Speech by Ukraine's Interior Minister on IDPs and Crime in Ukraine, September 2016, http://nv.ua/ukr/ukraine/events/avakov-nazvav-tri-kljuchovi-prichini-rostu-kriminogennosti-v-ukrajini-227444.html

Baron, N. and Gatrell, P. eds. *Homelands: War, Population, and Statehood in Eastern Europe and Russia, 1918–1924*, London: Anthem Press, 2004.

Batrin, S. "War Against Russia: The Legal Front," *Dzerkalo Tyzhnia*, 10 April 2015, http://gazeta.dt.ua/internal/viyna-proti-rosiyi-yuridichniy-front-_.html

Bogardus, E.S. "Measuring Social Distances," *Journal of Applied Sociology* 9 (1925): 299-308, https://www.brocku.ca/MeadProject/Bogardus/Bogardus_1925c.html

Bohnet, H., Cottier, F., Hug, S. "Conflict-Induced IDPs and the Spread of Conflict" (paper presented at the European Political Science Association (EPSA) in Barcelona, 20-22 June 2013) http://www.unige.ch/ses/spo/static/simonhug/ciasc/BohnetCottierHug2013_EPSA_Barcelone.pdf

Bradley, M. ed. *Forced Migration, Reconciliation and Justice*, Montreal: McGill-Queen's University Press, 2015.

Brettel, C., Holifield J. *Migration Theory: Talking Across Disciplines*, New York, London: Routledge, 2015.

Collier, P. *Exodus: How Migration is Changing Our World*. Oxford, New York: Oxford University Press, 2013.

CRIMEA SOS, UNHRC, and the Embassy of Canada in Ukraine, "Relationships Between Host Communities and IDPs in Ukraine: Overcoming the Negative Effects of Stigma of IDPs, including the Community of Crimean

Tatars and the Roma community in Kharkiv (2015), http://krymsos.com/files/5/9/59137aa----------------------------------------eng.pdf

Diken B., Lausten C.B. *The Culture of Exception: Sociology Facing the Camp*, New York, London: Routledge, 2005.

EU Commission DG Employment, Social Affairs, and Inclusion, *Social Impact of Emigration and Rural-Urban Migration in Central and Eastern Europe: Ukraine* (April 2012), http://ec.europa.eu/social/BlobServlet?docId=8820&langId=en

EUROSTAT, *Asylum Quarterly Report*, 15 June 2016, http://ec.europa.eu/eurostat/statistics-explained/index.php/Asylum_quarterly_report#Where_do_they_come_from.3F

Forostyna, O. "Poaching, Simmering, and Boiling: The Declining Relevance of Identity Discourse in Ukraine, 2015, http://www.ecfr.eu/page/-/WHAT_DOES_UKRAINE_THINK_pdf.pdf

Haider, H. *Refugee, IDP and host community radicalization (GSDRC Helpdesk Research Report 1162)*, Birmingham, UK: GSDRC, University of Birmingham (2014), http://www.gsdrc.org/docs/open/hdq1162.pdf.

Hébert, Y., & Sears, A. "Citizenship education," Canadian Educational Association (2001), accessed 20 July 2016, http://www.cea-ace.ca/sites/cea-ace.ca/files/cea-2004-citizenship-education.pdf

Hrytsak Y. *Passions Around Nationalism: Old History in a New Manner Essays*, Kyiv: Krytyka, 2011: 284-297.

Internal Displacement Monitoring Centre, *GRID 2016: Global Report on Internal Displacement* (2016), http://www.internal-displacement.org/globalreport2016/

International Organization for Migration, *National Monitoring System of the Situation with IDPs*. Round 1-2 (March/April 2016), http://www.iom.org.ua/sites/default/files/iom_nms_r1_eng.pdf and http://www.iom.org.ua/sites/default/files/iom_nms_r2-v.pdf

Ivashchenko-Stadnik, K. "Too Close or Too Far: Contemporary Challenges and Opportunities of the 'Near Diasporas' from a Country of Origin Perspective," Wien, ERSTE Foundation Working Paper Series (forthcoming)

Іващенко, К., Стегній О. «Між близькістю та відчуженням: ставлення населення України до вимушених переселенців з Криму та Донбасу (проблеми, тенденції та рекомендації), Українське суспільство: моніторинг соціальних змін (під ред. Ворони В., Шульги М.). Київ: Інститут соціології НАНУ, с.295." [Between closeness and alienation: the attitudes of the Ukraine's population towards IDPs from Crimea and Donbas: problems, tendencies and policy recommendation] [in Ukrainian]," 2015.

Kudelia, S. and Kuzio, T. "Nothing Personal: Explaining the Rise and Decline of Political Machines in Ukraine," *Post-Soviet Affairs* 31, no.3 (2015): 254-255, 274.

Leshchenko, S. "Sunset and/or Sunrise of the Ukrainian Oligarchs after the Maidan: What Does Ukraine Think?" European Council of Foreign Relations, 2015: 100-101.

Lischer, S.K. "Causes and Consequences of Conflict-Induced Displacement," *Civil Wars*, vol. 9 issue 2 (2007) 142-155.

Meynatyan, S. "Nuclear Disasters and Displacement," *Forced Migration Review*, no. 45 (February 2014), http://www.fmreview.org/sites/fmr/files/FMRdownloads/en/crisis/meybatyan.pdf

Міхеєва, О., Середа, В. «Сучасні українські внутрішньо переміщені особи: основні причини, стратегії переселення та проблеми адаптації," Стратегії трансформації і превенції прикордонних конфліктів в Україні Збірка аналітичних матеріалів 2014-2015. Львів: Галицька видавнича спілка, 9-49. [Contemporary Ukrainian IDPs: main causes, resettlement strategies and adaptation problems [in Ukrainian] (2015), http://peace.in.ua/wp-content/uploads/2016/02/%D1%83%D0%BC%D1%88-%D0%B2%D0%B5%D0%BB%D0%B8%D0%BA%D0%B0-%D0%BA%D0%BD%D0%B8%D0%B8%D0%B3%D0%B0.pdf

Milakovsky, B. "Understanding the 'Under Control' Donbas," *Kennan Cable* 16 (2016), https://www.wilsoncenter.org/publication/kennan-cable-no16-understanding-the-under-control-donbas#sthash.0MRj9lyj.dpuf

Ministry of Social Policy of Ukraine, "Report of the Ministry of Social Policy of Ukraine, http://www.ukrinform.net/rubric-society_and_culture/2042256-number-of-idps-in-ukraine-shrinks.html

Мукомель, В. "Ксенофобия как стержень российского общества," Фундаментальные проблемы модернизации полиэтничного макрорегиона в условиях роста напряженности: *сборник рефератов*. [Xenophobia as a pivot of the Russia's society] (2015), http://www.usd.cas.cz/wp-content/uploads/2014/12/referaty1.pdf

National Museum of War and History of Ukraine, "War Casualties Database," http://nvimu.com.ua/

*Novoje Vremia*, "What if Donbas is Ours Tomorrow?" 9 February 2016, http://nv.ua/ukr/project/Donbas-nash.html

NUMBEO, "Cost of Living in Ukraine," http://www.numbeo.com/cost-of-living/country_result.jsp?country=Ukraine

Obozrevatel, "War Casualties Across the Regions of Ukraine," 11 April 2016, http://ukr.obozrevatel.com/society/24915-u-merezhi-zyavivsya-poimennij-spisok-vsih-ukrainskih-voiniv-yaki-zaginuli-v-zoni-ato.html

Паніотто, В., Харченко, Н. «Актуальний стан справ в українському суспільстві." Звіт результатів опитування за травень 2015. Київський міжнародний інститут соціології. [The current situation in the Ukrainian society. Data of the survey conducted in May 2015] [in Ukrainian], http://kiis.com.ua/?lang=ukr&cat=reports&id=529&page=1

Паніна, Н. «Чинники національної ідентичності, толерантності, ксенофобії та антисемітизму в сучасній Україні,» Соціологія: теорія, методи, маркетинг. Київ: Інститут соціології НАНУ, №4, 26–45 (2005) [Factors of national identity, tolerance, xenophobia and anti-Semitism in the contemporary Ukraine] [in Ukrainian]

Прибыткова, И. "Помаранчевый мир над Майданом: социальная дистанция как индикатор консолидации общества," Социологические исследования современного общества: методология, теория, методы, № 723, 133-139 (2006) [The Orange Peace over Maidan: social distance as society's consolidation indicator [in Russian]

Прибыткова, И. "Хроники миграционных событий в Украине до и после распада СССР," Социология: теория, методы, маркетинг. Киев: Институт социологии НАНУ, №1. (2009) [Chronicles of migration events in Ukraine before and after the collapse of the USSR] [in Russian]

Rajput, S.G. "Internal Displacement: Simplifying a Complex Social Phenomenon," *Beyond Intractability* (2013), http://www.beyondintractability.org/rajput-internal-displacement

Rajput, S. "Displacement of the Kashmiri Pandits: Dynamics of Policies and Perspectives of Policymakers, Host Communities, and the Internally Displaced Persons (IDPs)," PhD diss., George Mason University, 2012.

Raphael, D. "The intolerable" in *Justifying Toleration: Conceptual and Historical Perspective*, Cambridge: Cambridge University Press, 1988.

Rothbart, D., Korostelina, K., Cherkaoui M.D. (eds.) *Civilians and Modern War: Armed Conflict and the Ideology of Violence*. New York, London: Routledge, 2012.

Rummel, R.J. *Understanding Conflict and War Vol. 1: The Dynamic Psychological Field*, Beverly Hills, California: Sage Publications, 1975.

Samayeva, Y. "VIZual Cruelty," *Zerkalo Nedeli*, 8-13 October 2016, http://m.zn.ua/internal/vizualnaya-zhestkost-_.html

*Science Daily*, "Hybrid War and the Conflict Between Russia and Ukraine," 3 October 2016, https://www.sciencedaily.com/releases/2016/10/161003092438.htm

Shlapentokh, V., Sendich, M., Payin, E. *The New Russian Diaspora: Russian Minorities in the Former Soviet Republics*, Armonk, N.Y.: M.E. Sharpe, 1994.

Smal, V. "A Great Migration: What is the Fate of Ukraine's Internally Displaced Persons," *Vox Ukraine* ( June 2016), http://voxukraine.org/2016/06/30/great-migration-how-many-internally-displaced-persons-are-there-in-ukraine-and-what-has-happened-to-them-en/

Spini, D., Elcheroth, G., Biruski, D. *War, Community, and Social Change. Collective Experience in the Former Yugoslavia*, New York: Springer, 2014.

Українське суспільство 1992-2015. Моніторинг соціальних змін. Соціологічний моніторинг. Київ: Інститут соціології НАНУ. [Ukrainian Society: 1992-2015: the dynamics of social change] [in Ukrainian]

UNHCR, "Internally Displaced People," 2011, http://unhcr.org/ua/en/2011-08-26-06-58-56/news-archive/1244-internal-displacement-map

UNHCR, *Ukrainians' Attitudes Towards IDPs from Donbas and Crimea. Summary of Opinion Polls* (2016), http://unhcr.org.ua/attachments/article/1605/Public%20Survey%20Report_ENG.pdf

USAID, "Conflict Fact Sheet: Ukraine, no. 1," 2016, http://www.cidi.org/wp-content/uploads/11.19.15-USG-Ukraine-Fact-Sheet-1.pdf

Vedernikova, I. "Dead Souls and Live Money," *Zerkalo Nedeli*, 26 April 2016, http://gazeta.zn.ua/internal/mertvye-dushi-i-zhivye-dengi-_.html

Zhurzhencko, T. "Ukraine's Eastern Borderlands: The End of Ambiguity?" in What Does Ukraine Think? Edited by Andrew Wilson, European Council of Foreign Relations, 2015: 46, http://www.ecfr.eu/page/-/WHAT_DOES_UKRAINE_THINK_pdf.pdf

# 3

# 'Strangers Among Ours': State and Civil Responses to the Phenomenon of Internal Displacement in Ukraine

TANIA BULAKH

Last summer I packed some household items to donate to a humanitarian centre for internally displaced persons (IDPs) in Kyiv. I called a taxi and when it arrived, a friend of mine volunteered to carry the bags to the car. As I was buckling my seatbelt, I noticed that my friend took a picture of the car's license plate. A minute later I received a text from her, saying: 'please, let me know when you arrive.' I was surprised by her concern for my safety. When I called and asked what was it about, she said: 'Didn't you see? He had a Donetsk number plate. I was worried about you.' In response, I told her that the driver offered me a free ride when he learned where we were heading. This incident is one of the signs of a growing tendency to categorise displaced people from the Donbas region of Ukraine as a social threat. In an exacerbated realm of hybrid war in Eastern Ukraine, increasing social tension could potentially escalate into more hostile confrontations. Thus, a critical examination and understanding of IDPs categorisation and its repercussions have significant importance.

In this chapter, I explore the transformations of responses toward the phenomenon of IDPs in Ukraine. My specific focus is the labelling of IDPs from Donbas, their acceptance and further alienation from a collective identity of 'ours.' Though the tendency to socially marginalise displaced people is a common problem all over the world (Malkki 1996, Pandolfi 2003, Calhoun 2008, Fassin 2012, Dunn 2012), my interest is to follow the dynamics from the de-terrorisation of people from Donbas to an accentuated image of Donbas; from a companionate acceptance as 'ours' (свої) to a growing rejection and outlawing. I aim to elucidate the internal diversity of Ukrainian IDPs, when those from Eastern Ukraine are perceived as less privileged, politically threatening subjects, while internal refugees from the annexed Crimea are often embraced as sufferers of political injustice. The hierarchy of othering and challenges of IDPs inclusion into a larger national community highlight nuances of identity politics in Ukraine, problematise equal access to social welfare, as well as jeopardise social stability in the country.

My analysis is based on fieldwork conducted in Ukraine in the summers of 2014 and 2015. This included participant observations at humanitarian centres, analysis of media discourses, and 13 in-depth interviews with aid providers for IDPs, such as representatives of the Ministry of Social Policy of Ukraine, local social welfare officers, representatives of international NGOs, and volunteers from Kyiv and Kharkiv. Exploring the perception of displaced people, I narrowed the pool of my informants to those who are directly involved in making decisions about welfare support. In this way, they have the power to translate emotionally charged negative or positive perceptions of IDPs into actions, for instance, influence the distribution of aid. In other words, their attitudes toward IDPs have tangible economic repercussions for the latter. However, I acknowledge that quite different perspectives can be obtained through studying how IDPs adapt in local communities and are perceived among them.

One of the major challenges I encountered while working on this project was the issue of prejudices and stereotypes in relation to IDPs. These generalisations are based on 'fixity' which Homi Bhabha defines as a central component 'in the ideological construction of otherness' (Bhabha 1996). Fixity induces reproduction of stereotypes, often without their critical examination. In this process, the Other is constructed as essentially or even ontologically different. Importantly, the knowledge about the Other is not grounded in actual experiences, but rather dissimilated and replicated through repetitions. Bhabha's explanation of fixity captures the danger that stereotypes present, namely that they produce an unchanging order, which is often taken for granted and maintained by constant reproductions of stereotypes. His observations were fundamental for the postcolonial critique and not so widely appropriated in studies of other discourses of power like social marginalisation of migrants. Though, when extrapolated for the situations with displaced populations, Bhabha's theorisations can highlight how IDPs are stigmatised and how their social marginalisation is normalised.

Expanding Bhabha's ideas, my observations showcase that the fixity can be challenged under certain critical circumstances, such as initial responses to emergencies. As Craig Calhoun observes, under the emergency imaginary of crisis, the relationships between people shift in the moral recognition of humans, where individuals are deemed as equivalent to each other (Calhoun 2010, 34). The initial compassion for displaced people, who are seen as victims, overshadows the prejudice and stereotypes about them. Even though, as I will discuss further, this appears to be a temporary phenomenon, a critical investigation of the variability of attitudes can challenge the unchangeable order that fixity produces. Accordingly, this implies that stereotypes can be transformed, which can lead to some practical application in the informational and media policies related to IDPs and forced migrants.

Methodologically, the reproduction of stereotypes presented a dilemma in the course of research. Guesses, assumptions, and generalised comments about IDPs can be often seen as an elusive knowledge that fades upon further inquiry, as it is not supported by actual facts or evidence. But rather then dismissing these beliefs, I found that they could be a prolific material for investigation. At the end, they illustrate a paradoxical situation when actors of state and humanitarian systems, who make political decisions related to IDPs, are guided by the epistemology of imagining, assuming not only beneficiaries' needs (Dunn 2012, 12), but their status and social identity.

Another methodological complication was the on-going transformation of attitudes toward IDPs. At the initial stage of the project in 2014, the phenomenon that drew my attention was the welcoming positive attitudes among Ukrainians that mobilised their resources to assist displaced people in need. However, in 2015, I documented reappearing unfavourable comments about IDPs, which was also the case in media publications. Thus, instead of investigating the positive perception of IDPs as 'one of us,' I faced more dynamic processes of how positive generalisations were replaced by negative prejudices. This transformation called for alterations in interviewing techniques. In most cases, state employees and representatives of international programs did not want our conversations to be recorded, as they were worried about the professional repercussions of talking negatively about IDPs on the record.

I recognise that my observations have a certain degree of generalisation as well. However, my intention to capture the prevailing opinions about displaced populations justifies a certain amount of generalisation for the purposes of giving a clear picture of the overall situation. At the same time, it is important to recognise that these generalisations are heuristic, and there are of course many nuances and variations to the perceptions.

## Initial Responses: How Displaced People Became 'Ours'

The initial civil responses to the needs of displaced people were highly praised as a prominent social phenomenon. Volunteer initiatives and grassroots engagement to assist IDPs were seen as a sign of an emerging civil society within a surge of political changes. Many of these responses originated from a self-coordinated grid of Euromaidan support (Euromaidan SOS, Automaidan, etc.). Already established and functioning networks of citizens refocused their activities either to support the Ukrainian army or to assist displaced populations.

In a way, volunteers were overtaking or complementing fundamental functions of the state to secure the safety and provisions for its citizens in need. This fact was especially important considering the major political reconfigurations, triggered by Euromaidan such as the introduction of a new cabinet of ministers, rotation and lustration of other state officials. These changes complicated even more the promptness of emergency responses from the inflexible and bureaucratically immobile state system. In this light, the impulse to assist the state was often seen as a part of citizens' responsibility on behalf of Euromaidan participants and activists.

From a broader perspective, support for displaced people is rooted in the ethical principle of shared humanity beyond social divisions (Pupavac 2010, Calhoun 2010). However, citizenship status is an important link that connects IDPs with volunteers. The idea of belonging to the same community of 'our fellow citizens' is at play, even though the nation-community is internally diversified (e.g. politically and ideologically). As it was rationalised by one of my informants, Anna: 'They are *our* people, *our* citizens and as we are building a new state, they should have faith in it' (Anna, volunteer).[1] In some cases, the acceptance into the category of 'our people' is rooted in the choice that displaced people have made. Some volunteers explained that from their point of view, IDPs fleeing to other regions of Ukraine were 'voting by their feet' in favour of a united Ukraine. It is particularly related to the displaced people from the Donbas region, where the conflict heightened political and ideological differences. However, it should be mentioned that in two volunteer centres that I visited, discussions on IDPs' war experiences and reasons that made people flee were restricted in 2014. This facilitated romanticism towards

---

[1] As research shows, even though significant support for displaced people came from the civil society sector and NGOs, displaced people's expectation was to receive assistance from the state (Semygina et al.). While a nuanced explanation can highlight different historical and ideological underpinnings of these expectations, in general, it was the status of citizenship that grants them entitlement and shaped their anticipation for the state's support.

the displaced people and ascribing a moral dimension to their decision. Accordingly, it accommodated IDPs acceptance into the imaginary national community by the volunteers and generally within the hosting environment.

Shared citizenship validated the volunteer assistance to the displaced people. Even though the first wave of displacement in 2014 was accompanied by critical narratives and some forms of housing and employment discrimination, the level of hostility toward IDPs remained comparatively low (KrymSOS 2015). The ideological differences and labelling IDPs as pro-Russian at that time did not translate into active confrontations or violence. Much like refugees, IDPs were perceived as 'stripped of the specificity of culture, place, and history' (Malkki 1995, 12), therefore their affiliation with the Donbas region was largely overshadowed.[2] Depoliticised and reduced to their status as citizens and humans, displaced people were categorised as victims, which meant that they were essentialised (Dunn 2012). Unlike refugees, displaced Ukrainians were not heavily labelled as distant or unknown Others. Citizenship affiliation granted them a place within a category of 'ours' (Ukrainian—свої), which has significant cultural implications in the post-Soviet milieu.

While the dichotomy of 'ours—others' has an extensive genealogy, I would like to focus on its function within the Soviet discourse, particularly because the semantic opposition of *sviy/nash* (ours/us) versus *other/they* obtained a strong political connotation during the Soviet times. In Catherine Wanner's definition, *sviy* signifies a common Soviet identity produced by 'shared experience with an oppressive state apparatus,' in which '[we] bond together against 'them,' the enemy, the state and its institutions' (Wanner 1998, 9; see also Yurchak 2006, 102-108). Bonding experiences of citizens in opposition to the oppressive state— or what would be more accurately described in this case as dysfunctional state— shaped the acceptance of displaced people by the volunteers and sympathisers. The recognition and acceptance of IDPs as 'ours' mitigated and silenced potential ideological discrepancies. An amplified sense of unity and a threatening state of emergency also reinforced generalisations of displaced people and made their suffering more salient than their regional differences.

**Changing Image and Alienation of 'Ours'**

The critical reevaluation of Euromaidan and recalibration of post-Euromaidan optimism have significantly affected civil and state responses to the needs of

---

[2] While it should be acknowledged that there were some social tensions and blaming of IDPs for the conflict in Eastern Ukraine took place, the critical narratives did not prevent the wave of compassionate responses from civilians and the state.

IDPs. The initial wave of compassion fuelled by the crisis and the anxiety from the unfolding war began to fade when the conflict shifted into a less active phase and when emergency displacement transitioned to a protracted one. Consequently, the narratives that criticised IDPs became more visible. These critical narratives were mostly directed towards the IDPs from Donbas and not to those from Crimea. People who fled Crimea after the Russian annexation were categorised as ideological refugees, who sacrificed their homes to resist the Russian occupation. In contrast, internal refugees from Eastern Ukraine were more commonly seen as those who 'were not able to defend Ukraine' (Olga, regional social welfare officer). This assumption was also reflected in gender biases, as male IDPs were often perceived as failed protectors or potential separatists.

This division between Crimean and Donbas IDPs can be seen as an internal Ukrainian 'hierarchy of othering,' where one type of Other is imagined as more threatening than another (Kaneva and Popescu 2014). The hostile and, accordingly, lower status of Donbas migrants is informed by the East-West division of Ukraine. Though the separation of pro-Russian Eastern Ukrainians and pro-European Western Ukrainians is highly debated and contested, the differing historical backgrounds and contrasting electoral preferences of these two parts of Ukraine cannot be ignored.

The areas that first reflected a negative image of displaced people were the real estate market and the job market. Typically, they are the most critical for resettled people and crucial for their social integration. Both markets started to openly filter IDPs from potential contacts and beneficiaries and the marker of displacement soon became a reappearing category in the rubrics for announcements. For instance, in spring 2015, six out of ten long-term rent announcements for moderately priced apartments in Kyiv had some kind of reference to displacement: 'displaced people and brokers, please do not disturb,' or in some cases 'displaced people might be considered' (data from olx.ua).

Even more damaging to their image is the growing tendency to criminalise displaced people. IDPs from Eastern Ukraine come from a region strongly associated with an industrial, underprivileged, and criminogenic environment. During the Euromaidan the hostility toward Eastern Ukrainians aggravated, particularly as the targets of the protests – former president Viktor Yanukovych and his Party of Regions – were from Donbas. The unfolding violence during Euromaidan was often extrapolated to the people from Eastern Ukraine. Not only were they blamed as supporters of brutality against Euromaidan protesters, but seen as a root cause for it because of the electoral choice they had made that led Yanukovych to presidency. The negative attitudes disseminated in media discourse, when, for instance, Donbas people were named as 'the most retrograde part of [Ukraine's] population' by historian Alexander Motyl (Radio Liberty 2014).

Furthermore, within the past year, the overall decreasing quality of life and well-being in Ukraine became more frequently blamed on IDPs. Thus, a so-called 'return of the 90s' is now often framed as IDPs' fault. Ukrainian media widely circulated the comment by sociologist Inna Bekeshkina, who explained the rise of crime rates in Ukraine by the pre-war high level of crimes in Donbas that has 'followed IDPs to other regions' (BBC 2016). Such comments imply displaced people's direct responsibility for this tendency. At the same time, Ukrainian police reported that the rise of crime rates started in 2012 and for the past two years increased only by 0.3 per cent (Korrespondent 2016). Even though the tendency of increased crime rates might be linked to the demographic changes triggered by the war, it is more likely to be caused by the spread of uncontrolled weapons, deterioration of the socio-economic situation, and more accurate reports on crime rates that followed the police reform (Korrespondent 2016).

According to a media monitoring survey conducted by Krym SOS, the regularity of media news reports that ascribed increasing crime rates as a result of IDPs influx has been constantly growing since the end of 2014 (Krym SOS, 2015). While regional media are not so biased, Kyiv news outlets do publish unproven and unchecked materials that have negative overtones for the construction of the IDPs' public image. A very recent example is related to a growing number of stolen cars in Kyiv. For the period of January-February 2016 this number tripled in comparison to the previous year. While experts express their concerns with a technical side of the issue—e.g. an introduction of a special devise that allows intercepting car key signal—the media with no evidence link the disturbing statistics to the influx of displaced people. For instance, one of the key media outlets reported: 'Among displaced people, many did not succeed in finding a job and normalising their lives, and some of them, to be honest, do not even want to do this. Stealing a car is a profitable alternative to official employment, especially under the unstable circumstances' (Nash Kiev 2015). The implication that stealing a car is as easy as shoplifting and that it is the work of displaced people does not leave any room for critical examination of the issue and puts the blame on IDPs' shoulders. The harming effects of reports like this result in alienation of displaced people and their further marginalisation.

Negative depictions of IDPs by media raise significant concerns, as they have a strong potential to shape both civil and state responses to IDPs' situation and influence policy decisions. Such media power is known as the 'CNN effect', as described by Steven Livingston (1997, see also Robinson 2005, Peksen et al. 2014). Analysing the role of television in the US foreign policy, Livingston named one of the types of the 'CNN effect' as 'policy agenda-setting' (Livingstone 1997, 1). He explained how emotional and dramatic reports necessitate political responses from governmental institutions. Drawing the parallel to the situation with internal displacement in Ukraine, we cannot dismiss the possibility that negative media discourse has had an impact on political responses from the state.

What I found especially disturbing is that these negative perceptions influence mid-level state workers who are responsible for the development and implementation of relief programmes. In my interviews, the reproduction of media narratives commonly occurred among these respondents. Accordingly, a reappearing theme was the replication of stereotypes about IDPs. For instance, one of the ministry workers reproduced a fake story about displaced children burning a Ukrainian flag – a widely circulated media report that was refuted a few days after the publication. Thus, the previously imperfect system of state assistance is further hindered by the functionaries of the state apparatus, who express their prejudices while developing and distributing assistance to displaced people. And although a direct correlation between personal preconceptions of state workers and larger political decisions regarding IDPs cannot be clearly identified, the circulation of stereotypes exposes an existing distance between how IDPs' experiences are imagined and what they actually are.

Recently, the Ministry of the Social Policy suspended financial assistance to IDPs that are suspected of forging their documents. The decision was made based on undisclosed lists of the Security Council of Ukraine (SBU) and affected 600,000 IDPs who are dependent on state payments (OCHA report from 24 June 2016). This situation was alarming for volunteers, as people they help were suddenly cut from state assistance with no prior notices or explanations, which significantly increased the amount of assistance they needed. At the same time, the state employees interpret this response as an urgent step because of the 'growing levels of fraud and crimes.' The payments were eventually resumed under requirement that IDPs' living conditions and places of actual residence would be inspected by special commissions (Cabinet of Ministry Decree №367). These forms of state responses damaged perceptions of IDPs, limited their mobility under strict state's control,[3] and are calling into question the state's ethical responsibilities

---

[3] In case IDPs are not at place of their official residence during the inspection, they are deprived of their status and social welfare payments. The decision can be appealed within three days from the date of inspection. For this, applicants should come to the state welfare office at the place of registration in person. NGO and human rights

to IDPs. Importantly, as follow-up interviews showed in summer 2016, volunteers who initially presented an alternative form of social support network for IDPs also introduced control measures to check the background of displaced people.

Thus, over the past year the generalised entity of displaced people was fragmented. The initial responses based on empathy and compassion blurred the social and ideological boundaries between IDPs and a larger national community. However, a post-euphoria syndrome and social tension associated with economic and political instability (Malyarenko 2016) along with a growing competition for scarce economic resources shifted the IDPs from falling within the category of 'ours' (*svoi*) to the domain 'they.' Consequent proliferation of negative media images of IDPs and profiling them as a social threat is one of the factors that contribute to shaping public opinions and institutional responses, such as meticulous background checks of IDPs, suspension of social payments, and everyday discrimination. However, it cannot be ruled out that demographic changes caused by the influx of IDPs contribute to the social instability, magnified attention to their lives and totalisation of them as criminals as well as increase social tensions within the country. As one of the volunteer activists mentioned, it triggers 'a road roller of repressions' that affects all IDPs. The fluctuation of attitudes demonstrates the emotional and highly perceptive nature of the sense of national community and questions critical rationalisations of these responses.

**Contamination with Donbas**

A growing stigma of displaced people is a discursive phenomenon. In popular narratives, the danger that IDPs carry often has no tangible or actual references and are embedded into a larger clichéd perception of Donbas. The volunteers describe the everyday hostility towards the displaced people in the following way: 'People say "You are guilty of what has happened in Donbas. And now you are coming here and *it* will start here (здесь будет то же самое)"' (Larisa, volunteer). These fears are often not rationalised, but emotional, and the threat is seen as an invisible, imaginary danger of '*it*' – some indistinguishable quality of regional identity that is ascribed to Donbas IDPs. Interestingly, this perception resembles the alienation of people who were displaced from the Chornobyl zone in the 1980s.

Conflict-driven displaced people are a new phenomenon in the history of independent Ukraine (Uehling, this volume). However, five years before the country's independence, in 1986, almost 100,000 people were internally

---

organisations alarmed that these conditions significantly restricted IDPs rights for movement and 'imprison' IDPs in their homes.

displaced from Chornobyl. The social marginalisation of nuclear disaster victims was heavily marked by social overreactions to the unknown consequences of the radioactive explosion. The lack of knowledge about the radioactive effects caused public anxiety, stress, and triggered the social exclusion of displaced people (Jaworowski 2010).

The invisible threat of radiation can be compared to the invisible threat of association with Donbas that affects the 'normalcy' of displaced populations. In this way, belonging to the national community becomes secondary, whereas the regional marker (either Chornobyl or Donbas) is amplified. In her research on refugees in Tanzania, Liisa Malkki emphasises the significance of the category of 'purity' for displaced people – both a purifying effect of suffering that populations have gone through and how hosting actors categorise them as 'pure,' depriving from social and political markers in order to rationalise assistance (Malkki 1996, 384-385). In the case of Ukraine, an 'impure' effect of radioactive or ideological 'contamination' is evident, as it converts the legal status of displaced people into a social label. The same effect can be seen as an important factor in the hierarchy of othering, as the 'impurity' of separatist movements in Donbas and the on-going war there are seen as more dangerous elements for Eastern Ukrainian IDPs' identity in contrast to the Crimean internal migrants.

Another parallel between Chornobyl and Donbas IDPs is their life-death experience that frames their social interactions and distances IDPs as 'them' (вони). Anthropologist Adriana Petryna in her study of post-Chornobyl life, politics and biological citizenship in Ukraine (2002), describes how victims of the nuclear catastrophe navigate their new social identities of survivors. For them, as Petryna argues, the idea of inclusion into a national community is 'charged with the superadded burden of survival' (Petryna 2002, 7). For IDPs from Donbas the survival is largely marked not only with the eruption of war, but also with an internal political conflict. Their experience is often silenced, for instance when volunteers are instructed not to talk with IDPs about the war. These measures are introduced not to disturb highly traumatic memories but also to avoid potential confrontations. The silenced past, this 'burden of survival,' conceals a possibility of being a political opponent or a supporter of separatist movements, which often contribute to othering and distancing of IDPs.

Drawing the parallel between Chornobyl and Donbas IDPs I aim not to equate their experiences, but rather to compare the emotional, uniformed, and somewhat superficial assumptions that shape responses to their situations of displacement. The danger of these assumptions is in magnifying IDPs as a social threat. This does not mean that the connection between the arrival of displaced population and social instability should be altogether dismissed. However, it calls for deeper critical examination of the process, reasons for IDPs' social exclusion, and the alteration of responses.

## Conclusion

In this paper, I highlight a shift on the axes of public perception of displaced people in Ukraine. The initial support of IDPs was celebrated as an indication of an important societal process, in which the regional belonging of IDPs was largely dismissed under the overarching concept of 'ours.' The same regional belonging became a marker of social stigmatisation over the past year. An accentuated image of Donbas ideological 'impurity' pictured IDPs from Eastern Ukraine in less favourable light than those from Crimea, creating internal hierarchisation of othering. Alienation and negative images of displaced people are reflected in the everyday discrimination and reinforce preconceptions about them. However, this fluctuation of attitudes questions the fixity of IDPs differentiation and demonstrates that the 'unchangeable order' can be more dynamic than unchangeable. Not only does it necessitate a revision of the conceptual framework of othering, but should be accounted for in the work of media communications, where often the generalised image of displaced people is generated.

The categorisation of uprooted people as impure and threatening is something that Lisa Malkki explores as a transcendent discursive phenomenon that affects public and academic languages about refugees (Malkki 1992). However, the danger of this tendency is particularly crucial in a larger context of ideological discrepancies within Ukraine, where the taken-for-granted separation between Eastern and Western Ukraine is heightened by displacement. Beyond the declarative statements about a unified Ukraine, the social standing of the displaced population remains complicated. Their inability to participate in local elections due to the legislative inconsistencies, meager and unstable social payments, as well as a growing tendency to social marginalisation make their inclusion into the larger national community quite complex.

This situation can potentially have significant political repercussions for displaced populations. The proliferation of negative images endangers their prospects of social inclusion and can affect future institutional actions and policy delivery (Zetter 1991, 2007). IDPs' limited leverages in these processes undermine their status as citizens – the one that initially granted them access to aid resources – and puts them on the margins of the 'state-citizens' relations, which is a prolific area for further ethnographic observation and examination.

# References

Calhoun, C. *The Imperative to Reduce Suffering: Charity, Progress, and Emergencies in the Field of Humanitarian Action*. Ithaca, New York: Cornell University Press, 2008.

Dunn, E. C. "The Chaos of Humanitarian Aid: Adhocracy in the Republic of Georgia," *Humanity: An International Journal of Human Rights, Humanitarianism, and Development* 3, no.1 (2012): 1-23.

Fassin, D. *Humanitarian Reason: A Moral History of the Present*, Berkeley: University of California Press, 2012.

Jaworowski, Z. "Observations on the Chernobyl Disaster and LNT," *Dose-Response* 8, no.2 (2010): 148-171.

Interview with Alexander Motyl, "The Benefits Of A Partitioned Ukraine," Radio Liberty, 20 February 2016, http://www.rferl.org/content/ukraine-split-partition-/25270988.html.

Kaneva, N. and Popescu, D. "'We are Romanian, not Roma': Nation Branding and Post-Socialist Discourses of Alterity," *Communication, Culture & Critique* 7, no.4 (2014): 506-523.

Livingston, S. "Clarifying the CNN effect: An Examination of Media Effects According to Type of Military Intervention," Research Paper R-18, June 1997, http://www.genocide-watch.org/images/1997ClarifyingtheCNNEffect-Livingston.pdf.

Malkki, L. "National Geographic: The Rooting of Peoples and the Territorialization of National Identity Among Scholars and Refugees," *Cultural Anthropology* 7, no.1 (1992): 24-44.

Malkki, L. H. "Speechless Emissaries: Refugees, Humanitarianism, and Dehistoricization," *Cultural Anthropology* 11, no.3 (1996): 377-404.

Malkki, L. H. *Purity and exile: Violence, Memory, and National Cosmology Among Hutu Refugees in Tanzania*, Chicago: University of Chicago Press, 1995.

Malyarenko, T. "Ukraine from the Euromaidan to the War with Russia," *The Routledge Handbook of Ethnic Conflict* (2016): 349-368.

Pandolfi, M. "Contract of Mutual (in) Difference: Governance and the Humanitarian Apparatus in Contemporary Albania and Kosovo," *Indiana Journal of Global Legal Studies* 10, no.1 (2003): 369-381.

Peksen, D., Peterson, T.M and Drury, A.C. "Media-Driven Humanitarianism? News Media Coverage of Human Rights Abuses and the Use of Economic Sanctions," *International Studies Quarterly* 58, no.4 (2014): 855-866.

Petryna, A. *Life Exposed: Biological Citizens After Chernobyl*, Princeton: Princeton University Press, 2013.

Pupavac, V. "Between Compassion and Conservatism: A Genealogy of British Humanitarian Sensibilities," in *Contemporary States of Emergency: Anthropology of Military and Humanitarian Intervention* edited by Didier Fassin and Mariella Pandolfi, New York: Zone Books (2010): 47-77.

Robinson, P. *The CNN Effect: The Myth of News, Foreign Policy and Intervention*, London: Routledge, 2005.

Wanner, C. *Burden of Dreams: History and Identity in Post-Soviet Ukraine*, Pennsylvania: Penn State Press, 2010.

Yurchak, A. *Everything Was Forever, Until It Was No More: The Last Soviet Generation*, Princeton: Princeton University Press, 2006.

Zetter, R. "Labelling Refugees: Forming and Transforming a Bureaucratic Identity," *Journal of Refugee Studies* 4, no.1 (1991): 39-62.

Zetter, R. "More Labels, Fewer Refugees: Remaking the Refugee Label in an Era of Globalization," *Journal of Refugee Studies* 20, no.2 (2007): 172-192.

"За час конфлікту ставлення до внутрішньо переміщених осіб погіршилось,"13 March 2015, *KrymSOS*, http://krymsos.com/settlers/news/55ba327458175/

# 4

# A Hybrid Deportation: Internally Displaced from Crimea in Ukraine

GRETA UEHLING

## Introduction

In February 2014, troops lacking military insignia invaded Crimea and swiftly took over key military and strategic sites. A referendum was hastily organised, even though this violated Ukrainian law and international norms. The Russian press claimed that 83 per cent of the electorate had turned out, and that 97 per cent of those who voted were in favour of annexation. While these figures are the ones featured by international news media sources, a report by the President of Russia's Council on Civil Society and Human Rights posted at the president-sovet.ru website showed that only 30 per cent turned out for the referendum, and of those who voted, only half were in favour of becoming part of Russian Federation (Gregory 2014).

With the bogus referendum swept under the rug, a treaty was signed between the newly proclaimed Republic of Crimea and the Russian Federation to initiate a process of integration. The peninsula was so radically transformed during this period that people describe the sudden change by saying they went to sleep in one country, and woke up in another. While the change in power and authority from Ukraine to Russia was greeted with a great deal of fanfare and enthusiasm by the pro-Russian part of the population, a significant pro-Ukrainian demographic felt sufficiently threatened to flee the peninsula. The first wave left very early when it was clear that Ukraine was not going to fight for the territory and the so-called 'little green men' were rapidly gaining control. A second wave followed after the 'referendum,' when the illegal occupation was declared an 'annexation.'

This chapter explores the experience of people from Crimea who became internally displaced within Ukraine. Unfortunately, there are no reliable statistics to tell us the exact number displaced by Russian occupation. In the beginning, statistics were captured by the State Emergency Services of Ukraine, a function that was subsequently transferred to the Ministry of Social Policy. The Deputy-Minister, Vitaliy Vadimovich Muschinin, points out that while some 20,000 IDPs from Crimea have been registered, this is only a fraction of the total number (Personal interview, 27 June 2016). Further calling the estimate of 20,000 IDPs from Crimea into question is the data of the Border Services, which have reported a net out migration from Crimea that is three times higher than the number being reported by the Ministry of Social Policy. IDPs who fled Crimea are now scattered across Ukraine.

In what follows, I first explain my methods in the absence of accurate statistics or a reliable sampling frame. Then, I explore the reasons people left, which suggest Russian policies are designed not only to eliminate dissent but also to remove people. The nation that received these migrants was unfortunately ill-equipped to welcome them. If the government lacked experience and resources to address internal displacement, the Ukrainian people, inspired by the 'Revolution of Dignity', had both the will and the desire to help those who arrived from Crimea. Two main findings stand out: first, population displacement contributed to the development of a new civic identity that has the potential to unite Ukrainians and fill a void that previously existed with regard to Ukrainian national identity. Second, there is deep disenchantment with the Ukrainian state that manifests itself most strongly in feelings of having been abandoned and betrayed by the government. The principal task ahead is to resolve the barriers and overcome challenges that stand in the way of IDP integration, so that state and society can function together.

**Methods**

To capture the experience of people displaced by the conflict in Ukraine, I carried out 125 interviews over a two-year period. Participant observation at cultural, social, political and educational events helped identify the most salient interview questions. Educational trainings for IDPs were a particularly valuable opportunity to 'hang out' with IDPs and listen to their concerns as they expressed them to one another. Monitoring of the Ukrainian press and social media further enriched my understanding.

The interviewing focused primarily on IDPs from Crimea (26 in 2015 and 18 in 2016). I also interviewed state officials, the staff of NGOs, psychologists, political and cultural leaders, and IDPs from the conflict in the eastern part of

Ukraine. People who were not displaced and chose to stay in Crimea were also consulted for this study. Because random sampling of IDPs is not possible,[1] I employed several non-random sampling techniques. Through quota sampling with NGOs that assist IDPs, respondents were selected according to gender, age and education. Gaps in demographic categories were then filled by snowball sampling with the assistance of three key respondents who were well-connected in their communities. I also used opportunistic sampling, inviting people I met at social, cultural, and educational events to respond to my questions. For these interviews, a semi-structured interview schedule was used to explore the IDPs' current thoughts and feelings about displacement. In 2016, follow-up interviews with 12 of the people interviewed in 2015 were carried out to assess the extent to which views changed over time. Since IDPs are dispersed widely across Ukraine, research was carried out in three cities favoured by IDPs and several small towns.

The experts interviewed for this study, some of whom were also IDPs, were selected through purposive sampling. These interviews were tailored to the individual's professional experience and expertise. All of the interview data was transcribed, translated, and analysed using Nvivo software for qualitative analysis. Monitoring of the Ukrainian press and social media sites further enriched the research.

Without an effective sampling frame, this research cannot claim to be representative. The methods combined, however, give the study as much validity as is possible under the circumstances. One important limitation to this research is that for ethical reasons, only the IDPs who felt ready to talk about their experience were interviewed. The thoughts and feelings of those with serious mental health challenges, for example, remain largely outside the scope of this study. This gap is partially filled by interviewing the psychologists and the social workers that serve IDPs. I also learned about people who were too affected by the events to talk about them from friends and family members. IDPs speculated that for the most part, their demographic differs from the one that stayed behind in being relatively more reflective, entrepreneurial and forward-thinking.

---

[1] Statistics are not disaggregated by ethnicity and only a subset, the most needy IDPs who need state assistance, register. NGOs have databases of beneficiaries, but I could not structure my sample around these data because they were said to be in bad repair (duplicate entries, gaps, omissions) and because they were unwilling to share these data.

## A Hybrid Deportation

Asked why they left, my respondents stated plainly and unequivocally that they disagreed with the change in power and would not live under the occupational authorities. Thus, a common denominator in the calculus of whether to stay or go is precisely the change in political regime. In addition to the most basic reason of not wanting to live in the Russian Federation, people leave to retain their human rights. Whether it was to have a political opinion, profess a faith, feel safe in their home, or avoid torture and death, all were seeking to preserve fundamental rights.

- **Right to a political opinion.** Individuals active in the Euromaidan protests or any form of pro-Ukrainian politics left to save their lives. The disappearances of colleagues prompted them to pack and leave. For Crimean Tatars, the death of Reshat Ametov is often mentioned. He was stuffed in an unmarked car after a one-man protest and later found dead with signs of torture. At least 20 disappearances of young Crimean Tatar men have followed. Expressing political opinion has become a risk. The Crimean Tatar political leadership, the *Mejlis* (a democratically elected representative body) was declared illegal and its top leadership barred from living in Crimea. Now, those who retain an allegiance are vulnerable to repression.

- **Right not to be tortured/right to a private life.** Many people, but especially academics and artists, left after their homes were searched for banned material, or they were invited for informal 'conversations' and subjected to psychological pressure. Searches of homes, in which the occupants must lay face down, and in which important property like computers and cell phones are confiscated, have become routine.

- **Right to religion.** The Ukrainian church was deprived of its premises and forced to operate underground. Similarly, devout and observant Muslims predicted they would be a target of the new Russian authorities. Searches of mosques, banning of even basic religious texts, detentions, and various forms of humiliation such as being booked and having to submit a DNA sample (obtained from urine and spit submitted at police stations) for attending a mosque have followed.

- **Right to education.** During the first two years of occupation, diplomas issued in Crimea were not recognised as valid in mainland Ukraine. Realising this separated them from any viable future outside Crimea, young people and their families left for education. Today there are plans for these diplomas to be translated and converted into official Ukrainian documents. Children in schools are pressured to become pro-Russian and inform on parents who are pro-Ukrainian. Some families stated they left to protect their children from this kind of abuse in the educational system and to preserve family unity.

Given these conditions, it is not surprising that Crimean Tatars label the policies of the *de facto* authorities as a hybrid or hidden deportation:

> If in 1944 the Soviet authorities selected the reason of collaboration with the Nazis, and the whole Soviet people just agreed with that, in the 21st century, to simply take a people and deport them is not going to be viewed favourably. Since they can't do that, they create the conditions to make people leave of their own accord. It would be too obvious to use trains' (No. 21, Crimean Tatar male IDP).

I think the 2014 occupation was interpreted through the metaphor of deportation in part because the process of mourning the 1944 deportation has never been completed. While governments may have rushed to proclaim the deportation a genocide in 2014, for over two decades it was proclaimed to be 'humane' by the pro-Russian authorities in Crimea. Thus, Crimea lacked a commonly agreed upon historical narrative. Without adequate ways to remember (memorials to those who perished were routinely vandalised) it remained contentious. The Russian Federation further disrupted the process of mourning when they occupied Crimea in 2014. Now the traumatic past is the present and termed 'hybrid deportation.' Whether or not it is scientifically accurate, the phrase transduces feelings of vulnerability and historical injustice, and captures the ways in which the choice to leave is a forced one.

**The Ukrainian Government's Response**

The Ukrainian government was not prepared to deal with flows of internally displaced persons. Ukrainian officials interviewed for this study readily admit a lack of experience that resulted in notable policy and protection gaps. Corruption has also undermined the government's ability to meet the needs of IDPs. Further complicating the ability to respond, recent years have been marked by restructuring and reorganisation, leading to staff turnover, loss of institutional memory and issues with coordination. For example, there has been disagreement between the Verkhovna Rada (the Ukrainian Parliament) and the Presidential administration on the best course of action for IDPs. The legislation put forward by Verkhovna Rada has lacked mechanisms for implementation.

There is also a significant problem with government officials passing responsibility to non-governmental organisations. For example, the government hotline established by the Ministry of Social Policy directed IDPs not to services provided by the Ukrainian government, but to volunteers. Even the process of registering as an IDP has been fraught with problems. Ambiguity in the law about whether or not the *spravka* or document identifying one as an IDP must have a stamp from the Migration Services led to a period of time in which it was impossible to register as an IDP. The Migration Services threw out their stamps according to one interpretation of the law, while regional authorities interpreted the law in a different way and required the stamp. Making matters worse, highly placed officials are rumoured to make negative statements about IDPs publically.

The government policy has led to a situation in which IDPs do not enjoy a full set of rights in mainland Ukraine. One manifestation of the issue is voting privileges. In July 2015, Ukraine's Parliament approved a law that excludes IDPs from participating in local elections. This obviously bars them from forming local councils and electing village and city mayors. Ukraine's displaced population has essentially been deprived of a voice in making policies, some of which are related to them, the IDPs.

Another example is that according to Ukrainian law, neither birth nor death certificates issued in the territory occupied or controlled by Russia are recognised. In other words, a baby born to Ukrainian parents in the occupied territory is not a Ukrainian citizen. When they bring their child to mainland Ukraine, IDPs are excluded from the stipend the Ukrainian government offers other families for the birth of a child until they go through a complicated legal process. The issues continue with death certificates that are not recognised in continental Ukraine. Although an attorney was able to win benefits for a child by presenting both the child and her medical records to a Ukrainian court, the matter is more complicated after death. 'A corpse?' he mused, 'much more difficult to transport' (Uehling 2015). This affects the ability to inherit property within families – a transaction that is only possible with a valid death certificate. In most countries of the world, the registration of births and deaths is accomplished through a simple administrative process. The Ukrainian government has taken steps to simplify and speed the process, but it is still only accomplished through time consuming and potentially costly court proceedings.

Banking is another example of a skewed policy response to IDPs. One of the first activities of the Ukrainian authorities after the occupation of Crimea was to freeze Crimeans' funds in Ukrainian banks in the occupied territory. Some were able to recover their funds through the painstaking intervention of

Diaspora, a Kyiv-based NGO, others lost them irretrievably. What is more, Ukrainian citizens with Crimean *propiskas* cannot open a new bank account in mainland Ukraine. They must first go through the long process of registering at an address in mainland Ukraine. The notion that she lacked the right to open a bank account in her own country led one IDP to exclaim she had been abandoned by Ukraine.

In short, IDPs from the occupied territories think Ukrainian government policies make them second-class citizens, attached to the body politic, but not fully joined as political subjects. The Ukrainian government seems to be 'saying' that the territory has been occupied unlawfully. What IDPs are 'hearing' however, is a form of rejection and condemnation. Thus, the current legal environment is one in which IDPs question whether they genuinely belong, and whether their hopes for incorporation will be fulfilled by a state that fails to offer them full rights.

Ong's insight (1996) that within the seemingly unitary category of citizenship there are in fact hierarchical schemes of difference that intersect in contingent ways is useful here. People holding valid Ukrainian citizenship but formerly residing in Crimea (and bearing a stamp called a *propiska* to that effect in their passports) have a different set of rights in independent Ukraine. Somewhat like the 'whitening' and 'blackening' processes described by Ong (1996, 741) there is a 'marking' by Russian occupation that sets these political subjects apart. IDPs from Crimea, whether Russian, Ukrainian, or indigenous Crimean Tatar, find themselves in a special status. Theoretically, citizenship is supposed to work against this (MacDonald 2012, Bosniak 2006) but Ukrainian citizens who come to the mainland from Crimea are viewed as politically tainted. IDPs said that in the beginning, they were called 'traitors' on account of the bogus referendum, whether they had voted in it or not.

In response to the gaps in services and the lack of harmonisation, the government of Ukraine has recently created a Ministry for the Temporarily Occupied Territories with two directives, one for the occupied territory of Crimea and another for the so-called Anti-terrorist operation (ATO) in the East. This Ministry is, however, only beginning its work. Officials interviewed in late June 2016 stated they see their primary role as coordination. They hope to identify gaps in legislation and services to IDPs. Their influence at this time is limited. Their current budget is limited to the administrative expenses related to supporting a staff of 35 people. They have a plan, which they have submitted for approval to the Ministry of Justice and the Ministry of the Economy.

## Work and Housing: Don't Build Us a Ghetto

In addition to civil liberties and legal protection, IDPs who have left homes, jobs, and personal belongings in Russian-occupied territory sometimes need financial assistance. At a time when the average monthly income is between 5000 and 6000 UAH, individuals who are registered as IDPs are entitled to a stipend of 440 UAH, the equivalent of 20 USD per month, to offset the cost of housing. Pensioners, invalids and children are eligible to receive 880 UAH a month, the equivalent of 40 USD, but there is a maximum payment of 2400 UAH per family per month. The limitation associated with these benefits is that they are highly contingent and there are a host of factors that make one ineligible. For example, if an individual is unemployed for one month the benefits are cut in half. At the end of two months, they are cut entirely. This results in a situation in which those most in need are least able to receive IDP benefits. Officials in the Ministry of Social Policy suggested the logic behind this policy is to avoid dependency syndromes and provide a reward or incentive to work.

Work is, however, hard to find. Crimean Tatars who left Crimea observe anecdotally that they are an extremely active demographic: none are sitting idle waiting for a handout. Ukrainian officials corroborate this, stating that most Crimean Tatar IDPs have simply found themselves work. NGOs have turned their attention from reception of IDPs to this very question of work, focusing on training IDPs to open small businesses and giving them grants and loans to do so. This is a wise approach; the Ministry of Social Policy observes that there are more job seekers than jobs, and the jobs that are available officially are low paying ones (interview, 27 June 2016).

Concern about their housing arrangement was a strong enough sentiment to appear in my interviewing as the primary reason IDPs stated they do not yet feel at home in mainland Ukraine. The vast majority of IDPs rent housing and are concerned with the high cost of accommodation, the looming possibility that they could be asked to move, and reluctance on the part of the host population to rent to them. IDPs from Crimea have not suffered nearly the stigma or discrimination as those from the East, who are stereotyped as wealthy, spoiled, arrogant, and uncultured. Those from Crimea who wore head covering told stories of repeatedly being denied housing.

Housing is a wedge that separates IDPs from the local population who live in homes and apartments that they own, having only to struggle with the rising cost of utilities, not rent. By contrast, IDPs must pay for housing and utilities while earning the same, and often lower, salaries. Unfortunately, the stipend to offset the cost of housing is too small to make an appreciable difference, and also became a justification for landlords to actually raise rent, further disadvantaging IDPs. Good solutions are still needed: in response to plans for an IDP settlement outside of Kyiv, one IDP exclaimed 'No, don't build us a ghetto.' Indeed, most of the social science literature shows that physical separation or special treatment is likely to impede, rather than facilitate integration.

With an eye toward the future, the government of Ukraine is collaborating with international organisations to resolve the issues of work and housing confronting the internally displaced. The World Bank and the United Nations Development Fund are perceived as the primary donors. In the last two years, the World Bank Group has provided a total of 4.7 billion USD to Ukraine (World Bank 2016). The International Organization for Migration and United Nations High Commissioner for Refugees have also been very active partners, distributing humanitarian aid to the neediest families, as well as grants and loans to start businesses to those with promising business proposals. The IOM has supported self-employment and micro-entrepreneurship with funding from the European Union, and the governments of Canada, Norway, Japan, and the United Kingdom (IOM 2016).

**Inventing Tradition**

In spite of the weak government response to IDPs, Ukrainian civil society was primed to receive them. The Euromaidan protests resulted in the formation of coordinated networks of citizens that turned their attention to IDPs once the Revolution was behind them. I suggest this is significant and could shape the outcome of population displacement far into the future.

Writing before the 'Revolution of Dignity', Shevel notes that unlike Russia, there was no domestic consensus on the definition of the Ukrainian nation (2006, 221). The only compromise among various viewpoints was that those with family origins on the territory of Ukraine were eligible to apply for Ukrainian citizenship, irrespective of ethnic, linguistic, or other characteristics (2006, 221). My research shows that after the conflict with Russia in the east and the occupation of Crimea in the south, there is a clearer sense of what it means to be Ukrainian emerging. This new civic identity, initially marked by the recognition of a common enemy in Vladimir Putin, has grown to encompass the identification of a common Ukrainian-Crimean Tatar history, the attenuation of the salience of ethnic and religious differences, and a new sense of political agency.

> After the Maidan, we began to construct a civic identity that was not there before. People began to say, 'Now I feel myself to be a citizen of Ukraine.' Most of the residents of Crimea never had the cause or the opportunity to think of themselves as being the citizen of ANY state (No. 32, Russian female IDP in Kyiv).

This statement was made by an ethnically Russian woman who left Sevastopol, underscoring that this is a politically not ethnically-motivated migration, and that the national identity is envisioned as subsuming multiple ethnic groups.

> We understood that to be Ukrainian isn't to be Ukrainian ETHNICALLY. It's more like the way the American mind sees things. It's not about NATIONALITY. It's a style of thinking, really. I'm Crimean Tatar [pointing to heart]. I'm Ukrainian [pointing to head] (No. 35, Crimean Tatar female IDP in Kyiv).

The pragmatics and gestural deixis of this conversation suggest that in the structure of feeling following the 'Revolution of Dignity', being Ukrainian and Crimean Tatar are different dimensions (head and heart) of the same body politic. These sentiments were echoed by Ukrainians coming to know the IDPs in their midst.

No longer just the inhabitants of a distant 'island,' IDPs from Crimea are in a unique position to educate. If the average Ukrainian knew very little about Crimea or Crimean Tatars before, they became very curious as a result of the occupation. Cooking clubs, master classes, common apartment block entryways, playgrounds, personal friendships, and the flush of new businesses opened by IDP-entrepreneurs are all bridging this gap. IDPs speculated that they have a special role to play, helping the Ukrainian population as a whole to become psychologically prepared for the day when Crimea is (hopefully) de-occupied.

This newfound sense of 'Ukrainian-ness' relies in part on separating itself from the Soviet and the Russian. Respondents in my study generated discourses that constructed Russians as being fundamentally different and 'other'. These conversations referenced genetic material, history, and values.

> They [Russians] are people who are ready to destroy any other people just in order to remain a superpower. That is not a part of who we are, we are free people and we would never

allow this to occur (No. 121, Crimean Tatar male IDP, Kherson).

This informant went deeper to hypothesise that Russians carry a genetically-based hatred for Crimean Tatars originating in the twelfth and thirteenth centuries. Discourses that essentialise the Other are prevalent in this region where the past has never been fully mourned or put away. As Etkind describes, post-Soviet memory 'operates as a living combination of various symbols, periods, and judgments which are experienced simultaneously' (2013, 11). It is specifically 'freedom' that is the primary marker of Ukrainian identity, which not only unites various peoples of Ukraine, but separates them from Russians who presumably do not value freedom of thought or conscience.

> FREEDOM! Ukrainians are a freedom loving people. This is a country in which there were no tsars or institutionalised slavery. Ukrainians always elected their khetmen. Then they killed them of course, but that's another story (No. 35, Crimean Tatar female IDP).

While discourses of freedom are hardly surprising in this post-revolutionary moment, the folding in of both Crimean Tatars and Ukrainians under this rubric represents a shift in comparison to the separation and suspicion between the two groups in the past. It is important to underscore that these feelings were not unique to Crimean Tatar IDPs. A common refrain was that whereas it used to be ethnicity that divided people of Ukraine, it is now political loyalty.

A crucial part of this civic identity relies on creating a collective past – a process that resonates with nation-building projects the world over as amply demonstrated in a volume edited by Hobsbawm and Ranger (1983). Held to be in common in today's Ukraine are fighting battles on the same side; common wedding rituals; the same melodies in music; common toponyms; styles of dress among Tatars and the Cossacks; and values.

> The history of the Crimean khanate, and the Crimean Tatars is closely tied to the history of Ukraine, to the people of Ukraine and to Europe, because among other things, it has been shown historically that the first khan was from what is now Poland. These relations are very deep. It's our common history. All the paraphernalia, sharovars [pants worn by Cossacks] the names of the clothes, the weapons, it is all 90 per cent Tatar (No. 39, Crimean Tatar male IDP, Kyiv).

> I had a project in which both Ukraine and Crimean Tatar music groups participated. We found that Crimean Tatar and Ukrainian melodies could be heard in the same piece. The music is identical. Yes. We never studied this before, and the [political] events inspired us (No. 6, Crimean Tatar male IDP).

These ideas about a common past from respondents only partially align with scholarly accounts. For example, Wilson places more weight on the social *distance* between Crimean Tatars and Ukrainians. In a discussion of how the Russian and Ukrainian Cossacks were allied with one another, Wilson states, 'Sometimes, the groups were in conflict with each other. At other times they joined forces to fight against their mutual enemy – the Crimean Tatars. In some respects, they were caught between slave-trading Islam and, as Orthodox, Counter-Reformation Catholicism' (2000, 59). Absent from Wilson's account is the acknowledgement that the Cossacks and the Crimean Tatars were on the same side.

There is more alignment when it comes to common cultural markers. As Wilson states, 'Still, the open steppe where they lived provided an opportunity to absorb the dress, vocabulary and methods of military organization from their Islamic enemies' (2000, 59). In other words, respondents in today's Ukraine were beginning to develop a counter-history to the version passed down to them, and are now casting Ukrainians and Crimean Tatars as friends rather than enemies. As one respondent put it:

> Well, firstly what I want to say, the object of Ukrainian peoples' pride are the Cossacks, because the Cossacks were the libertines, they loved freedom, and they provided the first seeds of statehood. And the Cossacks, their mode of life, their costumes, their weapons – all of these were Crimean Tatar (No. 25, non-IDP female, Lviv).

How far this reframing of history will proceed will be important to analyse as it continues. It is an open question whether this Ukrainian counter-history will withstand the pressure of Russian narratives and propaganda.

**No Longer Victims**

This new sense of Ukrainian-ness was strengthened by a growing awareness of their own political agency, which represents a departure from the past when the dominant narratives had to do with victimisation at the hands of the Soviets, either in the form of the collectivisation, the 1944 deportation or the Holodomor.

> The idea for the exhibit arose in conversations in which we said: 'wait a minute. We are used to victimising ourselves – talking about ourselves as victims. We may have been deported, but we emerged victorious, we are strong, and we are going to survive' (No. 43, Crimean Tatar male non-IDP, Kyiv).

To a certain extent, IDPs saw their displacement as a loss that also contained an opportunity. If discourses have the power to create the things of which they speak, IDPs were socially constructing themselves as resilient and creating openings for experiencing themselves as empowered.

> I am more than certain that in my generation there will be many notable people. Whether or not they are stars of the screen, they are going to be stars in the human rights field, in the field of management, in politics, because that is what is happening with us. Someone will get a Pulitzer, someone will become a Nobel Prize laureate (No. 3, Crimean Tatar male IDP, Kyiv)

These narratives, rich in the sense of individual political agency, represent an intriguing departure from the kinds of narratives that prevailed when I did research in Crimea in the 1990s. Political agency, defined here as seeing oneself as having and making choices to act or not act politically in the world, was a preoccupation of IDPs and is a theme in a majority of my interviews. While the theme of deportation and its legacy of discrimination surfaced in the metaphor of a hybrid deportation, these IDPs problematised any discourse of victimisation or victimhood, and spoke rather of crossing thresholds, turning pages, and otherwise moving forward, based on their own choices.

## Loyalty and Betrayal

The fact that Ukraine did not defend Crimea from Russian incursion, coupled with the lack of rights and lack of benefits in mainland Ukraine have led many IDPs to say they have been betrayed by Ukraine. The word used to describe this, *predatelstvo*, is heavily saturated with meanings because it is also the word that has been used to discredit and disenfranchise Crimean Tatars since the Second World War. After the 2014 occupation, Ukrainians asked why the Crimean Tatars had not stepped forward to do the work of the Ukrainian army and defend the peninsula against Russian takeover. There were also announcements that anyone who voted in the referendum was a traitor. There is a deeply painful irony in this choice of words because of the (unreciprocated) loyalty to Ukraine that Crimean Tatars demonstrated for over two decades in independent Ukraine. In the last 12 months, thoughts of leaving entirely have become more possible. Some IDPs rationalised that with time, the political environment would be improved and the economy would grow. Others lost the hope that led them out of Crimea into mainland Ukraine:

> Now I do not feel like a patriot of Ukraine, I am less tied to this country than ever before. Some of my friends have left already and others are planning to leave to Europe or wherever because they don't see a future or any possibilities. This is the very unpleasant effect of all these events (No. 109, Russian female IDP, Lviv).

Indeed, according to the IOM, 11 per cent of the Ukrainian population is located outside of Ukraine (IOM 2011). The displacement of people from Crimea to mainland Ukraine occurred as a result of an unlawful occupation. While traumatic and disruptive to the lives of individual IDPs, this migratory flow also presented Ukraine with an unexpected opportunity to generate its own traditions and become more integrated. It will take concerted effort on the part of state officials, civil society, and of course IDPs themselves to create positive momentum.

**Conclusion: A Double-Edged Sword**

It is difficult to predict whether the solidification of Ukrainian national identity occurring in 2015 and 2016 will continue to be ascendant, or whether tropes of treason and betrayal will undermine the forging of new political culture. Concerns that they could be labelled 'traitors,' undergo deportation at the hands of *Ukraine*, or become divided amongst themselves are sobering reminders that the structures of feeling following the 'Revolution of Dignity' are still in solution and have yet to precipitate into robust and longstanding institutions of civil society.

Upon returning from a short visit to aging parents in occupied Crimea, one IDP captured the ambivalence of being displaced in mainland Ukraine by highlighting that it is uncomfortable for migrants whether they return to occupied Crimea or stay in 'free' Ukraine.

> I went to visit and when I am home, among my own, on my land, in the house of my birth. Everything is the same, but not the same. There is an inexplicable pressure that's so intense you can't think. I told my husband I was either tired or going crazy. When I come back to mainland Ukraine, I can say anything I want, I can do anything I want, I can go anywhere I

want, but my loved ones and my native land are still missing. It's like a double-edged sword (No. 57, Crimean Tatar female IDP, Lviv).

This double-edged sword provides a good cipher for understanding IDP psychology. The hope for loyalty and the fear of betrayal run alongside a celebration of agency and unity, forming the complicated ground upon which state policies and institutions will continue to take shape. While IDPs from Crimea may be relatively small in number, they provide an important window, perhaps even a magnifying glass, on contemporary Ukraine.

## References

*Anthropoliteia*, "Birth, Death, and Fictive Citizenship: Political Agency in War-Torn Ukraine," 20 July 2015, http://anthropoliteia.net/2015/07/20/birth-death-and-fictive-citizenship-citizenship-and-political-agency-in-war-torn-ukraine/

Barabantseva, E. and Sutherland, C. "Diaspora and Citizenship: Introduction," *Nationalism and Ethnic Politics* 17, no. 1 (2011): 1-13.

Bosniak, L. *The Citizen and the Alien*, Princeton, NJ: Princeton University Press, 2006.

Etkind, A. *Warped Mourning: Stories of the Undead in the Land of the Unburied*, Stanford, CA: Stanford University Press, 2013.

Gregory, P.R. "Putin's 'Human Rights Council' Accidentally Posts Real Crimean Election Results," *Forbes*, 5 May 2014, http://www.forbes.com/sites/paulroderickgregory/2014/05/05/putins-human-rights-council-accidentally-posts-real-crimean-election-results-only-15-voted-for-annexation/#6ab3645810ff

Hobsbawm, E. and Ranger, T. eds. *The Invention of Tradition.* Cambridge: Cambridge University Press, 1983.

International Organization for Migration, *Migration in Ukraine: Facts and Figures,* September 2011, https://www.iom.int/jahia/webdav/shared/shared/mainsite/activities/countries/docs/Ukraine/Migration-in-Ukraine-Facts-and-Figures.pdf

International Organization for Migration, "Ukraine Displacement: Rise to the Challenge," 26 April 2016, http://www.iom.int/video/ukraine-displacement-rise-challenge

Marshall, Th. "Citizenship and Social Class," in *States and Societies* edited by Held, D. Oxford: Basil Blackwell, 1983: 248-260.

Ong, A. *Flexible Citizenship: The Cultural Logics of Transnationality*. Durham: Duke University Press, 1999.

Wilson, A. *Ukrainians: The Unexpected Nation*, New Haven: Yale University Press, 2000.

World Bank, "World Bank Vice President Reaffirms Support for Ukraine on First Visit to Kyiv," 3 June 2016, http://www.worldbank.org/en/news/press-release/2016/06/03/world-bank-vice-president-reaffirms-support-for-ukraine-on-his-first-visit-to-kyiv

# 5

# Economic Migration of Ukrainians to the European Union: A View from Poland

JOANNA FOMINA

The present chapter aims to analyse several aspects of economic migration from Ukraine to Poland in the context of the military conflict on Ukraine's territory. It looks at how the Euromaidan and the ensuing war with Russia impacted the dynamics of migration to Poland, which has been for a long time one of the most popular destinations for Ukrainians. It seeks to debunk the myth of the influx of Ukrainian refugees to Poland, promulgated by the Polish authorities, as a way to excuse their unwillingness to share the burden of the international migration crisis faced by the European Union. The chapter looks at the dynamics and significance of economic remittances from Poland. Finally, it discusses the unprecedented socio-political mobilisation of Ukrainian migrants in response to the Revolution of Dignity and the armed conflict on its territory that has resulted in increased consolidation of the Ukrainian migrant population and contributed to the development of migrants' social capital. The article employs the official data received upon request by the author from several state institutions including the Office for Foreigners, Polish Ministry of Foreign Affairs, National Bank of Poland and Ministry for Labour and Social Policy; a series of in-depth interviews with Ukrainian civic activists in Poland collected by the Institute of Public Affairs (Warsaw) and Institut für Europäische Politik (Berlin) as well as additional interviews with stake-holders conducted by the author as part of ongoing research on Ukrainian migration to Poland.

The Polish government has been supportive of the pro-democratic forces during the Revolution of Dignity and has backed Ukraine in the Russian-Ukrainian conflict from the start. Public opinion has also been relatively open towards the acceptance of Ukrainian refugees – around half of the population agreed that Poland should admit Ukrainian refugees arriving from the conflict zone (CBOS 2016). Poland organised the resettlement of about 200 Ukrainian citizens of Polish ancestry from the military conflict area, bringing them to Poland and granting permanent residence.

The increased migration flows from Ukraine triggered by the war in Donbas have become embedded into the wider debate on the EU's response to the unprecedented influx of migrants from Africa and Asia, in particular from Syria, and exploited by some public figures for their political ends. The Polish Prime Minister, in a speech in the European Parliament, claimed that Poland did not have the capacity to accept any Syrian refugees, as it has already accepted one million Ukrainian refugees (Chapman 2016). However, while the migration flow has indeed increased, neither the purported volume, nor the declared character of migration has been reflected by the official data. The vast majority of Ukrainians coming to Poland seek gainful employment and are not a burden on the Polish taxpayer, but rather contribute to the country's economic growth.

The number of applications for asylum from Ukrainians has indeed increased after 2013 in relative terms, yet even the total number of applications does not come close to the purported one million. If in 2013 there were 46 applications, in 2014 the number rose to 2318 and in 2015 it reached 2305. In 2016, until July, 709 asylum claims were registered. The Office for Foreigners (UDSC) distinguished several main groups: the Crimea, the Euromaidan, and the Eastern Ukraine profile. In terms of the number of submitted applications, currently Ukraine is second only to Russia, as the vast majority of applications come from Chechens. What is more significant, however, the vast majority of applications have been unsuccessful: the number of persons who were granted refugee status or subsidiary protection is just several dozen (Table 1) (UDSC 2016).

**Table 1: Number of persons granted refugee status or subsidiary protection in years 2013-2016**

|  | 2013 | 2014 | 2015 | 2016 |
|---|---|---|---|---|
| **Refugee status** | 2 | 0 | 2 | 32 |
| **Tolerated stay** | 8 | 11 | 6 | 1 |
| **Subsidiary protection** | 5 | 6 | 24 | 63 |
| **Total** | 15 | 17 | 32 | 96 |

*Source: Office for Foreigners, 2016, own elaboration of the data.*

Altogether between the year 2013 and 2016 almost 6000 Ukrainians applied for asylum and only 36 persons were granted refugee status, and 161 persons received international protection. As of 4 April 2016, 1600 citizens of Ukraine were receiving social aid (UDSC 2016). While claims about the gigantic number of refugees from Ukraine are vastly overstated, there has been a pronounced increase in the migration flow from Ukraine in the aftermath of the Euromaidan and the ensuing military conflict.

One could wonder where the quoted number of one million comes from. Most likely it refers to the number of Polish visas issued to Ukrainian citizens in the past year. Visa statistics shed some light on the dynamics of short-term, seasonal and circular migration, yet the cumulative numbers are not fully illustrative of migration trends for several reasons. First of all, the almost one million visas encompasses all visas issued to Ukrainians coming to Poland for various purposes, including business, tourism, family visits, conferences, often for just a few days[1].

**Table 2: All visas issued to Ukrainian citizens (C+D)[2] in years 2013-2015**

| Ukraine | 2013 | | 2014 | | 2015 | |
|---|---|---|---|---|---|---|
| | C | D | C | D | C | D |
| | 528,274 | 192,401 | 556,511 | 276,748 | 457,885 | 466,791 |
| | 720,675 | | 833,259 | | 924,676 | |

*Source: own elaboration of the data received from the Ministry of Foreign Affairs, 2016*

The number of all visas issued by Polish consulates has increased. In 2015, around 200,000 more visas were issued in comparison to 2013.[3] Notably,

---

[1] Not all visa holders cross the border, as it is explained below.
[2] It should be noted that persons undertaking business activity, studies or work in Poland may be issued both C or D visas. The decision on the type of visa issued depends on the duration of the intended stay. While a holder of a C-type visa is allowed to stay on the territory of the EU for not longer than 90 days over a 180-days period (yet such a visa may be valid for up to five years), D-type visas are granted for stays that are longer than 90 days, with the maximum stay of one year. Those intending to stay longer need to apply for a residence permit.
[3] It is worth pointing out that the dynamics of visas issuance numbers are related to the term of validity of C visas issued: the issuance of multi-entry visas with long-term validity (up to five years). According to the statistics collected by the European Commission around 70 per cent of C visas issued by Polish consulates are multi-entry, yet their validity may vary from six months to five years. If people who travel to Poland on a regular basis are granted visas with relatively short validity, visas granted to them artificially boost statistics.

there has also been a considerable increase in the number of work-related visas (Table 4). If in 2013 the number of visas issued on the basis of employer's declaration of intent to entrust a job was 125,871, in 2015 it has almost tripled (362,889). The share of study-related visas has also increased almost two-fold.

**Table 3: Visas issued to Ukrainian citizens by Polish consulates in years 2013 – 2015, selected purposes of visit (C and D visas combined)**

| Purpose | 2013 | 2014 | 2015 |
|---|---|---|---|
| Business activity | 182,649 | 185,021 | 133,570 |
| Work on the basis of employer's declaration of the intent to entrust a job | 125,871 | 192,614 | 362,889 |
| Work on the basis of work permit | 17,241 | 29,481 | 40,299 |
| Study | 12,093 | 17,258 | 20,243 |

*Source: own elaboration of the data received from the Ministry of Foreign Affairs, 2016*

One needs to be cautious, however, when interpreting these numbers. While they undoubtedly reflect an increased flow of Ukrainians to Poland following the military conflict in the east of Ukraine, the number of visas issued does not necessarily directly correspond to the number of persons coming to Poland or undertaking work in the country. While some visa holders never actually cross the border during the period of validity of their visa, often wishing to have a Schengen visa 'just in case', others use the services of fake employers in order to secure a visa and later seek employment after their arrival in Poland, possibly in other EU countries.[4] Notably, the share of irregular migration, contrary to conventional wisdom, is relatively low and according to a large-scale IOM survey study amounts up to 13 per cent of all

---

[4] As it turns out, the declaration of intent to entrust work system, while considerably liberalising the access to the labour market for Ukrainian workers, is prone to various abuses and malpractices. In general, it is perceived that getting a visa on the basis of a work declaration is relatively easy, and thus an option chosen by many Ukrainians. This is especially the case if one uses the services of intermediary Ukrainian companies cooperating with Polish companies whose main source of income is precisely issuing declarations of intent. According to the data collected during the State Labour Inspectorate investigation of companies that had issued work declarations in 2014, only 69 per cent of Ukrainians who were issued declarations actually entered the territory of Poland. Out of those who entered Poland in 2014 on the basis of visa issued on grounds of declaration of intent, only 37 per cent took up jobs with the employer who issued the declaration. For more, see the State Labour Inspection report, 2015.

Ukrainian migrants in Poland (IOM 2016).

The volume of long-term migration has also increased. As the data collected in Table 2 demonstrates, the number of residence permits (usually valid for one to two years) has almost quadrupled (from 9595 issued in 2013 to 37833 issued in 2015). The majority of temporary permits in 2015 (63 per cent) were issued on the basis of work. This increase also reflects the effects of the Law on Foreigners from 12 December 2013 (art. 114 and 126) introducing a single work and residence permit for stays longer than three months.

**Table 4: Temporary Residence permits issued to Ukrainian citizens, according to purpose of stay**

| Purpose of stay | 2012 | 2013 | 2014 | 2015 | 2016 – until 30.04.2016 |
|---|---|---|---|---|---|
| Family | 2482 | 2450 | 2726 | 3888 | 3236 |
| Education | 1649 | 2351 | 3798 | 7054 | 2668 |
| Work | 3323 | 8718 | 8307 | 23,925 | 11,327 |
| Other | 2373 | 931 | 2277 | 2997 | NA |
| Total | 9827 | 9595 | 17,108 | 37,833 | 17,231 |

Source: own elaboration of data by Office for Foreigners, 2016.

As of 1 July 2016, Ukrainian citizens were holding 83,000 residence permits (31 per cent of all foreigners in Poland). This number also corresponds to the IOM estimations of long-term Ukrainian migrants in Poland at the level of 90,000 (IOM 2016). Out of this number 22,500 were permanent residence permits, 57,500 were temporary residence permits and almost 3000 were long-term EU resident permits. In addition, the state issued 143 permits for EU citizen family members, 229 humanitarian protection permits, ten permits based on tolerated status and 17 based on refugee status (UDSC 2016).

Apart from the changes in sheer volume, there has been a significant change in the ratio of men to women, which is often interpreted as evidence that men migrate to escape army conscription. If in 2013 women clearly dominated over men among holders of temporary residence permits (5760 to 4036), in 2015 the situation was opposite: 22,817 men and 15,165 women were granted temporary residence and in the first half of 2016 – 15,672 men and 10,603 women. Moreover, the number of permits on the basis of family reunion, in particular marriage to a Polish citizen and membership of the family of Ukrainian citizen holding a residence permit, has increased considerably compared to the pre-2013 period. Around one in three of these documents are issued to first-time holders while the rest are granted to persons continuing their stay in Poland (UDSC data 2016).

The data on age and gender of visa holders is not available, nonetheless the survey conducted by the National Bank of Poland (NBP) confirms previously mentioned changes in gender mix and also demonstrates that the recent migrants tend to be younger. According to the survey results – which should not be treated literally, but rather as illustrative of the trends – among the new migrants 58 per cent are men, compared to 33 per cent among experienced migrants. In addition, the mean age of the new migrants is 33, as compared to 43 in the experienced migrants group. Moreover, the share of persons originally coming from eastern parts of Ukraine has also considerably increased (28 per cent in the studied group of post-conflict migrants, as compared to six per cent) (NBP 2016).[5]

Ukrainian workers most often work in domestic services, building, construction and remodelling and agriculture (NBP 2016). But there is also an increasing number of highly-skilled Ukrainian workers in IT and communication, science and education, and health care, often graduates of Polish universities.

The number of Ukrainians studying in Poland has also notably increased. According to the IOM survey, Poland is for Ukrainians a top destination for education purposes – 31 per cent of students studying abroad study in the country (as compared to ten per cent studying in Russia and eight per cent in Spain). Student fees and costs of living in Poland are not prohibitive, besides, holders of the Pole's Card study for free. The number of students enrolled in full-time programmes in 2014/2015 (20,693) has doubled in comparison to 2012/2013 (9620) (Stadnyi 2015). This increase is also reflected in the number of visas and residence permits issued on the basis of undertaking studies in Poland (an increase from 12,093 visas in 2013 to 20,243 visas in 2015 and from 2351 residence permits in 2013 to 7054 residence permits in 2015) (Tables 3 and 4). Students are an important group in the context of economic migration, as considerable part of them will seek employment in Poland or other EU countries after graduation. The law on foreigners from 2013 (art. 187(2)) allows graduates of Polish universities to stay in the country for one year to look for employment.

---

[5] Importantly, this data is not fully representative of the whole population and thus should not be treated literally. Yet it illustrates some trends characteristic of this group of migrants. The survey study was implemented by the Migration Studies Centre Foundation using the Respondent Driven Sampling (RDS) on a sample of 710 respondents employed in the area of Mazovian voivodship in the Warsaw metropolitan area and localities specialising in agricultural produce.

Significantly, according to the NBP estimates, the presence of Ukrainians on the Polish labour market so far has not impacted either the level of unemployment or salaries (NBP 2016). In other words, they have neither been a burden on the tax payer, nor have negatively impacted the situation of Polish employees.

**Remittances**

The increase in migration flows from Ukraine to Poland translates into increase of remittances by long-term migrants as well as the size of salaries earned by Ukrainian short-term migrants (and supposedly their remittances as well). While in 2013, according to the National Bank of Poland non-resident Ukrainians earned 3.6 billion PLN (1.2 billion USD), in 2014 it was 5.4 billion (1.5 billion USD) and in 2015 – 8.4 billion PLN (2.1 billion USD[6]) (NBP 2016). While the total amount in Polish zloty more than doubled in 2015 in comparison to 2013, the differences in American dollars are slightly less considerable due changes in exchange rates. There is no clear data on what share of this sum is transferred to Ukraine, as part of it is spent on their sustenance in Poland. If we assume that one third of the salary is spent in Poland on living expenses, around 5.5 billion PLN (1.4 billion USD) was transferred to Ukraine as remittances, savings, and in-kind contributions.

Long-term migrants are less likely to regularly transfer considerable amounts back home – only a share of them have transnational families relying on their support. The remittances by long-term Ukrainian workers via banks and international financial institutions amounted to 55.1 million USD (also an increase, as compared to previous years: 39.9 million in 2012, 40.5 million in 2013, and 39.2 million in 2014) (NBU data 2016). However, this number does not include in-kind contributions, savings and remittances through informal channels made by long-term migrants. However, the official and estimated remittances of Ukrainians in Poland are considerably smaller than the numbers quoted publically by the Polish Foreign Minister, who claimed that Ukrainians sent to Ukraine about five billion EUR to Ukraine last year.[7]

---

[6]   According to the exchange rates from 30.12.2013, 30.12.2014 and 30.12.2015, respectively.

[7]   'More than a million of Ukrainians who live in Poland annually transfer – only through official bank channels – about ten billion PLN, and the same amount in cash they transfers when visiting their families in Ukraine. This means that last year, according to the NBP, as a result of their work in Poland, Ukrainian citizens transported about five million EUR. This is an important support for the Ukrainian economy' (my translation of the quotation from Minister Waszczykowski's speech at the IX Europe-Ukraine Forum in Łódź): http://wpolityce.pl/polityka/279295-minister-waszczykowski-polska-bedzie-wspierac-suwerenne-decyzje-ukrainy

While remittances on macro-level may not play such a significant role as compared to some other countries, they contribute about 50 per cent of long-term migrants' and 60 per cent of short-term migrants' household income. The funds are mainly used for basic daily needs (food, clothing), improving the living conditions (furniture and household appliances), and expanding or building a house. Education or investing in business are also mentioned (IOM 2016). Some remittance researchers emphasise that remittances contribute to economic inequality (Kupets 2012, Malynovska 2014), yet the funds received from abroad are spent on domestic products and services, contributing to the overall development.[8]

**The Rise of Ukrainian Civil Society in Poland**

One of the significant consequences of the Euromaidan for the Ukrainian population in Poland has been an unprecedented civic mobilisation. It has contributed to the integration of the migrant population, the settled Ukrainian minority as well as the wider Polish society. The Ukrainian civil society existed in Poland well before; the Ukrainian minority has had a well-developed organisational structure focused on promoting Ukrainian language and culture for many decades. There also were a number of NGOs supporting Ukrainian migrants, run by both Ukrainians and Poles in Poland, with the largest share of them in Warsaw (for a comprehensive review of formal and informal Ukrainian civil society initiatives see Łada and Böttger 2016). However – as the in-depth interviews with Ukrainian civic activists demonstrate[9] – the dramatic events in Ukraine have motivated many Ukrainians with no prior civil society participation experience to engage in formal and informal civic initiatives, as well as prompted closer cooperation between various existing organisations.

---

[8] Other negative side-effects, apart from typical problems of transnational families, include both official (bank accounts and loans) and unofficial (household savings) dollarisation, which in turn limits the effectiveness of monetary policy, makes the banking system more vulnerable to economic crisis and currency depreciation; increasing inequalities; and reducing political will to undertake necessary reforms (Kupets 2012; Grotte 2012; IOM 2016).

[9] I would like to thank the Institute of Public Affairs and the Institut für Europäische Politik for sharing the transcripts of in-depth interviews with representatives of formal and informal civil society initiatives of Ukrainian migrants, the Ukrainian minority as well as their Polish partners conducted as part of the project „Ukraińcy w Polsce i w Niemczech – zaangażowanie społeczno-polityczne, oczekiwania, możliwości, działania", supported by the Polish-German Foundation for Science and PZU Foundation.

During the Euromaidan in Kyiv and after the annexation of Crimea, Ukrainian NGOs as well as unaffiliated activists organised protests in front of the Russian embassy as well as rallies and public events in support of the pro-democratic civic opposition in Ukraine. These events gathered rank-and-file Ukrainian workers, students, settled Ukrainian academics, civil society activists, representatives of the Ukrainian minority in Poland, as well as many Poles, including politicians and other well-known public figures. A Civic Committee for Solidarity with Ukraine united outstanding Polish public figures, including some representatives of the Ukrainian minority in Poland, as well as settled Ukrainians. Its activities have also helped to draw the attention of the Polish elites and the wider public to the events in Ukraine.

Apart from more formal fundraising initiatives (organised by various groups) there has been a considerable number of smaller, but equally important informal initiates. Funds and in-kind donations have been raised in order to aid the families of Ukrainian soldiers and refugees from the east of Ukraine as well as buy food, clothes, vehicles, equipment and medicine for Ukrainian soldiers. It is next to impossible to calculate the precise amount of funds collected and transferred to Ukraine, because these initiatives have been irregular, often unofficial and sometimes very small. Social media have played a very important role in mobilising Ukrainians, integrating different circles as well as making the fundraising initiatives effective. Many of those initiatives have been run almost solely through social media platforms, in particular through Facebook, benefitting from large transnational networks that include not only other Ukrainian migrants in Poland, but also Poles, Ukrainians in other countries as well as volunteers based in Ukraine, in a way creating a virtual civil society (Kittilson and Dalton 2011). Many of these initiatives have been promoted through dedicated Facebook groups, such as 'Ukraiński wolontariat w Polsce'. The newly developed social capital will contribute to further integration of the Ukrainian population in Poland.

The period of the Euromaidan and shortly afterwards was also the time when representatives of the Ukrainian community – often PhD students and graduates of Polish universities – were invited to comment and explain the ongoing events in the media. It has become an opportunity to not only provide a better understanding of what was happening in Ukraine, but also to reshape the image of Ukrainians in Poland, who are not only domestic help and builders but also well-educated and knowledgeable experts.

The civic engagement of Ukrainians during and after the Euromaidan has helped to draw the attention of the local authorities and to secure three new centres for the Ukrainian community: the Ukrainian World (*Ukrainsky Svit*), run by the Open Dialogue Foundation and Euromaidan Warsaw Foundation, the Ukrainian House (*Ukrainsky Dim*), run by Our Choice (*Nash Vybir*) Foundation and more recently – the Association of Friends of Ukraine Centre. These institutions provide legal and psychological help to Ukrainian migrants, raise funds and organise public events hosting Ukrainian public figures as well as various artistic events and initiatives, including experimental theatre at the Centre.

The unprecedented mobilisation of the Ukrainian migrant community in Poland has also boosted their self-esteem and increased their sense of agency. Many study participants believe that it has contributed to a more positive perception of Ukrainians by the Polish public opinion (Lada and Böttger 2016). Opinion poll results demonstrate, however, that the overall perception of Ukrainians as a people has not considerably changed in the past few years. Nevertheless, there has been a steady improvement from 15 per cent of Poles having a positive attitude towards Ukrainians in the 1990s to 31 per cent in 2013 and 36 per cent in 2015 (CBOS 2015).

**Conclusion**

The military conflict on the Ukrainian territory has considerably increased migration flows into Poland as well as made previously seasonal migrants take a more long-term stay. The gender and age mix of the Ukrainian migrant population has also changed, with a considerably increased share of young men. However, it is wrong to assume that Ukrainians arriving in Poland as a result of the conflict are refugees living on government handouts. Only a tiny minority has claimed asylum and just a few dozen persons have actually received a refugee status over the period of the past three years. The vast majority of Ukrainians in Poland are economic migrants earning their livelihoods, contributing to the Polish economy as well as supporting their families via financial and in-kind remittances. The military crisis in Ukraine has not produced an influx of asylum seekers, but resulted in an increase of economic migration.

The financial remittances do not play such a significant role for Ukraine on the macro-scale, as compared to other countries where they comprise a very significant share of the country's GDP (IOM 2016). Yet, they are a very important source of income for individual households. The total volume of remittances is hard to establish. According to official data 55.1 million USD were transferred through banks and international money transfer institutions by Ukrainians who worked in Poland for longer than a year. But the estimated income of non-resident Ukrainians in Poland for the last year has amounted 2.1 billion USD (8.4 billion PLN). If the assumption that the living costs comprise about one third of their salaries is correct, Ukrainian non-resident workers may have transferred to Ukraine up to 5.5 billion PLN (1.4 billion USD) through informal channels and in-kind contributions.

The Euromaidan and the Russian-Ukrainian war have led to an unprecedented mobilisation of the Ukrainian population in Poland and contributed to the greater institutionalisation of the civil society as well as the development of new Ukrainian centres. Ukrainian migrants' active engagement in various civic initiatives has boosted their self-esteem and helped to develop their bridging and bonding social capital. It also has contributed to some extent to reshaping the perception of Ukrainians in Poland by native Poles. Further research is needed to see how these developments affect the integration of Ukrainian migrant population into Polish society.

Thus, contrary to the statements of key Polish politicians, the increased presence of Ukrainian migrants in Poland has not been a burden on the Polish taxpayer. On the contrary, it contributed to the overall economic growth as well as public finances (through various official fees and taxes). Not only has the presence of a large number of Ukrainians proved politically uncontroversial, but it also provided political backup for Poland's tough stand against Russian aggression against Ukraine.

**References**

Association of Friends of Ukraine, http://www.tpu.org.pl/pl/towarzystwo/

CBOS, "Stosunek Do Innych Narodów," *Komunikat z Badań*, NR 14/2015.

Chapman, A. "Poland Quibbles Over Who's a Refugee and Who's a Migrant," *Politico*, 22 January 2016, http://www.politico.eu/article/poland-quibbles-over-whos-a-refugee-and-whos-a-migrant-beata-szydlo-asylum-schengen/

Civic Committee for Solidarity with Ukraine, http://www.solidarnosczukraina.pl/index.php/pl/home-page/jak-dziala-komitet

Grotte, M. "Transfer dochodów ukraińskich migrantów," in *Migracje obywateli Ukrainy do Polski w kontekście rozwoju społeczno-gospodarczego: stan obecny, polityka, transfery pieniężne* edited by Brunarska, Zuzanna, Grotte, Małgorzata and Magdalena Lesińska, Warsaw: Centre for Migration Research Working Papers, 2012: 58-84.

Kittilson, M. and Dalton, R. "Virtual Civil Society: The New Frontier of Social Capital?" *Political Behavior* 33 (2011): 625–644.

Kupets, O. "The Development and the Side Effects of Remittances in the CIS Countries: The Case of Ukraine," CARIM-East Research Report, Migration Policy Centre, February 2012.

Łada, A. and Böttger, K. (eds.) *#EngagEUkraine: zaangażowanie społeczne Ukraińców w Polsce i w Niemczech*, Warsaw: Institute of Public Affairs, 2016.

Malynovska, O. Перекази мігрантів з-за кордону: обсяги, канали, соціально-економічне значення, Київ: Національний інститут стратегічних досліджень, 2014.

Narodowy Bank Polski (NBP), "Bilans Płatniczy Rzeczypospolitej Polskiej za IV kwartał 2015 r.," Warszawa: NBP, 2016.

Nash Vybir Foundation, http://pl.naszwybir.pl/

Open Dialogue Foundation, http://odfoundation.eu/

Stadnyi, Y. "Українські студенти в польських внз (2008-2015), [Ukrainian Students in Polish Higher Education Institutions], CEDOS think tank (2015), http://www.cedos.org.ua/en/osvita/ukrainski-studenty-v-polskykh-vnz-2008-2015

State Labour Inspection, "PIP (2015) Sprawozdanie z działalności Państwowej Inspekcji Pracy w 2014 roku," Warszawa, 2015.

UDSC Office for Foreigners, "Raport na temat obywateli Ukrainy," Warszawa, 2016.

Ukraiński Wolontariat w Polsce: https://www.facebook.com/groups/303247243198607/?fref=ts

# 6

# Moving out of 'Their' Places: 1991–2016 Migration of Ukrainians to Australia

OLGA OLEINIKOVA

**Introduction**

Ukraine, like many other Central and Eastern European nations in the 20th Century, went through several sharp turns and endured many tragic twists. This chapter will look into two important historical turning points in the context of the migration of Ukrainians to Australia. The first is the collapse of the Soviet rule in August 1991 and the resulting massive emigration. The second is the 2014 Euromaidan protests and the associated intensification of migration caused by political unrest, economic downturn and the war in eastern Ukraine. These events touched every Ukrainian family deeply and will produce ripple effects for decades to come, both for those who migrated and those who stayed at home.

Ukrainian immigration to Australia has a long history. The first ethnic Ukrainians from western Ukraine are known to have settled in Australia as early as 1860. Then the First World War and the Russian Civil War led to the first massive political emigration, which strengthened the existing Ukrainian communities in Australia by infusing them with people with political, scientific, and cultural backgrounds. During the second wave of political emigration from 1945 through the 1950s, the Ukrainian diaspora in Australia also reasonably increased. The 1990s saw a third wave of Ukrainian immigration to Australia. Today, more than 35,000 people of Ukrainian origin live in Australia, half of whom were born in Ukraine.

Given the dramatic swelling of the Ukrainian community in Australia in the early 1990s and the complete change in Ukrainian migration patterns from 2004 onwards, understanding the larger context of the recent migration flows to Australia is critical. This chapter emphasises the structural variables that shape Ukrainian migration, particularly the events in Ukraine and the shifts in Australian migration policy in the period between 1991 and 2016. Depending on the combination of structural and individual factors, the profile of Ukrainian migrants varies across three periods of migration: (1) 1991–2003, (2) 2004–2013 and (3) 2014–2016. The profile of 1991–2003 arrivals, hereafter called 'transition migrants', is characterised by survival life trajectories and dominated by the arrival of blue-collar working class migrants through humanitarian and family reunion migration streams. Between 2004 and 2013 the character of Ukrainian migration changed towards the arrival of skilled professionals from the white-collar working class families through the skilled migration stream and marriage, and this cohort is addressed as 'dividend migrants'. Since 2014 the profile of Ukrainian migrants in Australia has experienced another shift back towards the dominance of survival aims and mechanisms, and the arrival through the humanitarian and skilled migration stream. These arrivals have been referred to as 'post-dream migrants', a reference to the situation where dreams for Ukraine's democratic and economically sustainable future are being destroyed by a reality that pushes its citizens to migrate.

The post-independence Ukrainian migration to Australia is an understudied phenomenon and this chapter seeks to address this gap. The analysis is based on the author's PhD research project that explored Ukrainian migration to Australia between 1991 and 2016. It did so by focusing on the bifurcation of migrant life strategies before, during and after migration. The study used a two-fold methodology. It began with the collection and assessment of secondary data on both Australian migration policy and Ukrainian migration from 1991 onwards. Later, qualitative fieldwork was conducted in Australia (NSW and Wollongong) between October 2012 and May 2013, which involved 51 semi-structured interviews with Ukrainians. A further five interviews with Ukrainians who arrived in Australia during or after 2014 (the Euromaidan protests) were conducted in June 2016. Hence, this chapter relies on a total of 56 interviews. Participants were stratified across Ukrainian regions. Of the participants, 32 were men and 24 were women. Regarding their social origins, 25 of the interviewees were born into white-collar working class families and 29 into blue-collar working class ones, while the remaining two interviewees originated from the class of cultural and scientific intelligentsia.

The empirical qualitative fieldwork garnered rich data that was then used to investigate the differences in migrants' profiles across the migration process as well as over the three time periods. Post-independence Ukrainian migration, our primary focus here, varied depending on a combination of structural and individual factors. Let us first sketch out the structural context and scrutinise the power of emigration dynamics to shape the profiles of 'transition migrants' (1991–2003), 'dividend migrants' (2004–2013) and 'post-dream migrants' (2014–2016) in Australia.

**Dynamics of Emigration from Ukraine to Australia: Structural Contexts**

*The 1991–2003 Migration Context*

The analysis of emigration dynamics between 1991 and 2003 are a direct reflection of Ukraine's period of instability and the country's negative economic, political and demographic situation during the first 12 years of independence. Ukraine faced a deep economic crisis, price hikes of basic consumer goods and transport, the commercialisation of education and the elimination of social benefits such as a guaranteed job, free health care and state housing. While these factors made migration more difficult, the economic problems forced people to look for opportunities to survive, which included migration. Hence, the huge difference in living standards between the post-Soviet Ukraine and the countries of the West significantly impacted the level of Ukrainian migration to the West for permanent residency.

Between 1991 and 2004, many countries experienced an influx of Ukrainian immigrants. According to official statistics, 2,537,400 individuals left Ukraine; 1,897,500 moved to other post-Soviet countries while 639,900 moved to other, mainly Western, states. More geographically distant countries, such as Australia, have only recently (in the second half of the 1990s and the beginning of the 2000s) become emigration destinations for Ukrainians. Based on the interviews, the choice of migrating to Australia was always associated with family ties, successful migration stories of friends and/or biographical circumstances.

The first five years of independence saw the most intensive flow of Ukrainians to Australia. Later, the flow of immigration decreased slightly, with 11 per cent arriving between 2001 and 2006, and 9.6 per cent during 2007–2011 (DIAC 2013). Between 1991 and 2003 a total of 3519 Ukrainians arrived in Australia with permanent residency status (DIAC 2014). Figure 1 summarises the data.

**Figure 1: Ukrainian-born arrivals in Australia**

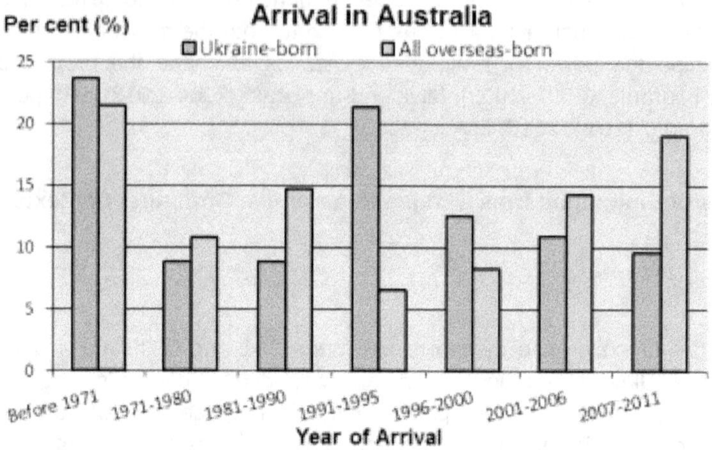

*Source: Department of Immigration and Citizenship (2013) Community Information Summary: Ukraine-born.* Australian Government: Canberra

Since the 1990s, key changes in Australia's migration policies have shaped the character of Ukrainian migration to the country. From 1970 to 1996 the government had made it increasingly more difficult for unskilled migrants to migrate to Australia outside of humanitarian and family reunion programmes (Larsen 2013). It encouraged family migration because it saw family migrants as bonding agents for the next migration wave, thereby assisting their cultural and economic integration (Larsen 2013). Only after 1996 were the first reforms to family migration introduced, resulting in a shift towards skilled migration, which was perceived to have earning potential (Boucher 2013; Hawthorne 2005; Markus et al. 2009). Therefore, at the beginning of the 1990s, Australia's migration policy created a number of barriers for Ukrainian migration. Given the policy, the majority of Ukrainians in the 1990s arrived as family and humanitarian (refugee) migrants. The UNHCR Statistical Online Population Database shows this clearly (see Table 1).

**Table 1: Ukrainian citizens granted refugee status in Australia and asylum applications submitted by Ukrainian citizens 1999-2009**

| Population type | 1999 | 2000 | 2001 | 2002 | 2003 | 2004 | 2005 | 2006 | 2007 | 2008 | 2009 |
|---|---|---|---|---|---|---|---|---|---|---|---|
| Refugees | 13 | 20 | 27 | 40 | 44 | 40 | 34 | 30 | 55 | 55 | 52 |
| Asylum seekers | 88 | 203 | 259 | 125 | 9 | 0 | 4 | 6 | 2 | 0 | 3 |

Source: UNHCR Statistical Online Population Database, United Nations High Commissioner for Refugees (UNHCR), Data extracted: 18 January 2014, www.unhcr.org/statistics/populationdatabase

As the situation of the mid 2000s changed, so did Australia's migration policy and in turn the migration trajectories of Ukrainians.

*The 2004–2013 Migration Context*

During this period, many Ukrainian citizens tried to find a legal opportunity to leave their country under any pretext—either for work or for permanent residence. Against the background of Yushchenko's myth-making and demagoguery about patriotism, more and more ordinary citizens lost any hope for a bright future in Ukraine and began looking for a better life abroad. The main destinations for Ukrainian labour migrants remained the same. In 2009 these were, firstly, Russia (48.1 per cent) and then the European Union countries (41.2 per cent) (State Statistics Service of Ukraine 2009, 33). However, between 2010 and 2013, migration research and statistics revealed a shift in the migration choices of Ukrainians towards Asia. Due to its geographical distance and the lack of an easy way for Ukrainians to access the country, Australia was still not among the most popular destinations. In addition, since 2004, there have been changes in the number and character of Ukrainian arrivals to Australia.

The number of Ukrainian arrivals into Australia during 2004–2013 decreased. The main feature of Ukrainian migration to the country during this period was the change in the quality of migrants since 2004: the skilled migration stream with permanent status came to outnumber humanitarian and family migrants. Out of the 2470 permanent arrivals between 2004 and 2013, a total of 1312 migrants came through the skilled stream while only 1005 came through the family stream (DIAC 2014)[10]. Between 1 January 2004 and 1 January 2014,

---

[10] As per the DIBP Settlement Database (SDB) data (extracted on 30 April 2014), the total number of Ukraine-born arrivals granted a permanent visa in Australia between 1 January 2004 and 1 January 2013 was 2470 people, out of which 1312 were skilled migrants, 1005 – family migrants, 6 – humanitarian migrants and 147 unknown.

only six Ukrainian migrants were granted a permanent visa through the humanitarian migration stream (DIAC 2014).

**Figure 2: Ukrainian permanent arrivals by migration stream (from 1 January 1991 to 1 January 2014)**

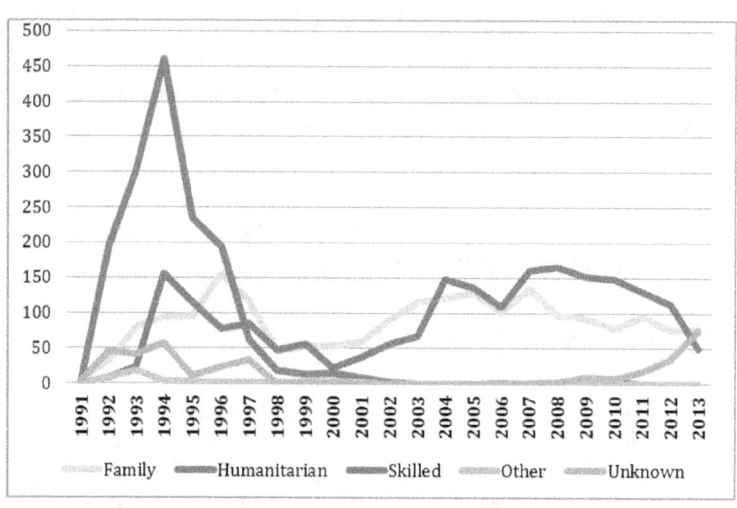

*Source: DIAC Settlement Reporting Facility*

This shift towards skilled arrivals from Ukraine was triggered by the change in the government's migration policy. In 2008 the Rudd Labor Government announced plans to increase the numbers of skilled migrants to Australia by 30 per cent compared to the previous year and this trend continues (Boucher 2013; Markus et al. 2009). The growing demand for highly skilled migrants attracted IT professionals and engineers from Ukraine. Hence, Australia's migration policies have evolved from focusing on attracting migrants for the purposes of increasing Australia's population to attracting migrants as temporary and permanent (skilled) workers in order to meet the needs of the economy.

*The 2014 – 2016 Migration Context*

Since the outbreak of mass protests against the Yanukovych regime in November 2013, Ukraine has been wracked by political and social unrest and violent conflict, especially with the annexation of Crimea in March 2014 and the outbreak of war in eastern Ukraine. In the years leading to the Euromaidan protests, political instability and pervasive corruption inspired not only a movement for democratisation and greater ties with the European

Union, but also the ambition to migrate among a significant portion of the population. The post-Euromaidan events have affected all Ukrainian migration flows, which can be broken down into three main categories: forced internal migration of internally displaced persons (IDPs) by the war in the Donetsk and Luhansk regions; international migration of asylum seekers driven by political motives, as well as the desire to avoid military conscription; and continuous emigration of skilled and professional Ukrainians, along with educational migration driven by a mix of political and economic motives.

During 2014 and 2015 there was a significant increase in the number of applications for refugee status submitted by Ukrainians to the EU countries, the US, Canada and Australia. In 2014, Ukrainians submitted 14,000 applications for refugee status, compared to 1120 in 2013. Given the increase in the number of applications for asylum from Ukrainian citizens in Australia between 2014 and 2015 (DIAC 2015), the country has become more restrictive in granting temporary tourist, study and business visas. Participants from this study who arrived in Australia in 2014 and 2016, mentioned that they know from their own experience and heard from their friends and relatives about instances where temporary visas for Ukrainians were refused. However, there are no open statistics to confirm the increase in the number of refusals from the DIAC.

Among the interviewed males, one of the main reasons for seeking asylum abroad was to avoid army conscription. As the conflict in the east escalated, the Ukrainian government reinstated a general draft with the power to conscript men between the ages of 20 and 27. As a result, many young men used diverse channels of migration to avoid conscription. This included employment, study, training programmes, internships and other available opportunities. It was in these different structural contexts and circumstances that Ukrainians made their decisions and plans to move to Australia. And these contexts have shaped the different migration profiles of Ukrainian migrants in Australia.

## Who Are They: Three Profiles of post-Independence Ukrainian Migrants to Australia

As stated above, the main finding of the 56 interviews of Ukrainians in Australia is that there are three waves of post-independence Ukrainian migration to Australia that correspond to three migration profiles: 'transition migrants', 'dividend migrants' and 'post-dream migrants'. These profiles vary depending on a combination of structural and individual factors (values, aims, needs, sense of agency and decision-making).

*Transition Migrants*

Analysis of the emotional, occupational, and class characteristics of the 'transition migrants' who arrived in Australia between 1991 and 2003, along with their professional, identity and emotional shifts after migration suggests that they created a set of personal and social characteristics which reflected a survival life trajectory. Drawing on the interview data, their survival-oriented, risk-minimising trajectory is mainly characterised by: (1) the aim to escape poverty and starvation and regain job status; (2) material values, values of traditionalism, family well-being, comfort and conformity; (3) the need for security (order and stability, living in a safe environment, avoiding threats), environmental needs (a healthy environment) and social needs (integrity of social and individual values); and (4) weak agency and behavioral passivity (meaning operation within the most accessible and safe opportunities, and not actively transforming their lives by extending their opportunities). These characteristics were found to be shaped in Ukraine before departure, and they are what defines and reinforces the survival life trajectory of 'transition migrants' in the post-migration stages.

The analysis of the motivations and aims for migration typical for 'transition migrants' shows that their choices are dominated by migration push factors. In the interviews, 'transition migrants' spoke about economic crisis and political turbulence as a push factor for their migration, and framed their emigration to Australia as being 'more forced than voluntary'. The main migration push factors found in their life stories were: (1) unemployment; (2) lack of occupational work; (3) low wages and arrears; and (4) the suppression of entrepreneurial activity.

The 'transition migrants' cohort mostly used the family reunion and humanitarian migration streams to assist their entry into Australia. The blue-collar workers and suppressed entrepreneurs formed a particular group of humanitarian 'transition migrants' comprised of regular and irregular short-term arrivals who tended to obtain their permanent residency in Australia by claiming asylum. This cohort was identified as using 'conspiracy' and 'maneuvering' tactics to enable their entry into the country and attempts to gain permanent residency. Their effective tactics were found to grow out of explicit social networks. Such networks were crucial for this group as they assisted them in managing the different types of precarity associated with the lack of life and work predictability and security, which affected their financial or psychological welfare.

The family reunion migration stream for 'transition migrants' was the second most popular way of entering Australia. Here, the economic rationale, in the form of a plan to escape poverty and unemployment in Ukraine, was the main driving force behind the participants' choice of family reunion. A connection to family and dependency on the resources that the family provided was found in many cases to encourage dependency on the Australian welfare system in the post-migration stage. It also tended to create a type of comfort zone that favoured the continuation of survival life patterns after migration.

Talking about migration as 'an ongoing emotional journey' (Ryan 2008, 301), the majority of 'transition migrant' interviewees emphasised the role of psychological discomfort and the depression that was induced by the social and economic conditions arising from post-Soviet unrest before migration that threaded through their post-migration life. The majority of 'transition migrants' showed disappointment, guilt, nostalgic depression and homesickness caused by their separation from home and those they left behind. Most of the stories expressed partial satisfaction with migration and demonstrated precarity, emotional insecurity and opportunism. These emotions were a deterrent to the success of their integration into and adaptation to Australia.

Influenced by occupational insecurity and 'structural disempowerment' (Mrozowicki 2011), a typical work experience for the 'transition migrants' was an occupational downgrade alongside an economic upgrade. Using Mrozowicki's (2011) terminology of 'dead-end careers', the occupational experiences of the majority of 'transition migrants' proved to be shaped by employment in non-professional jobs (dead-end careers) which were associated with the absence of occupational mobility in the new, changed environment. Thus, the survival life trajectory of the 'transition migrants' was reflected in their experience of a sharp downgrade of professional and social status after migration.

This cohort demonstrated a low level of English proficiency and a strong national identification with Ukraine, which created barriers for successful social adaptation and integration into Australian society. As the most powerful and important motivation to work, material orientation facilitated their quick economic adaptation to life in Australia. 'Transition migrants' tended to start their employment in the first available job, typically a manual job in construction, painting, or teaching Ukrainian at the Ukrainian language schools. Material values were also found to guide their behaviors and consumption practices.

Being born into blue-collar working class families and in majority having a secondary education, the 'transition migrants' do not attach much importance to professional growth and self-development. However, all of them mentioned that back in Ukraine they would never have believed that they would have had to wake up at 4 am in the morning and work as hard as they did in the construction industry, with only short breaks for holidays. Furthermore, the future plans of 'transition migrants' tend to be retrospectively oriented towards their past life in Ukraine. They continued to invest money in Ukraine and some of them cherished plans to return to the country for their retirement.

*Dividend Migrants*

On the contrary, the 'dividend migrants' who arrived in Australia between 2004 and 2013 approach their migration as a kind of investment. Their narratives show that their choice of Australia as a destination was informed and driven by calculated advantages–socio-economic dividends from migration – i.e. social, ethical, cultural, aesthetic, educational and civic capital.

Unlike 'transition migrants', 'dividend migrants' are motivated by Australian pull factors. Economic push factors are not the primary ones for these migrants—they all come from the class of professionals or scientific and cultural intelligentsia, and said they felt economically secure back in Ukraine and only went abroad seeking, to use one interviewee's words, an *upgrade in life*. Here, an 'upgrade' means professional growth and self-realisation, better money and an improvement in the quality of life, with interesting work with social mobility. The life trajectory of this cohort is defined as achievement life strategy.

Based on the interviews, the achievement life trajectory of 'dividend migrants' is characterised by the following: (1) long-term aims for professional success and self-realisation oriented at opening new opportunities (extensive goals) and the extended recreation of social and economic status; (2) socially-oriented needs for professional and cultural success and individually-oriented needs for creative self-expression and professional self-realisation; (3) instrumental values, aimed at achieving the goals accompanied by a set of non-material values, such as the prospects and opportunities for self-realisation and a favorable environment for developing their own initiative, freedom and independence.

Compared to the 'transition migrants', financial welfare comes second and is a minor value. 'Dividend migrants' demonstrate strong agency that is expressed through their active life position and the internal capacity to take responsibility for themselves instead of relying on external circumstances. Youth (the average age of the cohort was 30) also played a role in their active life position and determined their focus on high performance and the ability to live and work in conditions of uncertainty and risk. 'Dividend migrants' value originality, as well as access to a variety of choices of cultural styles and ways to implement them. The cohort is dominated by the young IT-skilled migrants from Ukraine who chose to be globally engaged through migration and used this strategy to achieve better pay, professional development and future alternative employment opportunities.

'Dividend migrants' arrived in Australia through the skilled and family migration streams. Both streams reflect how this cohort was affected by the lack of opportunities for development and professional self-realisation in Ukraine. Skilled migration during the 2003–2014 period was found to be mostly male and structured by IT market growth in Australia and Ukraine, as well as the international exposure of Ukrainian professionals, linked to global orders, services and corporations, to parts of the IT industry outside their country. Marriage migration in the cohort of the 'dividend migrants' is characterised by the involvement of highly educated (Master degree and PhD), middle-aged (in their 30s–40s) women in highly skilled professions such as law, banking and research. Despite the elite character of the participants' marriage migration, this cohort expressed their suffering from being stereotyped as 'mail-order brides'.

All the interviewed 'dividend migrants' have successfully adapted and integrated into Australian society both socially and professionally. They have an Australian and/or cosmopolitan identity, high levels of English and complete satisfaction with migration, with future plans to succeed in terms of professional self-realisation, career growth and personal development. Given their capacity to successfully maintain their social status after migration, they are the group of migrants who are positively contributing to Australian society in terms of social cohesion, innovation and economic production.

*Post-Dream Migrants*

For 'post-dream migrants', the most recent cohort to arrive in Australia between 2014 and 2016, survival life trajectories dominate. The values, needs and aims that were found in the five stories of the 'post-dream migrants' were very much similar to those of 'transition migrants', where material values dominated and family welfare and security, financial freedom and independence came first. The popularity of security needs, along with the needs for self-realisation and self-expression, are explained by the fact that before migration, the interviewees supported the 2014 Euromaidan protests and were investing emotionally and financially in Ukraine's democratic future. Significantly, this cohort is dominated by people under the age of 29 from the white-collar social class. Due to the absence of the promised reforms and changes in Ukraine, they experienced disappointment and the loss of hope for future changes. Ultimately the reality of their faded dreams pushed them to migrate. Such a reactionary behavioral response, spontaneous choice of migration and short-term aims drive the lives of the interviewed 'post-dream migrants'.

All participants in this cohort mentioned that their decision to migrate was reactionary and quick, rather than strategic. 'Conspiracy' and 'maneuvering' tactics to turn their Australian temporary visas (study and business) into permanent ones was the case for the majority of the interviewed 'post-dream migrants'. Their emotional sphere is threaded with precarity, emotional insecurity, opportunism and concerns about the future of Ukraine, as well as their future in Australia. Despite the negative attitudes and emotions associated with the events in Ukraine, all the 'post-dream migrants' express satisfaction with their choice to migrate. They enjoy their new life in Australia and do not plan to return to Ukraine.

'Post-dream migrants' have cosmopolitan identities as well as a rediscovered Ukrainian identification. Social networks played the most important role in their integration. In Australia they often found new acquaintances and first jobs through relatives or friends. 'Post-dream migrants' tend to settle with or near Ukrainian friends and Ukrainian neighborhoods in Sydney. Their involvement in primary groups is also high, as with the 'transition migrants'. The effect that all the interviewees experienced is a rather slower integration into Australian society compared with the fast and successful integration of the 'dividend migrants'. Moderate and high levels of English language proficiency dominate and play an important role in the first years of the 'post-dream migrants'' lives in Australia.

## Conclusion

The post-independence Ukrainian community in Australia is a mixed group. Based on 56 interviews, three profiles of Ukrainian migrants were identified and described as 'transition migrants', 'dividend migrants' and 'post-dream migrants'. These three profiles vary depending on the combination of individual values, aims, needs, agencies and the structural factors at the time of the migrant's departure from Ukraine.

A key point is the discovery that Ukrainian migration to Australia has changed since 2004, when the representatives of the professional class and the class of the cultural and scientific intelligentsia began using the skilled and marriage migration stream. At that point, Ukrainian immigrants in this group outnumbered the blue-collar working class and entrepreneurs of the earlier period who arrived through the humanitarian and family reunion programmes.

In 2004, for the first time in the history of Ukrainian migration to Australia, the number of skilled arrivals outnumbered those who arrived using the family reunion and humanitarian streams. The 2014 post-Euromaidan events also impacted on the life trajectories of Ukrainians, whose motives for migration into Australia underwent another shift, this time towards survival: economic, political and physical. As a result, the number of asylum seeker applications from Ukrainians increased in 2014 in comparison with the last ten years. Hence, the changed structural context of Ukraine in 2014–2016 has again reshaped the profile of Ukrainian migrants and their migration pathways in the last two years.

Given the small scope of the study and the number of respondents, the findings presented here should not be regarded as exhaustive. Migration situations are mobile and dynamic, and further research is needed on post-independence Ukrainian migrants, their profiles and adaptation to the structure of contemporary Australian society.

## References

ABS, "QuickStats," Canberra: Australian Bureau of Statistics, 2012.

ABS, "QuickStats," Canberra: Australian Bureau of Statistics, 2001.

Belyaeva, L.A. "Strategii vyzhivaniya, adaptacii, preuspevaniya," [Strategies of Survival, Adaptation, Prosperity], *Socis 6* (2001): 44-53.

Boucher, A. "Bureaucratic Control and Policy Change: A Comparative Venue Shopping Approach to Skilled Immigration Policies in Australia and Canada," *Journal of Comparative Policy Analysis: Research and Practice*, 15, no.4 (2013): 349-367.

Department of Immigration and Citizenship (DIAC), "Reduction of Certain Student Visa Assessment Levels," Canberra: Australia, 2012, https://www.immi.gov.au/students/reduction-student-visa-assessment-level.htm

Department of Immigration and Citizenship (DIAC), "Community Information Summary: Ukraine-born," Canberra: Australia, 2013, www.immi.gov.au/media/publications/statistics/comm-summ/summary.html

Department of Immigration and Citizenship (DIAC), "Settlement Database (SDB)," Canberra: Australia, 2014, http://www.immi.gov.au/living-in-australia/delivering-assistance/settlementreporting-facility/index.htm

Hawthorne, L. "Picking Winners: The Recent Transformation of Australia's Skilled Migration Policy," *International Migration Review* 39, no.3 (2005): 663–696.

Larsen, G. "Family migration to Australia," *Parliament Research Paper Series (2013-2014),* Canberra: Australia, 2013, http://parlinfo.aph.gov.au/parlInfo/download/library/prspub/2931915/upload_binary/2931915.pdf;fileType=application/pdf

Markus, A.B., Jupp, J., & McDonald, P. *Australia's Immigration Revolution.* Sydney: Allen and Unwin, 2009.

Mrozowicki, A. *Coping with Social Change: Life Strategies of Workers in Poland's New Capitalism*, Leuven: Leuven University Press, 2011.

Ryan, L. "Navigating the Emotional Terrain of Families 'Here' and 'There': Women, Migration and the Management of Emotions," *Journal of Intercultural Studies,* 29, no.3 (2008): 299–313.

State Statistics Service of Ukraine and the Ukrainian Center for Social Reforms, *Foreign Labour Migration of Ukraine's Population*, Open Ukraine, 2009.

United Nations High Commissioner for Refugees (UNHCR), "Ukraine Extended Migration Profile," *UNHCR Statistical Online Population Database* (2014), www.unhcr.org/statistics/populationdatabase

Part Two
# RUSSIA

# 7

# Migration of Ukrainians to Russia in 2014–2015. Discourses and Perceptions of the Local Population

VLADIMIR MUKOMEL

## Introduction

Migration flows between Ukraine and Russia have always been high, but they increased particularly in the 2000s when Russia became one of the main directions for labour migrants from Ukraine. As of 2 February 2014, shortly before the Ukraine crisis began, there were 1.6 million Ukrainian citizens living in Russia. Labour migrants, chiefly circular, comprised two thirds of this number. Since Ukrainian labour migrants do not belong to 'visible minorities' that are targets of xenophobia, they did not attract a particular attention from Russians. If the issue of labour migration from Ukraine began to be discussed among Russian society, it happened solely due to the influx of migrants from the east of Ukraine.

The large influx of individuals seeking asylum in Russia began in July 2014 when the most intensive hostilities evolved. By the end of 2014 (data from 5 December 2014) the number of Ukrainian citizens who stayed in the territory of Russia increased by more than 0.9 million and went up to 2.5 million persons.[1] Deterioration of living conditions in the territory of the so-called Novorossiya and bitter fighting which flared up in the region of Debal'tsevo

---

[1] Hereinafter references are made to data of the Central Database of Foreign Citizens and Stateless Persons' Registration of the Federal Migration Service of Russia (FMS).

and Mariupol in January–February 2015, further increased the number of people who fled from the war. By March 2015 the number of Ukrainian citizens in Russia increased to 2.6 million and afterwards stabilised at that level.

The necessary help was provided to the people who left Ukraine[2] and the migrants were offered preferential treatment. The local populations perceived the support ambiguously, particularly in the near-border regions where many natives from Ukraine had relatives and friends. How were the problems of people who left Ukraine covered by mass media and articulated by the authorities? What discourses dominated? And how did the recipient population react to the influx of people seeking asylum? This chapter seeks to address these questions.

## Methodology

The study is based on the following data: 1) Automated real-time media monitoring and analysis called Medialogia information and analytical system; 2) Sociological studies carried out by the Institute of Sociology of the Russian Academy of Sciences in summer and autumn of 2015. These included 40 focus groups and 25 in-depth interviews, conducted in five regions of Russia, with the local and migrant youth aged between 20 and 29 years, belonging to the higher strata of the middle class and the lower class[3]; 3) Data collected in the course of the Russia Longitudinal Monitoring Survey, RLMS-HSE. The twenty-fourth wave of RLMS-HSE was conducted between October 2015 and February 2016 and included 18,400 respondents[4]; 4) Department statistics of the FMS (the Central Database of Foreign Citizens' and Stateless Persons' Registration).

## Dominant Discourses in Russia

The issue of refugees has been considered by the producers of the discourse

---

[2] The Government of the Russian Federation allocated 4.94 billion RUB (about 140 million USD) as early as July 2014.

[3] Studies were carried out within the framework of a project supported by the Russian Scientific Fund, grant #15-18-00138.

[4] Russia Longitudinal Monitoring survey, RLMS-HSE conducted by the National Research University Higher School of Economics and Demoscope closed joint-stock company together with Carolina Population Center, University of North Carolina at Chapel Hill and the Institute of Sociology of the Russian Academy of Sciences. The RLMS-HSE is a series of nationally representative surveys designed to monitor the effects of health and economic welfare reforms on households and individuals in the Russian Federation.

(first of all the mass media and political figures) in the context of the assessment of Russia's actions in Crimea and south-east Ukraine. The cleavage within Russian society ran along the *pro et contra* line.

In the news and information programmes controlled by the state, compassion toward people who left Ukraine was accompanied by references to 'Kyiv junta', 'Fascists' and 'Bandera's followers' who were accused of waging 'war against their own people'. Federal TV channels every day transmitted talkshows on Ukraine where the above terms were used. Few liberal mass media attempted to present an alternative version of the events.

Personalities of mass culture who have had an enormous influence on the formation of public opinion were also divided on the matter.[5] When the popular singer Andrei Makarevich sang to the children of Ukrainian refugees in Ukraine, cultural figures[6] as well as the authorities turned against him and imposed a secret ban on his music performances and those of other singers who opposed the war. Some State Duma members suggested depriving Makarevich of all his titles and state rewards. Later, a suggestion to deprive Makarevich of Russian citizenship followed (Vesti.ru 2014; Izvestia 2015).

The discourse of authorities that backed the mass media propaganda campaign had two main components: the articulation of messages conveyed by propagandists ('citizens of Ukraine... are fleeing from the enemy which turned out to be the army of their own country' – as Sergey Naryshkin, the speaker of the Russian parliament stated, TASS 2014) and the demonstration of their actions' success ('It was done quietly, with no political outcry, buzz, and scandals. The people [refugees] are accommodated, the people work, their children take classes', RIA Novosti 2015).

The civil society was also split. On the one hand, the pro-government Public Chamber reproduced propaganda messages of success[7], but on the other

---

[5] One pole is represented by Aleksey Kortnev ('inflamed with the fraternal love the people applauds the fraternal war') and the other by the song 'Our Cossacks go, go through Slavyansk' which was changed into 'And our Cossacks will reach Kharkov... and Kiev' (the song was propagandised as the 'Hymn of the Russian spring').

[6] A quotation from a song by Andrey Makarevich ('My former brothers have obediently become helminths').

[7] Speaking of people coming from south-east Ukraine Vladimir Slepak, the member of the Russian Federation Public Chamber, said: 'The genuine gist of events will be understood in all countries of the world and people will rally against mendacious Ukrainian politicians who wage war against their own people. The world public will finally discern outright fascists in Ukrainian nationalists' [Public Chamber 2014a]. See also [Public Chamber 2015].

hand the Council for Human Rights under the President of Russia focused on the socio-economic problems of Ukrainian refugees. It drafted a well-researched report, many recommendations of which were implemented (The Consolidated Report 2014).

For all parties involved in the dispute the issue of refugees was just a pretext to influence the public. The struggle for the man in the street began in the summer of 2014 when the influx of people from Eastern Ukraine sharply rose. Of 70,000 publications in mass media and the Internet between June 2014 and June 2016 related to people who fled Ukraine, 64 per cent were written between June and September 2014 and 22 per cent between October 2014 and May 2015. Subsequently, the attention of the media in relation to refugees fell drastically; according to Medialogia only 9 per cent of publications on the issue appeared in the period from June to November 2015 and mere 5 per cent of publications in the period between December 2015 and June 2016.

The interest in the problems of refugees rose in times of active hostilities when the attention of the media was drawn to Ukraine, and fell after the conclusion of the Minsk and Minsk-2 agreements. The change in policy with respect to Ukrainian migrants at the end of 2015 played an important role in the decline of the media's interest in refugees. Namely, special privileges were abandoned and the requirements to legalise a refugee's stay in the territory of Russia were made more stringent. As a result, the continuation of a propaganda campaign was no longer needed.

The issue of migrants from Ukraine split internet communities too. About 460 thematic groups related to helping Ukrainians who had fled to Russia were formed on social networks. These groups organised fundraising and in-kind support for the displaced individuals as well as advertised job and accommodation offers. The expression 'help for refugees'[8] stood at the level of 105,000–115,000 of requests made in retrieval systems throughout summer months of 2014 (Public Chamber 2014b, 10). At the same time, from the summer of 2014 onwards groups that were actively opposed to people who came from Ukraine formed online via patriotic websites (for instance http://politicus.ru, http://pravda.ru etc.). Headlines of articles published on those websites provide a good summary of their content and include the following: 'Unfortunately, many refugees from Donetsk region proved to be cads, swindlers, and bottom-feeders' (politicus.ru 2014a) and 'The Ukrainian refugees: brothers or freeloaders?' (Pravda.ru 2014). Specialised blogs under symptomatic names 'We are against #Ukrainian refugees in Russia!!!', using

---

[8]  In the Russian discourse, all those who came from the south-east of Ukraine were treated as refugees regardless of their status.

foul language, were created.

The issue of people who fled from Ukraine attracted attention of scientific circles as early as 2014. The first publications were written predominantly by specialists from the Russian regions closest to Ukraine: Belgorod, Rostov and Volgograd. Later, the circle of authors had expanded up to Primorski region. The influx of refugees is considered in these publications in the context of challenges to security and social stability (Popova, Timofeeva 2015, Boiko 2015), communications (Borisova 2014, Olenitskaya 2015, Golub', Timofeeva 2015) regional finances (Vergun 2014) and socio-psychological and economic aspects of adaptation (Golub', Bezrukova et al. 2015, Yakimov et.al 2015).

**Perception of Forced Migrants from Ukraine by the Receiving Population**

The first wave of people who left the east of Ukraine settled in regions located close to the border: Rostov, Belgorod, Voronezh and Crimea. According to Konstantin Romodanovsky, the Director of the Federal Migration Service of Russia, over 80 per cent of the 515,000 inhabitants of east Ukraine who arrived to Russia between 1 April 2014 and 21 July 2014, stayed in the near-border territories (RF Government 2014). Striving to avoid gathering of migrants from east Ukraine in these regions, the authorities organised migrants' movement to other areas, up to the Far East, the Kaliningrad exclave, the Volga basin and to the Urals. At the same time, a ban on accommodating refugees in the near-border regions, Moscow, Saint Petersburg and some other areas was imposed.

The first migrants from Ukraine were received with a genuine enthusiasm on the part of Russian citizens, which was fed by vigorous propaganda spread by state media. With Ukrainian refugees arriving to other regions of Russia, the enthusiasm of Russian citizens has decreased. In 2014 the share of Russians who spoke in favour of providing the migrants from Ukraine with all necessities and propitious living conditions decreased considerably, from 50 per cent in July to 40 per cent in September. The share of respondents who thought that it was necessary to send refugees back to Ukraine as soon as conditions were favourable increased from 39 per cent in July to 45 per cent in September (VCIOM 2014).

The influx of refugees has affected the everyday life of the recipient population, particularly in the regions of Russia near the borders: 'The Ukrainians have settled in all our yards' (Belgorod). The attitude of the part of migrants who think that the recipient population is bound to help them provoked rejection: 'The Ukrainians think that because their country is ravaged by war it is precisely we who ought to help them' (Belgorod); and 'As if somebody owes them' (Kaluga).

Migrants have been accused of taking the jobs of local people and contributing to the decrease of local salaries: 'Our people who are looking for jobs cannot find employment because refugees are the first ones who are hired' (Rostov). The authorities' demand to provide the refugees with employment caused discontent: 'I work at a state institution... and we were obliged to allocate between ten and 15 per cent of jobs to Ukrainians' (Rostov); 'When it was ordered to allocate jobs for refugees from Ukraine our people were just fired. The administration simply found some pretext and fired people' (Belgorod).

Many local inhabitants were irritated by claims put forward by some migrants and by their willingness to live at other people's or the state's expense: 'We are refugees and you have to provide housing, prosperity, jobs for us; you have to do everything for us. It is certainly a problem' (Crimea).

The lack of gratitude on the part of refugees was also widely emphasised by respondents: 'My boss helps orphan homes, brings clothes there... And they [refugees] scrutinise these clothes and say: what did you bring to us? We will not wear these clothes. At first we feel pity for refugees and then...we felt no pity' (Kaluga).

Some refugees aroused bewilderment and doubts in their genuineness among local inhabitants: 'A taxi driver from Donetsk said: well, I have come here and I want to get an apartment at the southern coast of Crimea' (Crimea).

Local people accused refugees of contributing to the overcrowding of pre-school institutions and universities: 'The refugees get places in children care centres while local people do not get places for their children' (Belgorod); 'People grumble not so much against migrants taking their jobs as against them taking places in schools and higher education institutions' (Rostov); 'The fact that refugees get places in schools and higher education institutions provokes greater talks' (Rostov). The last claim is true, as the government has created preferential conditions for migrants from Ukraine. Moreover, local people have complained about refugees begging: 'Refugees go door to door and say: "I am a refugee, give me alms please"' (Belgorod).

An opinion that more is being done for refugees than for the local people has become widespread: 'People got angry not so much with refugees as with our state because refugees got subsidies and everything as if we, local inhabitants, were not humans' (Kaluga). Surveys carried out in the Volgograd region demonstrate that irrespective of amiable or negative attitude to refugees, respondents were convinced that the state behaved better towards refugees than its own citizens. 75 per cent of respondents shared this opinion (Golub', Timofeeva 2015, 67).

The state-imposed methods of supporting refugees have been clumsy. The supposedly voluntary, but in fact compulsory, nature of this help has caused particular concern among the recipient population. Employees of state-funded organisations came across dubious practices: '... a daily earning was taken from every employee as a help to refugees' (Belgorod). Such practices (taking away from one group in order to give to another) are unthinkable in other countries, and naturally raised concerns among those affected in the Russian Federation '... it has to be done not in a compulsory way but on a voluntary basis' (Kaluga).

Rumours that a daily allowance of 800 RUB (at that time the sum was the equivalent of about 23 USD) was allocated to every refugee caused a particular frustration. Comments from the internet are illustrative: 'A friend of mine works at a plant. Now they have to work two days a week for free in order to pay 800 roubles daily allowance to refugees' (We are against it... 2014). However, it was a misapprehension, as the money was allocated to the maintenance of migrants in temporary accommodation facilities, their food, transport and running of facilities.

Migrants were accused of unwillingness to work and of having excessive and unreasonable demands from the host community: 'The refugees say "But Vladimir Putin promised us?" They think that we owe them something' (Belgorod); 'Moms with children must come and not fathers in rough and tough cars. Let men protect their motherland. And they fear doing that' (Belgorod).

Accusations that the massive influx of refugees has led to the increase in criminal activity have been widespread; 'They plundered the local church... These people have nothing sacred'; 'They do nothing. They steal hens and pigs from their neighbours' (Rostov). 'Yes, Ukrainians pillaged. That really occurred'; 'It was the first wave of refugees. People say it was the most dreadful wave'; '... people who were stealing in Ukraine, now came to us' (Belgorod). Increased criminal activity is not an unusual outcome when a society is unable to fully integrate refugees. In some instances, it is a media effect: local media outlets may single out refugee activities while omitting similar reporting with regard to the general population. Even though the accusations are unlikely to be pure fiction, it is still a far cry from objective reporting.

On their part, migrants have complained about the difficulties finding jobs and housing. They have displayed four main reactions to the anti-migrant resentment. The first one was that of acknowledgment that some of the complaints of the local population have been substantiated: 'It is simply unpleasant to hear that because local people do not know what we had experienced... Yet the greater part of the population is loyal to us and understands us...' (Belgorod). The second reaction is that of 'deafness', reflecting resignation: 'Trivial matters not worthy of acute conflicts, it is silly'; 'Well, they have said and made their point, it is no big deal' (Belgorod). The third position is a position of agreement that there are serious problems with the behaviour of some fellow-countrymen: 'We ourselves are the source of problems' (Ukrainians from Belgorod).

The fourth position is very similar to the position of local residents' majority. It is characteristic for those Ukrainians who have settled down in Russia and received Russian citizenship. The proponents of the fourth position blame the newcomers for the deterioration of their living conditions: 'The most important thing is: their coming should not create problems for us' (Belgorod). At the same time, local Ukrainians have been dissatisfied with the need to turn down claims of relatives who live in Ukraine: 'All relatives in Ukraine think that we have to support them, that we have to dispatch something to them, remit money to them... They think we owe them' (Ukrainians from Belgorod).

However, when comparing the situation in Russia and in Ukraine, many Ukrainian refugees have expressed gratitude to inhabitants of Belgorod: 'There is a lot of kind and sympathetic people here. I meet primarily good people'; 'The people are simply good and less prone to conflicts' (Ukrainians from Belgorod).

## Conclusion

For many years, Russians were open to Ukrainians and saw them as desirable neighbours. However, in recent years the attitudes have deteriorated: in the course of a longitudinal poll of 18,400 respondents, 16.2 per cent expressed negative attitudes towards the idea of having Ukrainian neighbours and 25.5 per cent of respondents expressed negative attitude to the possibility of having a Ukrainian boss.[9] Thus, there is evidence to suggest that the recent geopolitical changes have had negative consequences on the ability to maintain good relations between the two nationalities.

The recipient population's attitude towards Ukrainian migrants and Ukrainians

---

[9] RLMS-HSE, 24 wave

in general began to worsen between 2014 and 2015; 14 per cent of respondents were ready to restrict Ukrainians' residence in the territory of Russia in August 2015 (versus five per cent in October 2013 and eight per cent in July 2014) (Levada-Center 2016). This shift in the public opinion can lead to more serious social problems, if the tension between Ukrainian refugees and the local population continues. There are some steps that could be taken to ameliorate this situation. First, those Ukrainians who intend to go back home, should adapt to the Russian realities while awaiting the change of circumstances in Ukraine. This means that they need a job, housing, and schooling for children within a Russian reality in which people rely predominantly on themselves. Second, people who came from south-east Ukraine and who do not intend to go back, as they connect their future with Russia, must be better integrated into the Russian society to avoid the negative social consequences associated with a factionalised society lacking in tolerance, empathy, and the ability to co-exist.

**References**

BFM, "The Federal Migration Service: Over 400 Thousand Ukrainians are Ready to Become a Part of the Russian Society," *bfm.ru* 2 января (2016), https://www.bfm.ru/news/312119

Boiko I. A. "Attitude of Belgorod Youth to Problems of Refugees from Ukraine and Syria," *Scientific Almanac* 12-3, no.14 (2015): 198-204

Borisova N.P. 2014. 'The Problem of Psychological Maintenance of Interaction of the Accepting Side with Refugees from Ukraine'. *Culture. Science. Integration* 2 (26): 18-21.

Chernysh, M.F. (ed.), *Socio-Economic Factors of Inter-Ethnic Tensions in the Regions of the Russian Federation*, Moscow: The Institute of Sociology of the Russian Academy of Sciences, 2015: 107.

Council for Development of Civic Society Under the President of the Russian Federation, "The Consolidated Report on Measures for Provision of Help to Persons Who Were Forced to Leave the Territory of Ukraine and Placed in the Territory of the Russian Federation," Consolidated Report, 31 October 2014, http://president-sovet.ru/documents/read/282/.

Golub' O.V., Timofeeva T. S. "Social Psychological Study of Volgograd City and Volgorad Region Residents' Attitude to Refugees from Ukraine," *Science and Modernity* 39 (2015): 66-73.

Golub' O. V., Bezrukova A. N., Timofeeva T. S., Popova A. R. *Social-Psychological Situation of Refugees from Ukraine: Regional Aspect*, Volgograd: Volgograd State University, 2015: 131.

*Izvestia*, "The Communists asked Andrei Makarevich to Renounce Citizenship," 7 May 2015, http://izvestia.ru/news/586192

Levada-Center, "Intolerance and Xenophobia" (2015), http://www.levada.ru/2016/10/11/intolerantnost-i-ksenofobiya/

Lyul'ko, L. "Where Do 'Bandera's Followers' Flee from Lugansk," Pravda.ru, 21 August 2014, http://www.pravda.ru/society/how/defendrights/21-08-2014/1222380-bejentsy-0/

Novikova, I. "Their Refugees Versus Our Invalids?" Pravda.ru, 19 August 2014, http://www.pravda.ru/news/expert/19-08-2014/1221979-novikova-0/ [

Olenitskaya, E.S. "From Ukraine in the Territory of Russia: Problems and Experience of Crisis Phenomena Management in Intercultural Communication," in *Russia in the Period of Transformation: Crisis Communication and Anti-Crisis Management*, Yaroslavl: Academy MUB&NT, 2014: 160.

Politikus, "Unfortunately Many Refugees from Donetsk Region Proved to be Cads, Swindlers, and Bottom-Feeders," *Politicus.ru,* 16 June 2014, http://politikus.ru/v-rossii/21736-k-sozhaleniyu-mnogie-bezhency-iz-doneckoy-oblasti-okazalis-hamami-moshennikami-i-lyubitelyami-halyavy.html

Politikus, "Who Are They? Refugees?" *Politicus.ru,* 3 July 2014, http://politikus.ru/v-rossii/23314-kto-eto-bezhency.html.

Popova A. R., Timofeeva T. S. "Problem of the Ukrainian Refugees' Relocation: Social and Economic Consequences for Russia," Volgograd State University, *Fundamental Research* 11-1 (2015): 179-184.

Pravda, "The Ukrainian Refugees: Brothers or Freeloaders?" pravda.ru, 22 August 2014, http://www.pravda.ru/news/world/formerussr/ukraine/22-08-2014/1222575-efir_bezhenci-0/.

Public Chamber Press Release, *The Russian Federation Public Chamber News*, 11 August 2014, https://www.oprf.ru/press/832/newsitem/25703.

Public Chamber, *The report on condition of the civic society in the Russian Federation 2014*, Moscow: The Russian Federation Public Chamber, 2014: 184

Public Chamber Press Release, "Refugees from Ukraine: International Judicial Protection," *The Russian Federation Public Chamber News*, 3 June 2015, https://www.oprf.ru/press/news/2015/newsitem/29617

Russian Federation Government, "Teleconference on Deployment and Social-Mundane Arrangement of Persons Who Were Forced to Leave Territory of Ukraine," *Russian Federation Government News*, 22 July 2014, http://government.ru/news/13896/.

RIA-Novosti, "Naryshkin: Russia Accepted Refugees from Ukraine with no 'Political Hollo," *The Russian Information Agency-News*, 1 October 2015, http://ria.ru/society/20151001/1294511627.html.

Telegraph Agency of the Soviet Union, "Naryshkin: For beginning of a Dialogue a Real Armistice is Needed," 1 July 2014, http://tass.ru/politika/1289903

Vesti.ru News, 18 August 2014, http://www.vesti.ru/doc.html?id=1901954

Vergun S. S. "Refugees from Ukraine as a Threat to Financial Stability of Rostov Region," *Economics and Entrepreneurship* 9, no.50 (2014): 259-262.

VCIOM, "Refugees from Ukraine: To Create All Conditions or Send Them Back?" *Russian Public Opinion Research Center (VCIOM) Press release 2682*, 26 September 2014, http://wciom.ru/index.php?id=236&uid=114994

VK.com, "WE ARE AGAINST UKRAINIAN REFUGEES IN RUSSIA!!!" https://new.vk.com/ukraina_go_out

Western Rus', "The Russian Spring song 'Our Cossacks go, go through Slavyansk," 2014, http://archive.ec/RPVjW#selection-1613.0-1613.52

Yakimov, Z., Shkodich I. and Ibragimova, M. "Problems of Social-Cultural and Legal Adaptation of Labor Migrants-Refugees from Ukraine in the Primorski Region," *Society and Economy* 3 (2015): 144-155.

# 8

# Russian Society and the Conflict in Ukraine: Masses, Elites and National Identity

VIACHESLAV MOROZOV

This chapter looks at how Russian society reacted to the conflict in and with Ukraine. The active phase of the conflict began in March 2014 with the annexation of Crimea and continued with Moscow's support for the separatist movements in the Donbas region of Eastern Ukraine. The main object of interest here is popular views of the conflict and its context, and in particular the way these views are conditioned by nationalism and the national identity discourse. At the same time, as I show in the first section, it is hardly possible to consider 'public opinion' as ontologically separate from the public debate waged mainly by the elites, as well as from the state's policies and the way they are legitimated. The issue is not just that public opinion is influenced by the state propaganda, but that both are part of the same broader discursive domain where meaning is constructed and reproduced.

Accordingly, this chapter starts with an analysis of Russian public opinion on the conflict and its relationship to the official propaganda. I then go on to discuss how the attitudes to Ukraine and the wider assessment of Russian foreign policy in recent years are related to the complex ways in which the Russian nation is defined and how the concept of the 'Russian world' plays into the picture. The final section focuses on the broader context of what Russians see as Western expansionism and how they justify Russia's conduct in terms of the need to defend the country's sovereignty and moral integrity against Western subversion. It is not my ambition in this chapter to present any original analysis of primary sources; rather, I see my task as summing up the findings of the existing studies (including my own) and highlighting the key issues that have come up in the scholarly debate so far.

## Russian Public Opinion on Ukraine and the Conflict

Russian society's response to the conflict in/with Ukraine must be analysed at different levels. The most easily accessible type of data are opinion polls. These, unsurprisingly, demonstrate that the Russian government enjoys the overwhelming support of its population. This phenomenon is most visible when it comes to the annexation of Crimea. Around half of the population 'definitely' supports this move, while the total share of positive attitudes has consistently remained above 80 per cent (Levada Centre 2016a). Similarly, as Denis Volkov (2015) points out, 'Russians are virtually unanimous (95-96 per cent) in denying their own country's responsibility for anything that's happening in Ukraine: the ongoing conflict, breaches of the Minsk Agreements, the shooting down of MH17 etc.' As highlighted by Lev Gudkov (2015b, 35-36), the annexation of Crimea produced a political transition among the relatively prosperous urban population, comprising about 20-25 per cent of the citizenry, who used to distance themselves from the regime but now fully support Putin and his foreign policy.

Even though the profound effect of the conflict with Ukraine on Russian public opinion is beyond doubt, this fact remains open to vastly different interpretations. Thus, Levada Centre scholars tend to explain Russia's stalled transition to democracy in general and the intervention in Ukraine in particular by referring to the lingering paternalistic attitudes, imprinted on the political culture by the 70 years of the Soviet rule (e.g. Levada 2004; for a critique, see Gabovich 2008). This reading implies that, in the final analysis, the role of the Kremlin's anti-Ukrainian propaganda consisted not so much in shaping the preferences of the audience as in voicing, legitimising and radicalising the views that the pro-Putin majority had held ever since the collapse of the Soviet Union. It seems that a similar view is embraced by Ted Hopf in his study of the interplay between mass common sense and elites' views in Russia. According to Hopf, while the elites strive to bring the country closer to the West, 'common sense is hindering any Russian movement from the semi-periphery to the core of Western hegemony' and thus 'has an effect on the distribution of power in the international system' (2013, 348). From this perspective, the conservative turn in Russian politics after 2012 could be interpreted as a result of the elites having finally embraced mass common sense. As Volkov (2015) puts it, the 'propaganda machine can only exploit sentiments and fears that are already present', 'a mistrust for the West ..., the passive consumption of television content by the majority of the population, and a nostalgia for lost superpower status' experienced by the typical *Homo Sovieticus*.

At the same time, both Hopf and Gudkov, a leading proponent of the *Homo*

*Soveticus* theory (see Gudkov 2009), are much more careful in their empirical analysis of the 'Crimean syndrome'. Gudkov, for instance, dismisses the implication that 'Russians have a metaphysical inclination toward traditionalism as such' and explains the surge in nationalism by 'a perceived lack of choice – a lack of alternative sources of authority and alternative ideas about the desirable and likely medium- and long-term future of the country' (2015b, 38). Similarly, in a later article, Hopf (2016) offers a more complex account of the discursive struggles that led up to the Crimean annexation, emphasising the role played by Putin and other leaders, as well as the impact of the Western expansion, which most Russians viewed as hostile.

The elites' agency comes out as an even more prominent factor in Peter Pomerantsev's influential account of the Kremlin's tactics: in his view, the goal is to infuse the public with a poisonous dose of cynicism by constantly exposing conspiracies and corruption – real and imagined – behind all political actors and institutions, in Russia and elsewhere, with only the Kremlin being immune to such disparagement. The resulting worldview is that 'nothing is true and everything is possible' (Pomerantsev 2015). Nuanced studies of public opinion consistently emphasise the complexity of this phenomenon: even though the anti-Western, anti-Ukrainian and xenophobic views clearly dominate, they go along with the reluctance to support direct military intervention in the neighbouring country and even the view that cooperation with the West on certain issues is desirable (Gerber 2015; Sherlock 2014; Volkov 2015).

This multifaceted discussion has direct bearing on the central argument of this chapter. It demonstrates that it would be wrong to reduce the consideration of Russian society's response to the Euromaidan revolution, the annexation of Crimea and the conflict in the Donbas to any individual factor. More specifically, while it must certainly be viewed through the prism of such concepts as nationalism and imperialism, these phenomena themselves are inherently contradictory and conditioned by radically dissimilar historical legacies. While imperialism is expansionist and inclusive, ethnic nationalism emphasises cultural homogeneity and thus treats even some Russian citizens as unwelcome strangers. The lasting impact of Soviet official internationalism makes the picture even more complex. Russian mass common sense is a mix of all these diverse elements: indeed, the concept of common sense itself, as it was introduced by Antonio Gramsci, presupposes a view of this phenomenon as necessarily protean, an incongruous combination of archaic and modern norms and values (Morton 2007, 62; Liguori 2009, 129). While the official ideology might be able, at times, to come up with a more consistent national identity narrative, it is also subject both to the demands of the political moment and the constraints imposed by the socially embedded popular views. As a result, many of the key political statements made by the

Russian leaders are deliberately ambiguous and open to multiple interpretations. Nowhere is this more evident than in the field of national identity politics.

## National Identity, Nationalism and Foreign Policy

It is common to point out the incompatibility between the ethnic, imperial and civic versions of Russian national identity (Tolz 1998, 2004; Shevel 2011). The first two appear to be conducive to some form of intervention in Ukraine, while the latter must, in principle, offer an alternative image of Russia and Russianness. Civic identity, however, has been in retreat since 2012, while the rise of ethnic nationalism was admittedly behind the perception of Russia as a divided nation and the image of 'the Russian world', used to legitimise the annexation of Crimea and the support for the Donbas insurgents (Zevelev 2014; Feklyunina 2015). Nevertheless, as Marlene Laruelle demonstrates,

> the status of this 'divided nation' line of argument remains instrumental: it is part of the discursive repertoire of Russia's foreign policy, deployed whenever the Kremlin needs to penalize a neighbor for its geopolitical or political disloyalty, but it does not appear as a driver of routine foreign policy decisions. (2015b, 95)

At the same time, ethnic nationalism is difficult to reconcile with the political reality of a multi-ethnic nation created on the ruins of empire. The problem is, however, that neither of the available alternatives can achieve unconditional hegemony (Laruelle 2015c). While nostalgic memories about the Soviet and imperial past seem to dominate mass common sense (Kozlov 2016) and are a useful resource for the propaganda machine, it is hard to directly translate them into a national identity for today's Russia.

A key, albeit not the only, reason for the limited utility of the imperial legacy is that the latter is, in itself, full of contradictions. Thus, the Soviet 'affirmative action empire' (Martin 2001) promoted the essentialised notion of ethnicity as the basis for nationhood, the principle of ethnic ownership of territories through the system of national autonomies (Miller 2007), the ideology of proletarian internationalism and equality of nations, combined, somewhat uneasily and with a varying degree of determination, with the imperial idea of ethnic Russians as 'the first among the equals'. If one adds to that the prominence of Orthodox Christianity and the romanticised view of family and other 'traditional values' usually associated with the pre-1917 Russia, the resulting mixture becomes utterly eclectic and untranslatable into a clear-cut dividing line between the national 'self' and the 'others'.

While the broad set of patriotic values promoted by the Kremlin is shared by a vast majority of the population, no specific definition of what it means to be a patriot enjoys the same universally accepted status. As revealed in a recent study by Paul Goode, when confronted with direct and specific questions, Russian citizens find it hard to agree on the meaning of patriotism and have to deploy various strategies to eliminate apparent contradictions. Importantly, for Goode's respondents, 'ethnic nationalism – though common in discussions of patriotism – rarely figured into evaluations of foreign policy or the Kremlin's policy toward Ukraine' (Goode 2016).

Opinion polls demonstrate that the Russian public is split down the middle on the question of whether Russians and Ukrainians are one people or two separate peoples, with the proportion of those who see Ukrainians as a separate nation steadily, but unevenly, increasing from 17 per cent in 2005 to 43 per cent in May 2016. The approval of the idea that Russia and Ukraine must merge into a single state peaked at 28 per cent at the moment of Crimean annexation, before dropping below ten per cent by the end of 2014 and remaining at more or less the same level ever since. On the contrary, a growing share of the population (36 per cent in May 2016) supports complete separation between the two states, with visas, customs controls and so on. In spite of this, those in favour of friendly relations with an independent Ukraine, without visas and customs barriers, have always remained a majority (Levada Centre 2016a). Generally, the Russian public does not support slogans of territorial expansion or intervention in the affairs of neighbouring states (Volkov 2015).

In other words, detailed studies looking at the relationship between the attitudes of the Russian masses and foreign policy, using both qualitative and quantitative methods and looking through the prism of public opinion as well as from the disciplinary perspective of international relations, tend to agree that Russian society remains divided with regard to any specific foreign policy issue. It would be equally wrong, however, to conclude that the masses are completely passive and ready to approve of any policy that the Kremlin might happen to select at any given moment. Any serious political choice still requires careful legitimation that needs to be constructed out of the existing eclectic elements of common sense.

Moscow's bold decision to intervene in Ukraine stands out as an exception against the overall background of Putin's presidency, which, at least prior to 2014, had been associated with prioritising the status quo and avoiding direct confrontation (with an important exception of the 2008 war with Georgia, see Astrov 2011). This decision needs to be understood as a reaction to what was perceived as an acute crisis of the international system, which in this view had lost its balance and required urgent action to prevent a genuine catastrophe. The point of origin of the crisis was easy to identify: predictably, it was seen as instigated by the irresponsible and expansionist West. The relationship with the West is important not just for Russian foreign policy makers, but for the society at large, and it needs to be explored in some detail.

**Looking in the Western Mirror**

What unites all definitions of the Russian nation examined in the previous section is that eventually they need the Western mirror to make sense in the wider context of the Russian political debate. The predominance of anti-Western attitudes is registered by all sociological instruments (Herber 2015, Volkov 2015, Goode 2015) as well as by discourse-analytical tools (Hopf 2016). It is also reflected in the recent conservative turn in Russian politics, ideology and legislation: such measures as the law banning 'propaganda of homosexuality', promotion of 'traditional family values' and other elements of Russia's 'spiritual sovereignty' seem to pay off in the sense of consolidating the social base of the regime (Sharafutdinova 2015).

It was the broad anti-Western consensus that made the annexation of Crimea and the support for the Donbas separatists possible and in some sense inevitable. It was prepared by a wide-ranging transformation of the Russian security discourse: while in the early Putin years Russians were inclined to see the weakness of their own state as the primary security challenge, by the end of the decade the external threats were seen as paramount and the domestic issues were redefined accordingly (Snetkov 2015). Even though, as Kingsbury shows in her chapter, the relative prominence of various threats varied with time and depended on the Kremlin's short-term priorities, Russian leadership never stopped worrying about subversive Western influence. Against the backdrop of the urban protest movement of 2011–2012, the Euromaidan came to be interpreted as anything but Ukraine's domestic matter: it was seen as instigated by the West and as a repetition of a future 'colour revolution' in Moscow.

This view, shared by the elites and by the pro-Putin masses alike, provided both the motivation and the legitimation for the dramatic foreign policy steps that followed. The Russian society sees itself as a victim of the West, which is aggressively promoting its own norms, institutions and values throughout post-Soviet space. The EU's Eastern Partnership initiative, NATO enlargement, US plans to create anti-ballistic missile defence, the supranational jurisdiction of the European Court for Human Rights, efforts at democracy promotion, support for LGBT rights movement and human rights in general are all seen as manifestations of Western expansionism. To defend its sovereignty, culture and independent moral standing, Russia needs to protect its sovereignty in all possible ways, but in particular by emphasising its unique values, strengthening 'spiritual bonds' within society (Putin 2012) and beefing up information security – a broad concept that includes control over media, social networks and private communications (Chernenko 2013; Morozov 2015, 103–134; Oliker 2016). If necessary, it also has to fight back to stave off the prospect of Ukraine's NATO membership and to make sure there are no NATO military bases in Crimea.

As a result, positive identification with Europe, which was dominant in Russia in the 1990s, was replaced by an equally forceful othering. While in late 1990s around two thirds of Russians believed their country must strive to become an EU member, this share dropped below 25 per cent after Putin's re-election in 2012, and the attitude to the EU underwent an even more drastic reversal in March 2014 (Gudkov 2015a; Levada Centre 2016c). In other Levada Centre polls, 59 per cent of respondents said they do not consider Russia a European country (Akopov 2016), while only 17 per cent believe that Russia must develop in the same way as Europe (Levada Centre 2016b, 46).

It would seem therefore that the Russian public shares the slogan 'Russia is not Europe', proclaimed by the Ministry of Culture in its April 2014 draft (Izvestia 2014). The reasoning behind this U-turn in identification is aptly summarised by the prominent nationalist historian Andrei Fursov:

> who would want to associate oneself with the zone of today's Europe, where traditional values are destroyed, homosexualism is on the rampage, there is a migration crisis etc. Europe today is, in essence, a dying zone, where the population is unable to defend its cultural and religious identity. It is a post-Christian and post-European world, a graveyard of European civilisation (quoted in Andreeva 2016).

As a radical intellectual who, in fact, had for a number of years been preparing the ground for the change of the official discourse, Fursov is probably more dismissive about Europe than most Russians would be. The same message, however, has been repeated by the official propaganda, which has exploited widely shared fears (xenophobia, homophobia etc.) in a situation where the defenders of individual rights and non-traditional lifestyles are silenced and sometimes even repressed (Sharafutdinova 2014; Stella and Nartova 2016).

Yet it would be wise not to exaggerate the significance of this reversal. Firstly, as already pointed out, Russian society would still prefer to see relations with both the West and Ukraine improve (even though it blames the other side for that not happening). The 'material' aspects of the European way of life, such as economic prosperity and rule of law, still remain hugely attractive to the majority of the Russian citizens (Volkov 2015; Levada Centre 2016b, 47, 130).

Secondly, and most importantly, even as the modality of the identification with Europe changes, Russian national identity discourse remains Eurocentric. While the overall success of the officially declared 'pivot to Asia' remains subject to a heated debate, identity-wise it has definitely not made Russia an Asian country. Likewise, there is no distinct 'Eurasian' identity so far, unless one would like to use this label to refer to the attempt to liberate the country from its normative and economic dependence on Europe – among other things, by building a Eurasian Union as an alternative integration project (cf. Morozova 2009; Laruelle 2015a; Schenk, this volume).

The latter example, however, highlights the Eurocentric nature of the attempts to establish 'Eurasia' as a separate political space, as the Eurasian Union is explicitly modelled on the EU both in its design and in the surrounding discourse about the usefulness of economic integration (Dragneva and Wolczyk 2015). Speaking in more general terms, the only way to insist on the uniqueness of Russian 'traditional values' and 'spirituality' is by contrast with what is perceived as Western or European values. Both Europe and the West thus remain indispensable as key Others against which Russia's identity continues to be defined (for a detailed analysis, see Morozov 2015, 118–134).

In sum, Russian society – both the elites and the masses – remains focused on Europe as the primary Other, which is seen as a geographical space where history unfolds and as a model (positive, negative or both) of social development and well-being. The Ukrainian conflict is viewed against this broad background, as resulting from the irresponsible expansionism of the West and as indisputable proof that Russia must remain firm in defending its interests and sovereignty. This is perhaps the main reason for the high levels of approval of the Crimean annexation and other foreign policy steps taken by the Kremlin since 2014: they are seen not as aggressive but as defensive, while the true aggressor is the West in its main incarnations as the US, NATO and the EU.

## Conclusion

Russian society remains fully behind President Putin's leadership. In particular, the decision to 'reunite' Crimea with Russia continues to enjoy overwhelming support, while all ensuing conflicts are blamed on the West. So far, this attitude has not been shattered by the economic crisis; confidence in the top leadership remains high in spite of omnipresent corruption, significant inflation eating away people's real income and blatant inequality.

As this chapter has argued, this phenomenon cannot be explained by simply reducing it to the effect of the official propaganda. The propaganda is certainly massive, but it hardly creates any new meanings: rather, it feeds on the mass common sense by picking certain elements from the vast and incongruous stock of popular beliefs and blowing them up, sometimes completely out of proportion.

The way the ordinary Russians comprehend the conflict in and with Ukraine is fundamentally conditioned by nationalism, but this nationalism is not necessarily xenophobic and aggressive. Kingsbury is right to point out in her chapter that the xenophobic attitudes are to a large extent deliberately promoted by the Kremlin at certain junctures and tend to subside when such campaigns are over. Besides, xenophobes are often racist and thus worry much less about Ukrainians than about labour migrants from Central Asia. In more general foreign policy terms, Russians would prefer to have good neighbourly relations with Ukraine, the EU and the US, but they are not happy with how their neighbours treat Russia as a nation, as well as their fellow 'compatriots' in post-Soviet states. While the concept of Russia as a divided nation is key to the understanding of Russian national identity and foreign policy, it is also extremely vague and open to a number of incompatible interpretations. It can be read in ethnic nationalist, imperialist and even civic terms, and all of these terms are present in the actual debate and policy documents. As a result, Russian nationalism can, in principle, be compatible with a rather broad range of actual policies.

Current Russian policy is both motivated and legitimised by the fear of Western expansionism. There is a serious and widely shared concern among Russians about the subversive effects of Westernisation for the spiritual integrity of the Russian nation. At the same time, Russian national identity discourse remains Eurocentric: all attempts to create an 'alternative' identity for Russia imply the need to explain how Russia is different from Europe.

## References

Andreeva, D. "Rossiya khochet byt Rossiei," *Russkaya Planeta*, 8 February 2016, http://rusplt.ru/society/Rossiya-hochet-byt-rossiey-21191.html.

Astrov, A. (ed.), *Great Power (mis)Management: The Russian–Georgian War and its Implications for Global Political Order*, Aldershot: Ashgate, 2011.

Dragneva, R. and Wolczuk, K. "European Union Emulation in the Design of Integration," in *The Eurasian Project and Europe Regional Discontinuities and Geopolitics*, edited by David Lane and Vsevolod Samokhvalov, Basingstoke: Palgrave Macmillan, 2015: 135-52.

Feklyunina, V. "Soft Power and Identity: Russia, Ukraine and the 'Russian World(s)," *European Journal of International Relations* (2015), DOI: 10.1177/1354066115601200.

Gabovich, M. "К дискуссии о теоретическом наследии Юрия Левады," *Vestnik obshchestvennogo mneniia* 2 (2008): 8–37.

Gerber, T. P. "Foreign Policy and the United States in Russian Public Opinion," *Problems of Post-Communism* 62, no.2 (2015): 98–111.

Goode, P.J. "Everyday Patriotism and Putin's Foreign Policy," *PONARS Eurasia Policy Memo 432*, July 2016, http://www.ponarseurasia.org/memo/everyday-patriotism-and-putins-foreign-policy.

Gudkov, L. "Usloviya vosproizvodstva 'sovetskogo cheloveka," *Vestnik obshchestvennogo mneniia* 2 (2009): 8–37.

Gudkov, L. "Rossiyane razliubili Evropu," *Novaya Gazeta*, 2 December 2015, http://www.novayagazeta.ru/politics/70997.html.

Gudkov, L. "Russian Public Opinion in the Aftermath of the Ukraine Crisis," *Russian Politics and Law* 53, no.4 (2015): 32–44.

Hopf, T. "Common-Sense Constructivism and Hegemony in World Politics," *International Organization* 67, no.2 (2013): 317–54.

Hopf, T. "Crimea is Ours: A Discursive History," *International Relations* 30, no.2 (2016): 227–55.

*Izvestia*, "Minkultury izlozhilo 'Osnovy gosudarstvennoi kulturnoi politiki," 10 April 2014, http://izvestia.ru/news/569016.

Kozlov, V. "Krizis vyzval u rossiyan depressiyu i nostalgiyu po SSSR," *RBC*, 4 February 2016, http://www.rbc.ru/politics/04/02/2016/56b241cb9a79470482dfe5bd.

Laruelle, M. "Eurasia, Eurasianism, Eurasian Union: Terminological Gaps and Overlaps," *PONARS Eurasia Policy Memo* 366, July 2015, http://www.ponarseurasia.org/memo/eurasia-eurasianism-eurasian-union-terminological-gaps-and-overlaps.

Laruelle, M. "Russia as a 'Divided Nation,' from Compatriots to Crimea: A Contribution to the Discussion on Nationalism and Foreign Policy," *Problems of Post-Communism* 62, no.2 (2015): 88–97.

Laruelle, M. "The Ukrainian Crisis and its Impact on Transforming Russian Nationalism Landscape," in *Ukraine and Russia: People, Politics, Propaganda and Perspectives* edited by Agnieszka Pikulicka-Wilczewska and Richard Sakwa, Bristol: E-International Relations, 2015: 123-28.

Levada, Y. "Chelovek sovetskii': chetvertaya volna," *Vestnik Obshchesvennogo Mnenia* 3, no.4 (2004): 8–18.

Levada Centre, "Monitoring rossiisko-ukrainskikh otnoshenii v predstavleniyakh zhitelei obeikh stran," 16 June 2016. http://www.levada.ru/2016/06/16/13639/.

Levada Centre, "*Obshchestvennoe mnenie – 2015*," Moscow: Levada-Tsentr, 2016.

Levada Centre, "Soyuzniki i 'vragi' Rossii, evropeiskaya integratsiya,"2 June 2016, http://www.levada.ru/2016/06/02/13400/.

Liguori, G. "Common Sense in Gramsci," in *Perspectives on Gramsci: Politics, Culture and Social Theory* edited by Joseph Francese, London, New York: Routledge, 2009: 134-144.

Martin, T. *The Affirmative Action Empire: Nations and Nationalism in the Soviet Union, 1923–1939*, Ithaca, New York: Cornell University Press, 2001.

Miller, A. "Natsiya kak ramka politicheskoi zhizni," *Pro et Contra* 11, no.3 (2007): 6–20.

Morozov, V. *Russia's Postcolonial Identity: A Subaltern Empire in a Eurocentric World*, Basingstoke: Palgrave Macmillan, 2015.

Morozova, N. "Geopolitics, Eurasianism and Russian Foreign Policy Under Putin," *Geopolitics* 14, no.4 (2009): 667–686.

Morton, A.D. *Unravelling Gramsci: Hegemony and Passive Revolution in the Global Political Economy*, London: Pluto Press, 2007.

Oliker, O. *Unpacking Russia's New National Security Strategy*, Center for Strategic and International Studies, 7 January 2016, http://csis.org/publication/unpacking-russias-new-national-security-strategy.

Pomerantsev, P. *Nothing Is True and Everything Is Possible: Adventures in Modern Russia*, London: Faber & Faber, 2015.

Putin, V. *Address to the Federal Assembly*, 12 December 2012, http://kremlin.ru/transcripts/17118.

Sharafutdinova, G. "The Pussy Riot Affair and Putin's Démarche from Sovereign Democracy to Sovereign Morality," *Nationalities Papers* 42, no.4 (2014): 615–21.

Sherlock, T. "Putin's Public Opinion Challenge," *The National Interest*, 21 August 2014, http://nationalinterest.org/feature/putins-public-opinion-challenge-11113.

Shevel, O. "Russian Nation-Building from Yeltsin to Medvedev: Ethnic, Civic, or Purposefully Ambiguous?" *Europe–Asia Studies* 63, no.1 (2011): 179–202.

Snetkov, A. *Russia's Security Policy Under Putin: A Critical Perspective*, London, New York: Routledge, 2015.

Stella, F. and Nartova, N. "Sexual Citizenship, Nationalism and Biopolitics in Putin's Russia," in *Sexuality, Citizenship and Belonging: Trans-National and Intersectional Perspectives* edited by Francesca Stella, Yvette Taylor, Tracey Reynolds and Antoine Rogers, New York, Abingdon: Routledge, 2016: 17-36.

Tolz, V. "Conflicting 'Homeland Myths' and Nation-State Building in Post-Communist Russia," *Slavic Review* 57, no.2 (1998): 267–94.

Tolz, V. "The Search for National Identity in the Russia of Yeltsin and Putin," in *Restructuring Post-Communist Russia* edited by Yitzhak Brudny, Jonathan Frankel and Stefani Hoffman, Cambridge, Cambridge University Press, 2004: 160-78.

Volkov, D. "Supporting a War that Isn't: Russian Public Opinion and the Ukraine Conflict," Carnegie Endowment for International Peace, 9 September 2015, http://carnegie.ru/2015/09/09/supporting-war-that-isn-t-russian-public-opinion-and-ukraine-conflict/ijt1.

Zevelev, I. "The Russian World Boundaries," *Russia in Global Affairs* 2 (2014), http://eng.globalaffairs.ru/number/The-Russian-World-Boundaries-16707.

# 9

# Migration to Russia and the Current Economic Crisis

MIKHAIL DENISENKO

## Introduction

The economic crisis in Russia, which began in 2014, was caused by a rapid fall in oil prices and the imposition of Western sanctions in connection with the events in Ukraine. Prior to the crisis, Russia was attracting a large number of both permanent and temporary labour migrants. International migration has become an important factor in the development of Russian labour market and overcoming demographic decline in the country. For the members of the Commonwealth of Independent States (CIS), from where large part of migrants originate, work in Russia was an important source of foreign currency, and a factor in poverty reduction. The current economic crisis, however, has had a significant impact on both permanent and temporary migration into Russia. Consequently, it has also affected the CIS countries and the region as a whole.

This chapter analyses the latest available statistical data to address the questions of how the volume and structure of migration flows in Russia has changed since the beginning of the recession, and how the crisis affected the remittances sent to the CIS countries. We shall try to answer these questions by looking at the statistics provided by the Federal Migration Service and Russia's Central Bank. I argue that changes in the migration law of Russia introduced in 2014–2015, and the creation of the Eurasian Economic Union in 2015 have had significant effects. While the economic crisis affects all migrants, the other factors influence only a subset of countries under consideration. It is advantageous here to be specific in explaining migration changes regarding migrants' origin countries, by examining particular components of those changes. Thus, the chapter starts with a description of general trends in labour and permanent migration between Russia and the CIS countries in the post-Soviet period.

## The Recent History

After the collapse of the Soviet Union and the emergence of new state borders in 1992, travel between the former Soviet republics changed from domestic to international. Therefore, Russia became one of the world's largest destinations for migrants overnight.[1] In 1994, migration growth in Russia reached its historical maximum of almost one million people (Figure 1). In the 1990s a significant portion of the movement into Russia involved the repatriation of persons who had once left this country, as well as their descendants. Additional strong factors pushing population from the former Soviet republics to Russia were the political events, especially laws about state languages and armed conflicts in the Caucasus, Transnistria, Tajikistan and others. The combined factors caused a flow of refugees and internally displaced persons of different nationalities. Ethnic Russians dominated this migration (constituting a little less than 60 per cent of all immigrants). According to current registration statistics and Census 2002 data, there was also a significant influx of other ethnic groups of Russia (nearly 15 per cent), Ukrainians (ten per cent), Armenians (more than six per cent) and Azerbaijanis (nearly three per cent). The proportion of indigenous peoples of Central Asia among immigrants was insignificant and did not exceed three per cent at that time.

In total, during the period between the censuses of 1989 and 2002, Russia gained an additional 5.5 million residents due to migration.

---

[1] According to estimates of experts from the Population Division of the United Nations, Russia is on the second place in terms of the number of migrants in the world after the United States. International migrant is defined as a person born in a country other than that in which he/she lives. In Russia, as in the other new states on the territory of the former USSR, Yugoslavia and Czechoslovakia, 'large numbers of international migrants appeared, literally from one day to the next, as persons who had moved within each of those countries and were born in a successor State different from that in which they resided at the moment of independence, became international migrants without necessarily having moved at that time' (UN Department of Economic and Social Affairs, Population Division. *Trends in Total Migrant Stock: The 2005 Revision*. United Nation 2006, 5)

**Figure 1: Migration increase in the Russian Federation, 1990-2015 (in thousands)**

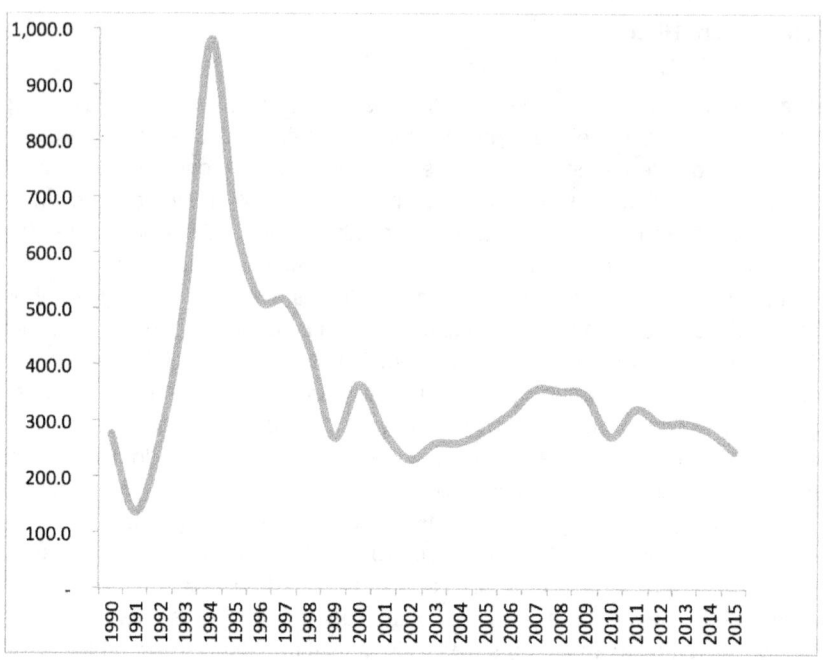

Source: Rosstat[2], Demographic Yearbook of Russia, 2014. Moscow; Rosstat, 2014; Rosstat, Total results of migration in Russia. http://www.gks.ru/wps/wcm/connect/rosstat main/rosstat/ru/statistics/population/demography/#

Since the beginning of the 2000s, economic factors strongly affected the volume and direction of migration flows in the post-Soviet territories. The rapid economic growth in Russia and Kazakhstan created a high demand for labour. The increasing difference between the CIS countries in their tempos of economic development and, as a result, in earnings (see Table 1) and standards of living also played a role. The number of temporary foreign workers in 2012-2013 in Russia reached seven million people, of which three to four million were undocumented migrants.[3] At the same time, the sizes of Russian-speaking populations outside of Russia significantly decreased.[4]

---

[2] Rosstat – The Federal State Statistical Service of the Russian Federation
[3] The Head of the Federal Migration Service, Konstantin Romodanosky, said there were more than 3.5 million undocumented migrants in 2013 (ww.rwbc.ru/rbcfreenews/20130730135511.shtml).
[4] According to the last Soviet census (1989) and the last national censuses, during 1989-2009 the number of Russians in Kazakhstan declined from 6.2 million to 3.8 million; in Kyrgyzstan, from 962,000 to 420,000; and in Tajikistan, from 388,500 to 34,500. The number of Ukrainians in Kazakhstan fell from 896,000 to 108,000; in

A distinctive feature of the 2000s compared to the previous decade was a marked increase in the number of migrants from three countries of Central Asia (Tajikistan, Uzbekistan and Kyrgyzstan), where the difficult economic situation was deepened by military and political conflicts. Almost 40 per cent of all permanent workers came from these countries in 2010-2011. Temporary migrants from the three Central Asian states received most (in 2012, nearly 60 per cent) of the issued documents permitting work (work permits and patents). Moreover, unlike in the past decade, migration from these countries to Russia was clearly dominated by people belonging to ethnic groups of Central Asia, rather than by people of European origin. The new post-Soviet generation of migrants from the countries of Central Asia and the Caucasus generally have lower levels of education, Russian language skills and vocational qualification training, as compared to the older generations. The majority of the young migrants perform heavy and dirty physical work. Therefore, Saodat Olimova, an expert from Tajikistan, characterised that situation as a *muscle drain,* rather than *brain drain*.[5]

In general, migration exchange has been beneficial for both Russia and the sending countries. In total, between 1992 and 2013 inclusive, Russia accepted over 8.4 million additional residents. The migration gain of over 60 per cent compensated the natural decrease of the population during this period. In the 1990s due to migration from the territory of the former Soviet Union, a significant redistribution of human capital took place, to the benefit of Russia, since the Russian-speaking migrants have higher levels of education and better skills.

Therefore, the loss of skilled labour that was earlier caused by mass migration from Russia to countries outside the former USSR was compensated.[6] Permanent and temporary migrants smoothed the imbalance in the labour market and solved labour shortages. However, while the immigrants worked where high or medium levels of qualifications were required, temporary migrant workers were mainly taking low-paid jobs with hard working conditions, unattractive for the Russian population. In 2013 almost 80 per cent of foreign workers were employed in construction or performed unskilled jobs in different sectors of the economy.

---

Kyrgyzstan, from 108,000 to 22,000; and in Tajikistan, from 41,000 to 1000.

[5] Money transfers and their influence on living standards in Khatlon oblast of Tajikistan. MOM-NITS, 'SHARK', Dushanbe, 2006, 30 (*Denezhnye perevody i ikh vliyanie na uroven zhizni v Khatlonskoi oblasti respubliki Tadkhikistan MOM-NITS*, 'SHARK', Dushanbe, 2006, 30)

[6] By the author's estimation over 1.5 million persons in 1990s had left Russia, of which more than 90 per cent for Germany, Israel and the US.

A significant flow of migrants and temporary workers from the CIS countries to Russia was accompanied by a counter-flow of money that migrants were remitting home to their families. According to the available data, between 2006 and 2013, the annual volume of money transfers from Russia to CIS countries increased by more than three times. In 2013 alone, the CIS countries and Georgia received 21.5 billion USD from Russia.[7] In addition to the money earned, migrants, especially those from rural areas of Central Asia, acquired professional training, improved their qualifications and work experience, and broadened their horizons.[8] This has contributed to the accumulation of human capital in their homelands.

**Factors of Migration in 2014–2016**

*Changes in the Economy*

Between 2000 and 2008 the Russian economy was rapidly developing: the average annual GDP growth amounted to seven per cent per year. The engine of development was the oil and gas sector, which was pulling other sectors of the economy, including services and construction. The unemployment rate was kept at five per cent and the state employment service was consistently showing one million vacancies. That pattern of growth was broken in 2009 by the financial crisis, when the GDP fell by 7.8 per cent. In 2010-2012 the economy started to recover, but again fell in 2013. Already in that year, economists were predicting a crisis caused by exorbitant social spending and declining investment.

The immediate cause of the new crisis in Russia was the fall in oil prices in the second half of 2014. As a result, in December 2015 the rouble depreciated by more than 50 per cent against the dollar. The current crisis was further exacerbated by external economic sanctions in connection with the events in Ukraine. In total, in 2015 the GDP decreased by 3.8 per cent. The most significant declines in output took place in the sectors involving predominantly migrant workers: construction (by seven per cent), wholesale and retail trade (by ten per cent), industry (by five per cent), hotels and restaurants (by five per cent).

One distinguishing feature of this crisis is the drop in Russian households'

---

[7] World Bank, Migration and Remittances data. http://www.worldbank.org/en/topic/migrationremittancesdiasporaissues/brief/migration-remittances-data

[8] Central Asian countries are poorly urbanised. According to the results of the last censuses the proportion of the total urban population in each country is as follows: in Kazakhstan (2009) – 54 per cent, Kyrgyzstan (2009) – 34 per cent, Tajikistan (2010) – 26.5 per cent. Rural youth predominates among migrants.

income (which fell by five per cent in 2015 alone), which did not decline during the previous crisis. Russian households employ at least half of all migrant workers. Many people prefer cheap labour of foreign workers – builders, motor mechanics, drivers, nurses, servants etc., to expensive services of the Russian firms. All of the above changes have led to a decline in demand for labour. Demographic factors have been partially counteracting these trends. For example, since 2007, the working age population of Russia has been declining by one million persons annually. Secondly, the imposition by the Russian government in August 2014 of a food embargo against Western countries has stimulated the development of the domestic agricultural sector.

These estimates do not include temporary foreign workers. However, as statistics show (and as will be discussed in the following section), in 2015 the proportion of foreign labour was significantly reduced. This was mainly caused by the fall of the rouble, which led to the reduction of wages in dollar terms. Thus, while in 2013 the average monthly salary in Russia was 963 USD, in 2015 it fell to 560 USD. The wages decreased not only against the dollar or euro, but also against the currencies of the former Soviet republics (Table 1). As a result, for part of population from the CIS countries, the incentives to go for work to Russia have diminished, especially given the fact that the Russian food embargo against the West has led to growth in the agriculture and food sectors in CIS countries. In this regard, Ukraine has been the exception, as due to the ongoing crisis, the living standards continue to decline, even compared with Russia. Therefore, the factors pushing Ukrainian workers abroad continue to intensify.

**Table 1: Average wages per month in CIS countries as share of average wages in Russia (%).**

| Country | 1990 | 2000 | 2007 | 2013 | 2015 |
|---|---|---|---|---|---|
| Russia (US $) | 170 | 80 | 532 | 963 | 560 |
| Russia (=100) | 100 | 100 | 100 | 100 | 100 |
| Azerbaijan | 64 | 63 | 47 | 38 | 81 |
| Armenia | 80 | 53 | 41 | 58 | 69 |
| Belarus | 89 | 63 | 61 | 60 | 74 |
| Georgia | 71 | 47 | 41 | 45 | 73 |
| Kazakhstan | 88 | 129 | 80 | 77 | 101 |
| Kyrgyzstan | 74 | 32 | 20 | 25 | 37 |
| Moldova | 78 | 42 | 32 | 31 | 44 |
| Tajikistan | 68 | 9 | 9 | 16 | 26 |
| Turkmenistan | 81 | … | … | … | … |
| Uzbekistan | 72 | … | … | … | … |
| Ukraine | 81 | 54 | 50 | 44 | 34 |

Source: CIS STAT[9], National Statistical Office of Georgia

It should be noted that we are not observing large-scale unemployment among migrants in Russia. A characteristic of the Russian labour market is that wages remains its main regulator. If wages become low, migrants either look for a new job, or leave Russia and go back to their home countries, where the costs of living are lower.

Studies show that in the countries of Central Asia, Moldova and Armenia, a circular migration mechanism has developed. Returning migrants are the most adventurous part of society; they look for and take up new economic niches. Migrants with years of experience abroad in construction, transport and industry offer their specific skills to the local labour markets. They are used to work more than those who did not participate in migration. But soon the former migrants realise that living on the earned money in their home country without significant savings is impossible. They again go to work in Russia, Kazakhstan and other countries (Marat 2009).

---

[9] CIS STAT – Interstate Statistical Committee of the Commonwealth Independent States

*The International Situation*

In addition to economic factors, in 2014 and 2015 migration processes were influenced by political circumstances. Since 1 January 2012 Belarus, Kazakhstan and Russia have been united in the Common Economic Space (CES). This form of interstate integration provides for the removal of restrictions on citizens' access to the labour markets of CES countries, the abolition of the quota system and compulsory work permits for migrant workers, and a more liberal procedure for migration registration. On 1 January 2015, the three states formed the Eurasian Economic Union (EAZS) and shortly after Armenia and – in August 2015 – Kyrgyzstan entered the organisation. As Armenia and Kyrgyzstan are significant exporters of labour to Russia, joining the EEU has created more opportunities for labour migration of their citizens.

Another group of political factors was generated by the military-political crisis in Ukraine. The armed conflict in the east of the country has caused a flood of asylum-seekers from Ukraine. With the beginning of the combat operations, Russia introduced preferential conditions in terms of residence and employment (no need for work permits) for the citizens of Ukraine who have left their homes and moved to Russia. However, at the end of 2015, Russia cancelled these benefits and instead gave persons of Ukrainian descent the same migration rights as are enjoyed by citizens of CIS countries that do not belong to the single economic space

*Changes in Migration Policy and Irregular Migration*

In June 2012, the Russian government adopted a new *Concept of the State Migration Policy until 2025*.[10] Its content reflects the experience of reforming migration policy in Canada, Australia, Germany, the UK, the US and other countries. The first phase of implementing the Concept was targeted towards preventing irregular migration. Between 2012 and 2015 more than 50 laws were adopted, almost half of which was aimed at strengthening the administrative and criminal penalties for violating migration laws. Let us now consider the laws that have the greatest direct impact on the size and structure of both legal and undocumented migration flows.

Under the new rules from 1 January 2014, a temporary stay in Russia is still limited to 90 days, but individuals can enter the country only once within a period of 180 days. After the introduction of the rule, the number of crossings

---

[10] *Concept of the State Migration Policy until 2025.* Adopted by the president of the Russian Federation on 13 June 2012. http://en.kremlin.ru/events/president/news/15635

of the Russian border fell and migrants from CIS countries coming with the purpose of work for a longer period have had to obtain authorisation to work. This policy was further supported by a ban to enter Russia introduced in 2013 for migrants who had overstayed in the country during their previous trip. This is the most common offense in the field of migration, which is directly related to illegal employment. Those who lived in Russia illegally for more than 270 days are forbidden to enter the country for ten years, whereas those who overstayed between 170 and 270 days cannot re-enter Russia for five years. Those who overstayed for less than 170 days are not allowed to enter the country for three years. In the middle of 2016 the total number of offenders approached two million persons.[11] Most of them were the citizens of Uzbekistan and Tajikistan. It means that almost ten per cent of the male population between the ages of 20 and 50 of those two countries is now barred from entering Russia.

Let us also note two important changes in the Russian migration legislation. Before 2015 there were two types of labour authorisation documents: work permits and the so-called patents (2010). Work permits are further divided into general permits, permits for qualified professionals and permits for highly qualified specialists. General work permits are subject to numeric quotas. Patents were introduced in 2010 to allow individuals (or households) to employ foreign nationals from CIS visa-free countries.

Under the new law, from 1 January 2015, foreigners who arrive from the CIS countries with visa-free entry to Russia do not have to obtain work permits.[12] Instead, they need to acquire patents for their work, whether they want to be employed by an individual, an organisation or an individual entrepreneur. By introducing patents, the government has eased the access of CIS citizens to the Russian labour market. Another policy change adopted on 1 January 2015 requires all foreigners who seek employment (except highly qualified professionals) to pass an exam in the Russian language, Russian history and the fundamentals of law of the Russian Federation.

According to estimates of the Federal Migration Service (FMS), as a result of the above changes the number of undocumented migrants decreased in 2015 by more than 900,000, from 3.6 to 2.7 million. The head of the Federal Migration Service, Konstantin Romodanovsky, noted that 'for the first time in many years the number of legally employed persons exceeded the number of

---

[11] Olga Kirillova (The head of the General Administration for Migration Issues of the Interior Ministry of Russia), Interview for Interfax. 1 July 2016. http://www.interfax.ru/interview/516300

[12] With the exception of students who must get work permits, provided they plan to work outside their universities.

workers without permits.'[13] In Russia, undocumented immigrants are mostly citizens of CIS countries, who work without appropriate permits. The tightening of migration legislation was reflected in their number.

**Permanent Migration from the CIS Countries**

The study of permanent migration into Russia is complicated by frequent changes in the statistical definitions of migrants. The last such change occurred in 2011. Until that time, permanent migrants were considered to be only those who were permanently registered in a new location (or were withdrawn from the migration registry at their former places of permanent residence). However, in 2011 the statistical category of permanent migrants was extended to include other long-term migrants who were registered at a given place of residence for a period of nine months or longer. Withdrawal from the register of this category of migrants is carried out automatically upon termination of their stay. As a result, large groups of foreigners started to be treated as migrants: students of academic programmes, workers with employment contracts for a period of over nine months and relatives of permanent residents of Russia who arrived for a longer period.[14] Obviously, these changes immediately increased the number of arrivals and after a year – the number of departures.[15]

As a result of the changes in the flows of arrivals and departures, migration gain in Russia between 2013 and 2015 decreased from 296,000 to 245,000. Especially significant changes occurred in the migration exchange between Russia and Uzbekistan. Prior to the crisis, over 20 per cent of migration gain to Russia was due to Uzbekistan. According to official statistics, in 2015 Russia has started to lose population in the migration exchange with this most populous Central Asian country. The only exception is Ukraine, which in 2015 provided more than half of the total migration gain in Russia, although in 2012–2013, i.e. before the Ukrainian economic and political crisis, its contribution to the Russian migration gain was limited to 12 per cent.

Whereas Uzbekistan demonstrates how significant economic factors are in explaining long-term migration, Ukraine underlines the importance of non-

---

[13] Romodanovski K.O., Mukomel' V.I., *Regulation of migration processes: problems of transition from reactive to system policy [Regulirovanie migratsionnykh protsessov: problem perekhoda ot reactivnoi k sistemnoi politike]. Obschestvennye nauki i sovremennost.* 2015, No 5:10.

[14] Those who seek temporary asylum in Russia are not included in the number. In 2015 circa 330,000 persons applied for asylum in Russia.

[15] The number of arrivals in 2011 was twice as large as in 2010, while the number of departures in 2012 was twice as large as in 2011.

economic factors. Long-term migrants, as already noted, are divided into several groups. The first group consists of immigrants, i.e. those who come to live in Russia. As a rule, such a decision is not taken spontaneously, but long before the move and is strongly influenced by the situation in the countries of origin. In many cases, statistical reports on migration cover those who have stayed in Russia long ago and in a given year received their permanent resident status i.e. temporary residence permit or a residence permit.

Some migrants arrive in Russia with their Russian citizenship already in hand. There are many such migrants from Moldova (45 per cent), or to be more precise – the territory of Transnistria, as well from Kyrgyzstan (41 per cent) and Kazakhstan (41 per cent), with which until 2011 Russia had an agreement about simplified procedure of citizenship acquisition.[16]

A separate group is composed of migrants who arrived within the framework of the *State Program of Assistance to Voluntary Resettlement to the Russian Federation of Compatriots Living Abroad*. Under this programme, the government provides certain immigrants who have strong ties to Russia (known as 'compatriots') with financial support and work. Between 2007 and 2016, over 400,000 persons arrived in Russia under this scheme and until 2014 most participants were from Kazakhstan and Uzbekistan. The situation changed in 2015, when out of 183,000 participants 110,000 (more than 60 per cent) were citizens of Ukraine. Thus, the majority of all 194,000 migrants from Ukraine in that year arrived in Russia as 'compatriots.' The use of this term is striking in light of the political conflict.

Among the migrants who have arrived for a longer term (nine months or more) and failed to receive permanent residence, students and migrant workers are highly represented. The number of students from the CIS countries, despite the crisis, has increased from 156,000 in 2013 to nearly 200,000 in 2016. In contrast, the economic crisis has directly affected the number of labour migrants from CIS countries. Below we shall examine these changes in temporary foreign labour migration in more detail.

**Labour Migration**

Statistics show that the highest number of work permits in Russia was granted to foreigners in 2014, the first year of the current crisis. The total number of such permits issued was 3.4 million, of which 1.3 million were work permits and 2.1 million – patents. Over 95 per cent of the documents were

---

[16] At the same time, those who have acquired Russian citizenship have also kept their former one.

granted to the citizens of CIS countries with visa-free entry to Russia.[17] Let us now consider how the flow of foreign workers has changed along the major channels of labour migration: work permits, patents and free movement within the single labour market of the Eurasian Economic Union (EAZS).

*Work Permits*

In 2014 there were three types of work permits in Russia: (1) general permits, (2) permits for skilled workers and (3) permits for highly qualified specialists. General Work Permit for a long time was the main channel for labour migration to Russia. They are granted for up to one year with a possibility of prolongation. The number of permits issued is subject to numeric quotas; in total, over the time period between 2010 and 2014, about six million such permits were issued. Most of them were granted to citizens of Uzbekistan (about 42 per cent), Tajikistan (15 per cent) and Ukraine (11 per cent). Non-CIS countries accounted for less than 15 per cent of permits. As noted above, from 1 January 2015, all foreign workers who arrive in the Russian Federation without a visa must acquire a patent. General work permits are granted only to foreign citizens who enter Russia with a visa.[18] In 2015, more than 140,000 such permits were granted (25 per cent less than in 2014), half of them to the citizens of China and Turkey.

Until 2015, work permits were granted to *skilled specialists* – representatives of certain professions, the list of which is approved annually by the Russian Federation Ministry of Labour. The first such list was drafted in 2009 and contained only 17 professions. By 2014, the list was expanded to include 62 positions, mainly executives of companies, engineers and technicians, as well as workers of culture and art. A contingent of qualified specialists was formed mainly by the citizens of CIS countries. The number of permits issued annually for permanent work increased and in 2014 reached its peak, amounting to 160,000. In 2015, about 25,000 of these permits were issued, only for workers who had Russian visas.

In 2010, another channel of labour migration opened up for *highly qualified professionals*. The main criterion in the definition of highly qualified specialist is the salary; it must not be less than two million roubles (about 66,000 USD) and for professors of universities and researchers – not less than one million

---

[17] Since the conclusion of the agreement on the creation in 1999 of 'The Union State', citizens of Russia and Belarus have equal rights to employment in both countries. From this year they have not been included in national statistics of external labour migration in both countries.

[18] International students must also obtain a work permit if their place of work is outside their universities.

roubles (about 33,000 USD) a year. Unlike other programmes, highly qualified professionals can obtain a residence permit for up to three years. In total, between 2010 and 2014 about 90,000 such work permits were granted, over 90 per cent of which were issued to citizens of non-CIS countries. Between 2014 and 2015 the number of highly qualified professionals from the European Union, the United States and Canada went down. However, at the same time, the number of work permits issued for this category of migrants increased due to China. At the end of 2015 there were about 36,000 highly qualified specialists in Russia, including over 8000 Chinese citizens, 7500 citizens of the EU countries, 3600 citizens of CIS countries and 3000 citizens of Turkey.

*Patents*

Since 2010, foreign workers from countries with visa-free entry to Russia may be employed by individuals. For this purpose, it is necessary to acquire a patent for the 'execution of works or services for personal, household and other similar purposes unrelated to business activities' and unlike work permits, the number of patents is not limited. Their initial price was up to 1000 RUB per month (about 32 USD), but by the end of 2014 it increased to 1200 RUB (about 21 USD). Initially patent-based migration complemented the work-permit based one which serves the needs of the government and private companies. However, since the beginning of 2015 patents have become the main channel for the inflow of foreign workers from countries with visa-free entry. Currently, patents are granted for a period of one to 12 months, after which they may be extended by up to a year. Their prices vary and have been regulated by regional authorities; the most expensive ones at the end of 2015 were in Moscow and costed 4200 RUB (about 65 USD).

In total, between 2010 and 2014, 12.7 million patents were granted, of which 48 per cent were bought by the citizens of Uzbekistan and 21 per cent – by the citizens of Tajikistan. The number of patents obtained in 2015 (1.7 million) was lower than in 2014 (2.1 million), partly due to the fact that citizens of Armenia (since January 2015) and Kyrgyzstan (second half 2015) gained the right to work without quotas and patents, following their countries' accession to EAZS. However, their share in the total number of patents during the previous years did not exceed 15 per cent. Importantly, the number of patents granted in 2015 should be compared to the number of both patents and work permits granted in 2014, and for the sake of accuracy should exclude Armenia and Kyrgyzstan.

**Table 2: Issued documents for work in Russia**

| Country | Document | 2013 | 2014 | 2015 |
|---|---|---|---|---|
| Azerbaijan | Patent | 59,300 | 96,800 | 5000 |
|  | Work permission | 16,900 | 14,700 | 1200 |
| Armenia | Patent | 92,500 | 148,700 | 100 |
|  | Work permission | 42,100 | 34,900 | 100 |
| Kazakhstan | Patent | 900 | 900 | - |
|  | Work permission | 800 | 400 | - |
| Kyrgyzstan | Patent | 90,400 | 157,400 | 31,100 |
|  | Work permission | 107,700 | 88,200 | 3,200 |
| Moldova | Patent | 48,800 | 180,300 | 96,700 |
|  | Work permission | 54,500 | 4700 | 2300 |
| Tajikistan | Patent | 301,900 | 443,500 | 421,800 |
|  | Work permission | 197,200 | 186,300 | 6500 |
| Uzbekistan | Patent | 720,700 | 848,500 | 869,200 |
|  | Work permission | 564,200 | 556,600 | 15,600 |
| Ukraine | Patent | 42,200 | 256,300 | 203,200 |
|  | Work permission | 144,700 | 165,500 | 6500 |
| Other Countries | Patent | - | - | - |
|  | Work permission | 286,500 | 229,500 | 183,800 |
| Total | Patent | 1,356,700 | 2,132,400 | 1,672,100 |
|  | Work permission | 1,414,600 | 1,323,100 | 219,200 |

Source: Database of The Federal Migration Service of the Ministry of Internal Affairs

If we take into account the total number of all work permits and patents issued, we will see (Table 2) that the inflow of migrant workers between 2014 and 2015 from Uzbekistan Tajikistan, Ukraine, Azerbaijan and Moldova declined. Not only labour migration has decreased, but also emigration to Russia from CIS countries, with the exception of Ukraine. The available data suggest that part of labour migrants changed their temporary status to permanent by receiving a temporary residence permit, citizenship, becoming students, etc. These data answer the important question of how the volume and structure of migration flows in Russia changed since the beginning of the recession.

*Free Movement of Labour Force*

The citizens of the Eurasian Economic Union's member states (Russia,

Belarus, Kazakhstan, Armenia and Kyrgyzstan) now participate in a single labour market, which means that they do not require any permits to work in Russia. However, for this same reason there is a problem of statistical accounting of this group of foreign workers. Indirect data (registration statistics, information from employers) show that in 2015 the flow of labour migrants from these countries did not significantly decrease. This is explained by the accession of these countries to a common labour market of the Eurasian Economic Union, the expansion of opportunities for finding and getting work, reduction of costs associated with migration, and a new amnesty for formerly irregular immigrants and those who had been denied entry to Russia for violating immigration laws.

**Remittances**

Russia is the main source of remittances for CIS countries. Between 2010 and 2015, according to the Central Bank of Russia, the volume of personal remittances to these countries reached 108 million USD.[19] The main recipient of remittances is Uzbekistan, which received 30 per cent of the above amount followed by Tajikistan and Ukraine (Figure 2). For a number of CIS countries, remittances are the most important factor of development. According to World Bank estimates, the ratio of the volume of cash remittances to GDP in 2014 was 36.6 per cent in Tajikistan, 30.3 per cent in Kyrgyzstan, 26.2 per cent in Moldova and 17.9 per cent in Armenia.[20]

---

[19] Personal remittances represent households' income received from their members temporarily employed abroad and nonresident households and are mostly related to temporary and permanent migration of population. Remittances can be made through both official channels (via banks, post offices, money transfer operators – MTOs), and direct transfers in cash or valuables from a member of a household temporarily employed abroad to his household or from one household to another. See: The Central Bank of the Russian Federation, General Notes Relating to Personal Remittances http://www.cbr.ru/eng/

[20] World Bank Group (2015). Migration and Remittances. Factbook 2016. Third Edition.

**Figure 2: Personal remittances from Russia to CIS countries, 2011-2015 (billions of US dollars).**

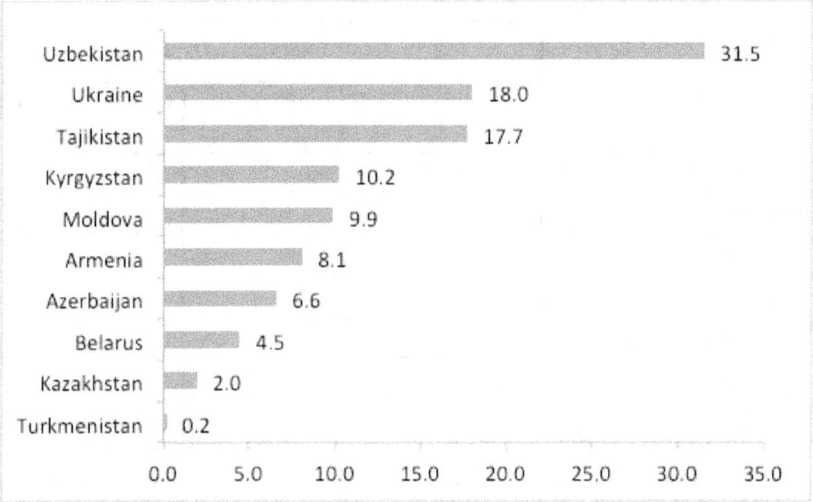

|  |  |
|---|---|
| Uzbekistan | 31.5 |
| Ukraine | 18.0 |
| Tajikistan | 17.7 |
| Kyrgyzstan | 10.2 |
| Moldova | 9.9 |
| Armenia | 8.1 |
| Azerbaijan | 6.6 |
| Belarus | 4.5 |
| Kazakhstan | 2.0 |
| Turkmenistan | 0.2 |

Source: The Central Bank of the Russian Federation http://www.cbr.ru/statistics/?Prtid=svs

The highest volume of remittances from Russia to CIS countries was reached in 2013, when their total volume amounted to 24.7 billion USD. However, in the second half of the following year the cash flows started to decrease. Personal remittances of migrants from Russia to CIS countries in 2015 were half as large as in 2013 (Table 4). The main reason was the fall of the rouble, which began in the middle of 2014. In early July, the exchange rate was 33.4 roubles per dollar. At the end of December 2014 one dollar was sold for 56 RUB, while at the end of December 2015 – for 72 RUB. Another reason was the reduction of the flow of migrant workers, both legal and undocumented.

The flow of remittances has fallen most to Uzbekistan and Moldova and least – to Kazakhstan and Kyrgyzstan (Table 3). Differences between countries in the reduction of remittances from Russia can be explained not only by the difference in migration flows, but also by the characteristics of their structure (i.e. the relationship between legal and undocumented migrants and migrant employment industry trade). Among the undocumented migrants, the citizens of Tajikistan and Uzbekistan predominated, while among the citizens of Kyrgyzstan and Tajikistan who have received permission to work before the crisis, almost one-third worked as unskilled workers. Among Ukrainian citizens that professional group comprised less than ten per cent.

**Table 3: Personal Remittances from Russia to CIS countries, 2013-2015 (billions of US dollars)**

| Countries | 2013 | 2014 | 2015 | Decrease in flows (%) | |
| --- | --- | --- | --- | --- | --- |
| | | | | remittances 2013-2015 | Labour migrants* 2014-2015 |
| CIS countries | 24,786 | 21,400 | 12,403 | 50 | 35 |
| Azerbaijan | 1378 | 1374 | 948 | 31 | 54 |
| Armenia | 1747 | 1752 | 1121 | 36 | ... |
| Belarus | 993 | 1000 | 581 | 41 | ... |
| Kazakhstan | 377 | 465 | 351 | 7 | ... |
| Kyrgyzstan | 2113 | 2239 | 1514 | 28 | ... |
| Moldova | 2248 | 1862 | 908 | 60 | 56 |
| Tajikistan | 3927 | 3662 | 2088 | 47 | 32 |
| Turkmenistan | 35 | 30 | 16 | 54 | ... |
| Uzbekistan | 7878 | 5828 | 3054 | 61 | 37 |
| Ukraine | 4090 | 3187 | 1823 | 55 | 50 |

*documents for work

*Source: The Central Bank of the Russian Federation http://www.cbr.ru/statistics/?PrtId=svs*

Based on the data, it is reasonable to say that economic factors have determined a significant reduction in the number of permanent and migrant workers in Russia from countries that are not included in the Eurasian Economic Union: Azerbaijan, Moldova, Uzbekistan and Tajikistan. The military-political conflict in Ukraine also caused a stream of people who sought and received asylum in Russia. Many of those persons have changed their migration status, which was accompanied by a significant increase in the number of permanent migrants from Ukraine to Russia. However, the flow of legal labour migrants in 2015 reduced almost twice.

The fall in the inflow of migrant workers and the value of the rouble against the dollar and euro have led to the reduction of remittances sent to the CIS countries. Their volume in 2015 was twice smaller than in 2013. Such a significant reduction in cash flows obviously affected the well-being of the population in those countries where remittances comprise a large part of the GDP (such as Tajikistan, Moldova, Kyrgyzstan, and Armenia). This is particularly significant considering that according to forecasts, the current crisis in Russia will continue until 2019–2020 (Center of Development Institute 2016). Thus, the reduction in population income will also continue. The decrease in labour demand due to the crisis in the coming years will be accompanied by the reduction in labour supply. According to the estimates of the UN Population Division, between 2015 and 2015, the number of persons between the ages of 15 and 60 in Russia will decrease by nine million (UNDESA 2015). Therefore, the need for a large number of foreign workers (most probably less than in 2013/2014) will continue.

However, the resources to meet this demand in traditional sources are likely to go down. Moreover, the decline of working age population in all the former Soviet republics in the coming years is expected.[21] Therefore, it is likely that the importance of migration from the three Central Asian countries for Russia will increase. Correspondingly, for Kyrgyzstan, Tajikistan and Uzbekistan migration to Russia remains vital due to the financial resources that exceed international aid. If the inflow of transfers of migrants continues to decline due to the Russian economic crisis, under the absence of significant economic progress, the well-being of the population of Central Asian countries will significantly deteriorate, which will complicate the internal political situation on the ground.

## Conclusion

This chapter has analysed the latest available statistical data to assess how the volume and structure of migration flows into Russia have changed since the beginning of the recession, and how the crisis affected the remittances sent to the CIS countries. The data show that while migration to Russia is determined by multiple and continuously changing factors, it is possible – and indeed important – to disaggregate the economic, policy, and geopolitical influences on migration and understand their relative significance. As discussed, whereas Uzbekistan demonstrates how significant economic factors are in explaining long-term migration, Ukraine underlines the importance of non-economic factors. After the collapse of the Soviet Union, strong migration links between Russia and other former Soviet republics remained. However, over time, the migration ties between Russia and the newly independent states have generally weakened. This is unlikely to bode well for either Russia or the countries in the region.

---

[21] According to the estimates of the UN Population Division, the population between the ages of 15 and 60 from 2015 to 2025 reduced: in Azerbaijan – by about five per cent, Armenia and Moldova – by nine per cent, in Belarus and Russia – by ten per cent, in Georgia and Ukraine – by 12 per cent.

## References

Central Bank of the Russian Federation, "General Notes Relating to Personal Remittances," http://www.cbr.ru/eng/

Central Bank of The Russian Federation, "Personal Remittances from Russia to CIS Countries, 2011-2015," http://www.cbr.ru/statistics/?Prtid=svs

Centre of Development Institute, "Our Economic Forecast," National Research University Higher School of Economics, March 2016, https://dcenter.hse.ru/data/2016/03/30/1126653929/NEP_2016_1.pdf

CIS STAT, "Interstate Statistical Committee of the Commonwealth Independent States," http://www.cisstat.com/eng/

Database of The Federal Migration Service of the Ministry of Internal Affairs

Kirillova, O. Interview with the Head of the General Administration for Migration Issues of the Interior Ministry of Russia, Interfax, 1 July 2016, http://www.interfax.ru/interview/516300

Marat, E. "Labor Migration in Central Asia: Implication of Global Economic Crisis," *Silk Road Papers*, Washington, DC: Central Asia-Caucasus Institute & Silk Road Studies Program, May 2009.

MOM-NITS, 'SHARK', and Dushanbe, *Denezhnye perevody i ikh vliyanie na uroven zhizni v Khatlonskoi oblasti respubliki Tadkhikistan MOM-NITS*, 'SHARK', Dushanbe," 2006: 30.

RBC Free News, "The Head of the Federal Migration Service Konstantin Romodanosky Said There Were More Than 3.5 Million Undocumented Migrants in 2013," July 2013, www.rwbc.ru/rbcfreenews/20130730135511.shtml.

Romodanovski K.O., Mukomel' V.I. "Regulation of Migration Processes: Problems of Transition from Reactive to System Policy [Regulirovanie migratsionnykh protsessov: problem perekhoda ot reactivnoi k sistemnoi politike]" *Obschestvennye Nauki i Sovremennost* 5 (2015): 10.

Rosstat, "Total Results of Migration in Russia," *Demographic Yearbook of Russia: 2014*, 2014, http://www.gks.ru/wps/wcm/connect/rosstat_main/rosstat/ru/statistics/population/demography/#

Russian Federation Government, *Concept of the State Migration Policy until 2025*, 13 June 2012, http://en.kremlin.ru/events/president/news/15635

United Nations, Department of Economic and Social Affairs, Population Division, "World Population Prospects: The 2015 Revision," 2015, http://www.un.org/en/development/desa/population/theme/trends/index.shtml

World Bank, "Migration and Remittances Data," last modified October 2016, http://www.worldbank.org/en/topic/migrationremittancesdiasporaissues/brief/migration-remittances-data

# 10

# Dangerous and Unwanted: Policy and Everyday Discourses of Migrants in Russia

IRINA KUZNETSOVA

**Introduction**

For many years, Russia was the second greatest world recipient of migrants after the United States and it currently holds the third position, after Germany, with 12 million newcomers a year. It is the main destination country for various categories of migrants from South-Eastern Europe, Eastern Europe and Central Asia (SEECA), with 38.4 per cent of all immigration directed towards this country (Migration facts and trends... 2015, 34). Citizens from post-Soviet states, specifically from the 1991-founded Commonwealth of Independent States (which includes Azerbaijan, Armenia, Belarus, Kazakhstan, Kyrgyzstan, Moldova, Tajikistan, Uzbekistan, and associated countries – Turkmenistan and Ukraine) have comprised the biggest number of migrants in Russia ever since the collapse of the Soviet Union.

Migration to Russia from these countries has been almost ten times higher than from other countries of the 'far abroad'. According to official statistics in 2013, 422,738 people arrived from the CIS and 59,503 from countries outside of the region. Such a mass migration from CIS states into Russia has been facilitated by the visa-free regime, but also by close economic, political and personal relations between the people – and later due to disparities in the economic development of CIS countries, which encouraged labour migration to the more developed Russia.

Over a span of 25 years, the character of migration, state policy and official rhetoric towards migrants have changed dramatically – being dependent on the Russian labour market and often forced to work informally, many migrants have suffered from the growing restrictions of migration law and the lack of policy to facilitate better integration.

This chapter will address the formation of the myth of a 'dangerous migrant' through politics' and mass-media constriction of migrants' image as connected with crime, disease and illegal work. The restrictions of migration legislation bring a lot of complications and contribute to the ambiguous position of migrants in the society. One of the main problems facing migrants in Russian society is racism and xenophobia, which often enjoy the support of the state and mass-media. Due to the armed conflict in Eastern Ukraine which began in April 2014, almost a million people have sought refuge in Russia, which according to the UN, is the ninth largest displaced group in the world. The chapter discusses the existing regulations and the main issues facing the refugees.

This paper is based on several years of the author's research on migration in Russia, including her Open Society Institute funded project 'The everyday lives of Central Asian migrants in Moscow and Kazan in the context of Russia's Migration 2025 Concept: from legislation to practice', during which she conducted about 300 in-depth interviews (with Dr. John Round) between 2013 and 2015; the 2012-2014 Russian Foundation for Humanities funded project titled 'Social integration of migrants in a context of social security' (with Prof. Laissan Mucharyamova), with a survey of 297 migrants, in-depth interviews with migrants and experts and discourse analysis; and the ongoing 2016-2017 British Academy Small Grant funded project titled 'Asylum seekers from Eastern Ukraine in Russia: identities, policies and discourse in the context of forced migration from the Ukraine conflict'.

## The Myth of a 'Dangerous Migrant' and Tightening of Migration Control

Portraying migrants as dangerous because of the supposedly high crime and unemployment levels among them and the fact that they contribute to the destruction of national identities, is common across the globe (Vertovec 2011). The rise of xenophobia and nationalism in Europe and the United States supported by political disourse (Wodak, Boukala 2015; Chavez 2013 etc.), has brought tremendous changes in political agenda. In Russia the rise of xenophobia towards migrants goes in parallel with increasing control in migration policy. As Shnirelman (2007) pointed out: 'if in the middle and second part of the 1990s Chechens were portrayed as the main enemy, in the beginning of the 2000s after announcing the new war as an 'antiterrorist operation', the mass-media started the active cultivation of a negative image of migrants.'

The changing official stance of President Putin in relation to the idea of a multi-ethnic society explains a lot. While in 2012 he spoke about a 'complex and multidimentional' country and argued that 'if a multi-ethnic society is struck by the bacilli of nationalism, it loses its strength and stability' (Putin 2012)[1], in 2014 his rhetoric reflected a very different view. He stated: 'we still have quite a few problems here that have to do with illegal, uncontrolled migration. We know that this breeds crime, interethnic tensions and extremism. We need a greater control over compliance with regulations covering migrants' stay in Russia, and we have to take practical measures to promote their social and cultural adaptation and protect their labour and other rights' (Putin 2014).

Thus, Putin has drawn an unsubstantiated connection between migrants' irregular status and crime, extremism, and ethnic tensions. The time period between these two statements saw an increase in xenophobic attitudes in Russia, the Moscow mayoral election (in which the candidates focused on demonising the Other), round-ups and public detention of migrants, and attempts to securitise migration policy. Inter-ethnic tensions have been exacerbated through the increase in the number of workplace raids, after which the 'illegal' migrants would be paraded through the streets. In addition, sweeps of the metro system in search for criminals (i.e. irregular migrants) have been well covered by the media. The migrants were also blamed for the poor health care system and rising crime levels.

The media has portrayed migrants as bringing disease to Russia, even though HIV infection rates, the most commonly discussed illness, in Central Asia are much lower. The first deputy of the State Duma Committee for Ethnic Affairs, Mikhail Starshinov, stated without citing any data that a 'huge number of migrants have dangerous diseases such as tuberculosis, HIV and various "shameful diseases"' (Chernov 2014). HIV in Russia has been viewed as an imported disease with authorities and doctors blaming migrants for the increasing number of infection cases (Pichugina 2012; State Duma 2013; TV Center 2013). Moreover, migrants are often portrayed as drug abusers lacking in health education, sexually promiscuous and unable to control themselves, thereby putting the native population in grave danger. The media has also focused on showing migrants accessing health care for free, attacking particularly Central Asian women who deliver babies in Russian hospitals (see Primor'e 2013). Blaming migrants accessing prenatal and

---

[1] In Russian: 'если многонациональное общество поражают бациллы национализма, оно теряет силу и прочность' (Putin 2012)

antenatal care for 'medical tourism' does not correspond with a reality when woman often have to go to their countries of origin to give birth as an alternative to dealing with often xenophobic attitudes in hospitals (Rocheva 2014).

The migrant-criminal figure is another standard othering tool in all migrant recipient countries. In Russia it was taken to the extreme when the mayor of Moscow, Sergey Sobyanin, stated that the city would be the world's safest capital if only migrants were not committing crimes (Sobyanin 2013). These constructions show migrants as a dangerous and superfluous flow towards what is, to employ Mbembe's theory of necropolitics, a 'let to die'. Our research demonstrates that migrants are simultaneously visible and invisible to the state; the legal uncertainty denies them access to welfare and a voice within society, but they are visible for exploitation both in terms of their labour and the political capital gained from their presence (Round and Kuznetsova 2016).

While they are often portrayed as dangerous, the reality is quite different: migrants often become subjects of hate crime attacks. The Comitee for Civil Assistance supported by the Sova Centre created a map at hatecrime.ru website which has reported on hate crime incidents in Moscow and Moscow Oblast since 2010, and registered 565 attacks. According to Sova Centre's data, migrants from Central Asia traditionally have constituted the largest group of victims (in 2014 one person was killed and 17 were injured). 11 victims (one killed, ten injured) were of unspecified 'non-Slavic' appearance, usually described as 'Asian'. In addition, there are five victims among migrants from the Caucasus (in 2014 three were killed and 13 injured) (Alperovich and Yudina 2016, 11).

From the beginning of 2000s, migration policy in Russia has been shifting towards increasing control of immigration and restriction of migrants' labour rights, enabled by new laws. Human rights activists and migrant rights advocates worry that most of the changes in Russian migration law will have a negative effect on the employment and living conditions in Russia and will also affect the citizens of post-Soviet states who can enter the country without a visa (see Figure 1 for a brief outline of some important changes in migration policy).

**Figure 1: Some key changes in Russian migration policy from 2002**

| 2003 | Introduction of work permits and regional quotas for foreign workers |
|---|---|
| 2008 | Restriction of migrants' mobility to their area of registration in the Russian Federation

Introduction of the compulsory 'free from infections' test to be provided within 30 days from the start of employment |
| 2010 | Introduction of patents for labour migrants granting the right to work in the private sector without work permit |
| 2012 | Introduction of the 'Concept of the State Migration Policy of the Russian Federation until 2025' |
| 2013 | Ban on entry to Russia for migrants who violated two administrative laws |
| 2014 | Restriction for stay in Russia for 90 days only without obtaining a permission

Compulsory registration in the country (work and home address) Refugee crisis in Ukraine due to armed conflict in Donbas |
| 2015 | Introduction of a new regulation, according to which after two administrative law violations or one migration law violation a migrant has to leave the country within five days

Compulsory registration of the address of stay in the country

Abolition of quotas for work permits for foreign migrants from countries with free visa regimes and introduction of patents

Citizens of CIS countries not included in the Custom Union (Azerbaijan, Moldova, Tajikistan, Turkmenistan, Uzbekistan) can come to Russia only with international passports, but do not need a visa. Citizens of Armenia, Belarus, Kazakhstan, Kyrgyzstan and Ukraine can cross the border with internal passports |
| 2016 | The closing down of the Federal Migration Service and transfer of its functions to the Ministry of Internal Affairs |

On 1 July 2010, patents for labour migrants were introduced, which gave migrants the right to work in the private sector without a work permit. According to Ryazantsev (2012), in the beginning this law helped to regularise the status of approximately half a million migrants who earlier preferred to work unofficially. The new measure was so popular that in the first six months from its introduction, the authorities received more than one million applications.

In 2013, Russia introduced an entry ban for those migrants who had committed two administrative law violations. In 2014, the allowed stay in the country without any permission document was limited to 90 days, down from 180. The new law introduced in 2015 requires migrants who have committed two or more administrative or one migration law violation to leave the country within five days. Administrative law violations include offences such as unpaid penalty for driving, violations of migration law – for instance being registered in one apartment, but living in another. Due to these measures from 2012 to 2014, the number of CIS citizens banned from entering Russia increased more than nine times (from 2013 to 2015, 1.6 million people received such a ban) (Troitsky 2015, 20). As a result, about four per cent of the total population of Tajikistan, or more than half of those who worked in Russia in 2015, were banned from the country, according to the Ministry of Labour, Employment and Migration of Tajikistan (cited in Troitsky 2015, 22). Civil rights activists reported mass violations of human rights. In most cases migrants were not allowed to read their court cases, as there were no interpreters available. The scale of abuse was huge; the Moscow court, for instance, considered 42 cases in one hour for migrant deportation (Troitsky 2015), which shows the lack of any in-depth consideration of individual situations.

In 2015 Russia experienced a massive decrease in international migration from post-Soviet countries. The greatest reduction in migration growth was in the case of Tajikistan (47.8 per cent compared with 2014) and Kyrgyzstan (41 per cent). Moreover, Russia experienced a 42.6 per cent decrease in the number of migrants from Uzbekistan (Social'no-jekonomicheskoe polozhenie Rossii 2015, 246).

While Russian citizens pay a penalty if they live in an apartment without registration, foreigners who do the same face deportation. Such a practice can be referred to as the 'ethnicisation' of politics (Gulina 2015). In addition, the new Russian migration laws affect the citizens of some CIS countries and significantly restrict their freedom of movement and opportunities to work. We can suppose that it is partly because the articles of the Convention of the CIS regarding human rights and freedoms in the area of employment do not have any control mechanisms (Davletgildiev 2016, 37), but more importantly, because of Russia's special role in the CIS and the lack of protest from Tajikistan and Moldova in response to these restrictions.

2015 was a crucial year for migration policy because of the new law introducing compulsory tests in the Russian language and Russian history, and additional laws for all foreigners who plan to work in Russia (with the exception of citizens from the EEU countries, highly skilled migrants, and several other categories). These exams not only increased the financial burden for labour migrants, as most of them have a salary which is lower than the regional average, but were immediately followed by administrative barriers. Respondents complained that 30 days to pass the exam was not enough considering the time needed to register and the waiting list. Moreover, certificates from exams passed on the regional level are not recognised in the rest of the country. At the same time, the costs of the federal exam have been much higher and the waiting time – much longer. The Presidential Council on Civil Society and Human Rights has suggested changes in the new law, such as getting rid of the history and law components in the exam, since such a knowledge is of no use to foreign citizens temporarily employed in Russia (Jekspertnoe zakljuchenie... 2015).

One of the most significant changes to migration policy has been the shutdown of the Federal Migration Service and the transfer of its functions to the Ministry of Internal Affairs (Ukaz... 5 April 2016). Even before this reform, analysts argued that 'courts have become part of the chain of migration policy implementation, focusing on regulating the number of foreign citizens in the Russian territory, especially from some countries' (Troitsky 2015, 51). The new change will bring an even greater turn of migration policy towards police control.

**Refugees from Eastern Ukraine in Russia**

The armed conflict in Eastern Ukraine began in April 2014, affecting an area with approximately 5.2 million inhabitants. An estimated 9000 people have died, 14,000 have been wounded, and over a million have been internally displaced within Ukraine as a result of fighting (UN reports 2015). In the first six months of the conflict over 835,000 Ukrainian citizens from the war-torn areas arrived in Russia to seek asylum (Svodnyj doklad 2014) and over half a million Ukrainian citizens received provisional asylum in 2015 and 2016 (Chislennost' vynuzhdennyh pereselencev... 2016).

Centers where people displaced from Ukraine could stay were set up, usually in former pioneer camps, health hotels etc. Soon after, however, several Russian regions were assigned refugee quotas and Moscow stopped inviting more people to settle in those areas. It is important to mention here that the influx of people from Ukraine saw the rise of volunteer activities and civil society groups to support the refugees and provide them with food, clothes and sometimes a place to live. The Civil Assistance Committee and Migration and Law NGOs provided free advocacy services in several Russian regions to assist refugees.

However, as one of the countries with the highest number of asylum claims in Europe, Russia has been more inclined to grant applicants provisional asylum rather than refugee status; between 2014 and 2016 only 505 Ukrainian citizens received it (Chislennost' vynuzhdennyh pereselencev... 2016). Data gathered during the author's research show that a number of Ukrainian citizens from war-affected territories do not have provisional asylum and live in Russia as labour or undocumented migrants. Some of those people moved to Russia before the war and others come from regions not included in the list of conflict-affected territories, which has been the requirement to receive asylum. Overall, in 2015 there were 2.6 million registered Ukrainian citizens living in Russia.

The situation of Ukrainians from war-affected territories is likely to change with the new law, adopted on 1 May 2016, introducing a simplified procedure for issuing residence permits to Ukrainians who have received a refugee status or provisional asylum. In addition, according to the new law, those who will take part in the federal programme of assistance for volunteer migration will be treated as compatriots living abroad. Previously, residence permits were issued often even a year after one moved to Russia (Federal Law 'On the amendments to the Article 8 of Federal Law "On the legal status of foreign citizens in the Russian Federation" from 1 May 2016 № 129').[2]

Despite a large volume of applications from Ukrainian citizens, there is an ongoing confusion in relation to the procedure they shall follow and the support they are entitled to. They can remain in Russia for 180 days without a visa and significant resources were initially allocated to providing living facilities for this group. However, from pilot research it has been clear that Ukrainian asylum seekers experience the same problem as other migrants, as they become mired in bureaucracy, corruption, and the general lack of recognition of migrants' human rights. Despite the allocated resources and administrative support to assist refugees, people have trouble finding official employment due to their status. Another problem is mental health. After dramatic events, in some cases followed by the loss of home and family, people need psychological support and, according to our research, there were not enough opportunities to receive it.

---

[2] Assistance to Ukrainian citizens coming to Russia due to armed conflict in Donbas became the priority of the State Programme for Voluntary Emigration of Compatriots Living Abroad to Russia. In 2014 and the first quarter of 2015, 70,900 Ukrainian citizens registered in Russia with the programme, which makes 47.5 per cent of all compatriots who migrated to Russia (Monitoring... 2015, 16).

## Undocumented or 'Illegal'?

In both the political and media discourse migrants have been commonly portrayed as 'illegal.' Following the words of Elie Wiesel, a Holocaust survivor and Nobel Peace Prize winner: 'No human being is illegal', human rights activists in many countries campaign to avoid using this term. The International Organization for Migration and the United Nations use the term 'irregular migration' and restrict the use of term 'illegal migration' to 'cases of smuggling of migrants and trafficking in persons' (International Organization of Migration 2011).

However, such nuances do not exist in the Russian state and media discourse, which promotes an extremely narrow definition of informal work, assuming that the workers take up unofficial employment for tax avoidance purposes, and thus by default are illegal. As Williams et al. (2013) have shown, many ethnic Russians struggle to operate fully in the formal labour market due to employers' practices, but in the case of labour migrants the situation is even more problematic. In Russia, various studies demonstrate that informal workers made up between one-fifth and one-third of the total employment in 2013 (Gimpelson and Kapeliushnikov 2014). It is unavoidable for both the labour market and for migrants as well. Labour migrants, as the interviews revealed, in many cases are offered either cash in hand payments, or extremely low formal salaries. According to our survey in Kazan in 2013, 54.5 per cent of labour migrants had neither a patent, nor a work permit (Kuznetsova and Mucharyamova 2014a, 47).

The issues surrounding employers' practices are perhaps the most pernicious in the whole process, as they force labour migrants to operate informally, thereby reducing their security and salaries and enabling the state to view them as 'illegal.' For example, a large number of migrants from post-Soviet countries worked in preparation for the Sochi Olympics. Human Rights Watch exposed a pattern of abuse across a number of major Olympic sites which included non-payment of wages or excessive delays in payments, employers' failure to provide written employment contracts or copies of contracts, excessive working hours, illegal withholding of passports and other abuses (Race to the Bottom... 2013). Our research showed also that migrants were often under attack by Cossacks and police raids, arrested and kept in humiliating conditions. Migrant and Law network has supported those who did not receive their wages by initiating court cases against the employers. Nevertheless, many of them have not been resolved, as it was impossible to track the chain of sub-contractors.

Even when labour migrants work formally, they still occasionally face legal obstacles. For instance, in November 2013 many cities in Russia experienced a collapse in public transportation services because of a new legislation which prohibited driving with licenses issued in other countries. Thus, 80 per cent of drivers in Yekaterinburg and 70 per cent of drivers in Petropavlovsk-on-Kamchatka have not been able to work on 5 November 2013 (Shipilov 2013). Neither the migration office, nor the municipal council informed bus companies about the new procedures. In the same year, the chief of the Russian Duma Committee on State Security, Irina Jarovaya, suggested to prohibit migrants' work in trade, but the initiative was never implemented (Jarovaya 2013).

The social construction of 'illegality' does not only block migrants' possibilities to receive a fair wage, but makes them 'invisible' for the state. Our analysis of data gathered by the Medical Information and Analytical Centre of the Republic of Tatarstan found that in 2012 the majority of foreigners did not have medical insurance (2560 migrants out of 2584) (Mucharymova, Kuznetsova and Vafina 2014; Kuznetsova and Mucharymova 2014b). The only accessible care without an insurance policy is emergency care (Postanovlenie Pravitel'stva ... 2013), but even this was questioned at the beginning of 2016 by Duma deputy Vladimir Sysoyev who requested that the Ministry of Health Care reconsiders providing migrants with free emergency assistance (Runkevich and Malay 2016). Working in Russia has become a challenge in terms of access to health care, especially for those employed in sectors such as construction and trade, due to the lack of safety regulations in the workplace, extremely long working hours and little time for relaxation. Both documented and undocumented workers have extremely limited access to Russia's health care system and thus they often turn to paid services they can barely afford, informal care or do not undertake any treatment.

The fear of being 'illegal' even among documented migrants negatively impacts on people's everyday lives, limits the available options for spending free time, affects community building and creates a huge psychological pressure (Round and Kuznetsova 2016).

**Conclusion**

After the collapse of the Soviet Union, Russia became one the largest migrant receiving countries. Most of the immigrants come from the post-Soviet states of Central Asia whose economies partly depend on remittances, as well as from Ukraine, Armenia, Azerbaijan and Belarus. Although the visa-free regime for citizens of the Commonwealth of Independent States made it relatively easy for people to work in Russia, restrictions in the migration law introduced in the last decade have created barriers for safe life and employment in the country, and contributed to the decrease of labour migration. The Russian state and society have made a lot of effort to support refugees from Eastern Ukraine by arranging special employment conditions for this group, however, the refugees still face issues related to integration. When it comes to labour migrants, the work and living conditions for foreigners from post-Soviet countries have been challenging. Those with non-Slavic appearance are often subject to xenophobia and racist attacks. Moreover, due to the large size of the informal economy, migrants face issues related to access to health care and work safety. They live under stress, having to cope with constant changes in regulation and the risk of exclusion.

*This work was supported by funding from the British Academy, Open Society Institute and the Russian Foundation for Humanities. The author would like to thank Agnieszka Pikulicka-Wilczewska and Dr Greta Uehling for their insightful comments on the paper.

**References**

Alperovich, V., Yudina, N. "The Ultra-Right Movement under Pressure: Xenophobia and Radical Nationalism in Russia, and Efforts to Counteract Them in 2015," in *Xenophobia, Freedom of Conscience, and Anti-Extremism in Russia in 2015: A collection of annual reports by the SOVA Center for Information and Analysis* edited by Alexander Verkhovsky, Moscow: SOVA Center, 2016: 7-66.

Chavez, L. *The Latino Threat: Constructing Immigrants, Citizens, and the Nation*, Stanford: Stanford University Press, 2013.

Council Under the President of the Russian Federation for the Development of Civil Society and Human Rights, "Svodnyj doklad o merah po okazaniju podderzhki licam, vynuzhdenno pokinuvshim teritoriju Ukrainy i razmeshhennym na territorii Rossijskoj Federacii ot 31 Oktjabrja 2014 [Report about measures for support to people had to leave Ukraine and had asylum in Russian Federation from 31 October 2014]," 2014, http://president-sovet.ru/documents/read/282/

Davletgildiev, R. "*Avtoreferat dissertacii na soiskanie stepeni doktora juridicheskih nauk po special'nosti 12.00.10 – Mezhdunarodnoe pravo. Evropejskoe pravo 'Mezhdunarodno-pravovoe regulirovanie truda na regional'nom urovne.'* [Abstract of the doctoral dissertation in Law in specialty 12.00.10 International Law. European Law 'International legal regulation of labor in regional level']," Kazan: Kazan University Publishing House, 2016.

Demoscope, "Vos'moj ezhegodnyj demograficheskij doklad Naselenie Rossii 2000. 5.7. Bezhency i vynuzhdennye pereselency'. [Eighth annual demographical report on population of Russia. 2000.5.7]," http://demoscope.ru/weekly/knigi/ns_r00/razdel5g5_7.html

Federal Service for State Statistics, "Chislennost' vynuzhdennyh pereselencev, bezhencev i lic, poluchivshih vremennoe ubezhishhe (chelovek, na 1 janvarja) [Number of displaced people, refugees and people received temporal asylum (persons for 1 January)]," 2016, http://www.gks.ru/free_doc/new_site/population/demo/tab-migr4.htm

Federal Service for State Statistics, "Social'no-jekonomicheskoe polozhenie Rossii, Federal'naja sluzhba gosudarstvennoj statistiki [Social and Economic state of Russia]," 2015, http://www.gks.ru/wps/wcm/connect/rosstat_main/rosstat/ru/statistics/publications/catalog/doc_1140086922125

Gimpelson, V. and Kapeliushnikov, R. "Between Light and Shadow: Informality in the Russian Labour Market," IZA Discussion Paper No. 8279, Moscow: Higher School of Economics, 2014.

Gulina, O. "Jetnizacija fenomena migracii v zakonodatel'stve [Ethnization of Phenomena of Migration in Law]," *Journal of Tomsk State University. History* 5, no.37 (2015): 24-33.

Human Rights Watch, "Olympic Games in Sochi," 2013, https://www.hrw.org/report/2013/02/06/race-bottom/exploitation-migrant-workers-ahead-russias-2014-winter-olympic-games

International Organization of Migration, "Key Migration Terms," 2011, http://www.iom.int/key-migration-terms

International Organization of Migration, "Migration Facts and Trends: South–Eastern Europe, Eastern Europe and Central Asia," 2015, https://publications.iom.int/system/files/pdf/migration_facts_and_trends_seeeca.pdf

Kuznetsova, I. and Muchyaramova, L. "Labor Migrants and Health Care Access in Russia: Formal and Informal Strategies," *The Journal for Social Policy Studies* 12, no.1 (2014): 7-20.

Kuznetsova, I. and Muchyaramova, L. *Social'naja integracija migrantov v kontekste obshhestvennoj bezopasnosti (na materialah Respubliki Tatarstan) [Social integration of migrants in a context of social security (case of Republic of Tatarstan)]*, Kazan: Kazan University Press, 2014.

Malakhov, V. "Russia as a New Immigration Country: Policy Response and Public Debate," *Europe-Asia Studies* 66, no. 7 (2014): 1062–1079.

Ministry of Foreign Affairs, "Gosudarstvennaja programma po okazaniju sodejstvija dobrovolnomu pereseleniju v rossijskuju federaciju sootechestvennikov, prozhivajushhih ZA rubezhom," https://guvm.mvd.ru/about/compatriots

Mucharyamova, L., Kuznetsova, I. and Gusel. V. 2014, «Sick, patient, client: the positions of labor migrants in the russian health care system (evidence from the Republic of Tatarstan),» *Vestnik Sovremennoi Klinicheskoi Mediciny [The Bulletin of Contemporary Clinical Medicine]* 7, no.1 (2014): 43-50.

Mukomel, V. "Rossijskie diskursy o migracii: 'nulevye gody'.' [Russian discussions about migration: 'zero' year]," in *Rossija reformirujushhajasja: Ezhegodnik-2011* (Vol 10), edited by Mikhail Gorshkov. Moscow, Saint-Petersburg: Institute of Sociology of Russian Academy of Sciences, 2011: 86–108.

Presidential Board of the Russian Federation, "Jekspertnoe zakljuchenie na proekt Federal'nogo zakona 'O vnesenii izmenenij v otdel'nye zakonodatel'nye akty Rossijskoj Federacii' (v chasti porjadka poluchenija patentov trudovymi migrantami). 2015. [Expertise on bill of Federal Law 'About ammendments in some legislation of Russian Federation (rules of patents' receiving)]," 18 August 2015, http://president-sovet.ru/documents/read/383/

Putin, V. "Vladimir Putin, Rossija: nacional'nyj vopros," *Nezavisimaya Gazeta*, 23 January 2012, http://www.ng.ru/politics/2012-01-23/1_national.html

Reeves, M. "Clean Fake: Authenticating Documents and Persons in Migrant Moscow," *American Ethnologist* 40, no.3 (2013): 508–524.

RIA Novosti, "Putin: nuzhno kontrolirovat' sobljudenie pravil prebyvanija migrantov [Putin: We must control following rules of migration regime]," 20 November 2014, http://ria.ru/society/20141120/1034333285.html

Rocheva, A. "A Swarm of Migrants in our Maternity Clinics!': The Study of Stratified Reproduction Regime in the Case of Kyrgyz Migrants in Moscow," *Journal of Social Policy Studies* 12, no.3 (2014): 367-380.

*Rossijskaya Gazeta*, "Postanovlenie Pravitel'stva Rossijskoj Federacii ot 6 marta 2013 g. N 186 g. Moskva 'Ob utverzhdenii Pravil okazanija medicinskoj pomoshhi inostrannym grazhdanam na territorii Rossijskoj Federacii," 11 March 2013, https://rg.ru/2013/03/11/inostr-med-site-dok.html

Round, J. and Kuznetsova, I. "Necropolitics and the Migrant as a Political Subject of Disgust: The Precarious Everyday of Russia's Labour Migrants," 2016, *Critical Sociology*, DOI 0896920516645934.

Runkevich, D. and Malay E. "Skoruju pomoshh' predlagajut sdelat' platnoj dlja migrantov," *Izvestya*, 14 January 2016, http://izvestia.ru/news/601529

Russian Informational Agency, "Jarovaja predlagaet zapretit' migrantam rabotat' v sfere torgovli," 3 September 2013, https://ria.ru/society/20130903/960371221.html

Ryazantsev, S. "Patenty vyveli 'iz teni' bol'she milliona migrantov.' [Patents revealed from shadow more than a million of migrants]," *Migratsia* 2, no.11 (2012): 45-47.

Shipilov, E. "Migrantov zapretili po oshibke," Gazeta, 5 November 2013, https://www.gazeta.ru/auto/2013/11/05_a_5737725.shtml

Shnirelman, V. "Jetnicheskaja prestupnost' i migrantofobija [Mass-media, 'ethnic crime' and migrantophobia]," in *Jazyk vrazhdy protiv obshhestva* edited by Alexander Verkhovsky, Moscow: Sova centre, 2007.

Sobjanin, S. "Rabota mjera interesnee prem'erstva' [Sergei Sobyanin: The work of the Mayor is an interesting premiership]," *Izvestia*, 13 July 2013, http://izvestia.ru/news/551895

Troitsky, K. "Administrativnye vydvorenija iz rossii: sudebnoe razbiratel"stvo ili massovoe izgnanie?" Moscow: Civil Assistance Committee, 2015, http://refugee.ru/wp-content/uploads/2016/05/doklad-o-vydvoreniyakh1.pdf

Ukaz Prezidenta Rossijskoj Federacii ot 5 aprelja 2016 g. № 156 'O sovershenstvovanii gosudarstvennogo upravlenija v sfere kontrolja za oborotom narkoticheskih sredstv, psihotropnyh veshhestv i ih prekursorov i v sfere migracii,"http://kremlin.ru/events/president/news/51649

Verhovsky, A. "*Jazyk moj... Problema jetnicheskoj i religioznoj neterpimosti v rossijskih SMI.* [My language... The issue of ethnic and religious intolerance in Russian mass-media]," Moscow: Sova Centre, 2002.

Verkhovsky, A. "The Rise of Nationalism in Putin's Russia," *Helsinki Monitor* 18(2) (2007): 125.

Vertovec, S. "The Cultural Politics of Nation and Migration," *Annual Review of Anthropology* 40 (2011): 241–256.

*Vesti*, "V Primor'e vyjasnjajut, pochemu vrachi ostavili migrantku rozhat' na poroge' roddoma [It is explained why doctors left a migrant to deliver a baby outside]," 7 November 2013, http://www.vesti.ru/doc.html?id=1151352

Wodak, R. and Boukala, S. "European Identities and the Revival of Nationalism in the European Union: A Discourse Historical Approach," *Journal of Language and Politics* 14.1 (2015): 87-109.

# 11

# Labour Migration in the Eurasian Economic Union

CARESS SCHENK

One of the key points of contention leading to the Ukrainian crisis was the debate over whether to sign the Association Agreement, aiming to increase Ukraine's integration with the European Union. The controversy came as a result of the perception that any agreements with the EU would necessarily be a move away from integration with Russia. In the end, Ukraine proceeded with the signing of the Association Agreement in 2014, and Russia moved forward with its plans to create the Eurasian Economic Union (EEU), which came into being on 1 January 2015. The management of labour migration in the framework of the EEU offers a glimpse at the inner workings of Russia's new integration project.

The Eurasian Economic Union is an extension of various integration projects between the countries of the former Soviet Union beginning with the Commonwealth of Independent States (CIS), Eurasian Economic Community, and Eurasian Customs Union. From the Western perspective, the EEU is often framed as a Russian imperial project, though in the region there are multiple meanings and justificatory frameworks tied to the participation of the non-Russian countries (Armenia, Belarus, Kazakhstan, and Kyrgyzstan). From the perspective of migration and labour market integration, the agreement is far more radical than anything that has existed since the fall of the Soviet Union. In many ways the EEU creates one of the most integrated labour markets in the world, clearly taking a page from the EU, though its provisions have been so far hardly realised in practice. Migration in the Eurasian region has long been dominated by informal processes that have little to do with the policies that aim to regulate them, and the EEU has done little to change the situation. In order to manage disparate goals at the domestic and international levels, member states do not fully implement EEU commitments into domestic law, leaving migration flows in the informal sector outside official data, and consequently out of the public eye.

This article looks at the gap between EEU obligations set out in the treaty text, domestic immigration laws and procedures in Kazakhstan and Russia, and migrant experience with state regulations. In order to assess these gaps, I consider government and legal texts, interviews with officials, diaspora leaders, and migrant rights activists in Russia and Kazakhstan. Media reports and official immigration statistics are also included in the analysis. These gaps serve strategic goals of member states because they allow countries to formally agree to EEU commitments while keeping domestic policy underdeveloped or bureaucratically unwieldy, which serves to keep the numbers of migrants who are officially taking advantage of the treaty provisions low.

**The Ukrainian Crisis and Economic Downturn in Eurasia**

The EEU migration system was profoundly impacted by the economic downturn in Russia that resulted from the crisis in Ukraine. In response to the Russian annexation of Crimea in 2014, Western countries imposed sanctions that compounded the economic difficulties Russia was already facing due to falling oil prices, sending the country into negative GDP growth (World Bank 2015, Dreyer and Popescu 2014). Beginning in August 2014, the rouble began to lose hold against the dollar and by December 2014 had fallen to half of its value.

At the same time, migration rates began to decline. The Russian media was especially keen to announce that migrants were leaving Russia as a result of the economic downturn. More specifically, the media reported lower numbers of documented labour migrants than in the immediately preceding years. For example, compared with 3.2 million documented labour migrants in 2014, 2015 saw a reduction of 40 per cent to 1.9 million legal labour migrants.

While media reports focused solely on economic explanations for the fall in the number of labour migrants, a major change in Russian migration policy also contributed significantly to the ability of migrants to achieve documented status. It is the combination of these factors together that contribute to a fuller picture of migration. While economic factors are a primary driver of migration flows, policies and their implementation determine how easily labour migrants will be able to regularise their status. While states often have little control over external economic shocks, their greatest point of control over immigration is the proportion of migrants who will be diverted to the informal sector through policies and their implementation.

Policy changes affected all migrants from the Commonwealth of Independent States countries who were not part of the EEU (including major sources of immigration: Tajikistan and Uzbekistan). New policies that took effect on 1 January 2015 required migrants to complete a standard set of procedures including passing a language, history, and legal norms exam in addition to undergoing a number of bureaucratic procedures, all within 30 days of arrival. These tasks proved difficult for migrants to complete within the allotted time. As a result, many migrants shifted into the informal labour market, demonstrating a veritable law of migration, according to which when policy becomes more restrictive, previously temporary or circular migration flows become more permanent (though in this case unofficial) stocks (Hollifield, Martin and Orrenius 2014; Martin P. L. 2014; Massey and Pren, 2012).

Yet, immigration trends indicate that migration policies are secondary to economic forces in determining migration flows. According to a migrant rights activist from Moscow, there was indeed an outflow of migrants as a result of recession in Russia, but it was temporary, lasting six months or so. Compared to the aftermath of the 2008 global financial crisis, which also saw decreased migration flows to Russia that recovered only within a few years, the 2014 recession had a relatively short-term impact on migration flows. In 2014, the rouble crisis began to affect Russia's Central Asian neighbours to the point that Russia quickly returned to its place as a comparatively advantageous destination for work and earning potential. Despite continued recession, both the supply of migrants and the demand for their labour remains robust in Russia, even if migrants are not able to legalise their status. The same is true in Kazakhstan, a secondary destination for migrants from Central Asia. Kazakhstan experienced significant currency devaluation in 2015 (losing nearly half of its value) but was able to stave off recession. The comparatively better economic position, combined with significant state construction projects requiring low-skilled labour (such as EXPO 2017), has increased Kazakhstan's relative importance as a migrant destination in the Eurasian region.

## Labour Migration Trends, Policies, and Barriers to a Common Labour Market

In the context of economic downturn and policy change, the entry into force of the EEU created a number of migration-related puzzles. Both in the Russian case (Schenk 2013) and more widely in the experience of migration countries such as Spain, Japan, South Korea, the US immigrant receiving states often erect protectionist policies such as reduced quota, hiring bans, and 'return bonuses' or pay-to-go schemes (cash settlements to migrants who agree to leave the country) in response to economic crisis (Fix, et al. 2009; Martin

2009; Ybarra, Sanchez and Sanchez 2016; Lopez-Sala 2013). Given these general principles of migration policy-making, the main puzzle herein concerns the decision to maximally open the labour market in a time of recession. A further puzzle is why open labour market policies would be pursued at the same time as other major migration policies were becoming increasingly closed and securitised.

In Russia, reforms of labour permits (called 'patents') beginning on 1 January 2015 for CIS citizens are a key example of migration restrictions that run in a counter direction to the EEU common labour market. In both Russia and Kazakhstan, we see increasingly securitised migration rhetoric (framing migrants as a threat), which both creates and reinforces anti-migrant attitudes in society, as well as policies and institutional reforms that follow the rhetoric. For example, in April 2016, Russia transferred the responsibility of migration regulation and policy development from the independent Federal Migration Service into the Ministry of Internal Affairs. In June 2016, Kazakhstan created a National Bureau of Migration within the Ministry of Internal Affairs specifically to address security-related migration problems including uncontrolled migration and illegal settlements.[1]

The fact that EEU migration policies run counter to the general migration orientation in Kazakhstan and Russia must be carefully managed by these countries' governments in order to manage the dual goals of regional integration (to serve geopolitical aims) and protecting local labour markets (to satisfy domestic populations). There are two primary ways that this management can proceed: in data collection and reporting, and in (non-)adherence to EEU agreement principles through implementation into domestic law and practice. Both of these mechanisms are instrumental in determining and reflecting how many migrants are able to formalise their labour status.

It is difficult, though not impossible, to measure the real impact of the EEU on migration trends because of a number of data deficits. First of all, data is scarce, and in some cases completely absent or unavailable from the government sources that collect them. Data in Russia are the most developed and publically available in the region, while Kazakhstan is marked by a remarkable dearth of data in spite of its position as the second largest migrant destination in the region. Second, official government data from the statistical services is typically issued with a significant delay. Therefore, at the time of writing, data for 2015 has yet to be released (see Table 1). The only available data for 2015 comes from Russia's General Directorate for Migration (the

---

[1] https://tengrinews.kz/kazakhstan_news/mvd-rk-poyavitsya-natsionalnoe-byuro-voprosam-migratsii-296329/

former Federal Migration Service). These data hint at a third problem: many labour migrants do not appear in the official statistics. This is not only because of irregular migration, but also due to the potential for labour migrants to be counted in different migration categories. As a result, even prior to the EEU labour migrants were underestimated for a variety of reasons.

Table 1: Documented labour migrants

|  | 2008 | 2009 | 2010 | 2011 | 2012 | 2013 | 2014 | 2015 |
|---|---|---|---|---|---|---|---|---|
| **Russia** | | | | | | | | |
| All | 2,425,900 | 2,223,600 | 1,640,800 | 1,792,800 | 2,229,100 | 2,468,200 | 3,177,900 | 1,931,957 |
| CIS countries[2] | 1,773,800 | 1,642,700 | 1,245,700 | 1,620,400 | 2,048,400 | 2,303,500 | 2,997,800 | 1,768,758 |
| Customs Union countries[3] | 10,400 | 11,200 | 8300 | 9300 | 1700 | 1600 | 1400 | 429[4] |
| EEU countries[5] | 295,100 | 249,300 | 185,800 | 220,000 | 255,800 | 302,700 | 410,700 | 246,649[6] |
| **Kazakhstan** | | | | | | | | |
| All[7] | 54,204 | 30,988 | 29,178 | 27,132 | 22,041 | -- | 31,600[8] | -- |
| CIS | -- | -- | 3122 | -- | 2160 | -- | -- | -- |

Source: (Rosstat, 2015; Rosstat, 2011; Sadovskaya; Sadovskaya, 2013)

[2] CIS countries include Armenia, Azerbaijan, Belarus, Moldova, Kazakhstan, Kyrgyzstan, Tajikistan, and Uzbekistan. Ukrainian citizens are also extended in the same entry and work privileges, though they are not an official member of the CIS. Ukrainians are recorded in migration statistics as part of the CIS. The 2008 figure includes Georgia (4,200 workers), which left the CIS in 2009.
[3] These figures reflect workers from Kazakhstan only, as there are no recorded labour migrants from Belarus during this period.
[4] Includes Belarus.
[5] Belarus, Kazakhstan, Kyrgyzstan, and Armenia.
[6] Number of contracts concluded and submitted to the migration services, plus the number of patents issued.
[7] The figures reported for Kazakhstan are based on the number of work invitations that are issued under migrant quotas (a task that is coordinated by the Ministry of Labour and Social Protection). The data are substantially different than those of the Ministry of Internal Affairs (which houses the migration police, in charge of migrant registration). According to the Ministry of Internal Affairs, Kazakhstan hosted between 350,000-430,000 annually from 2009-2014 (Aliev 2016).
[8] As of November: http://economy.gov.kz/ru/gosudarstvennye-uslugi/detail.php?ELEMENT_ID=68772&

One of the primary reasons why labour migrants are underestimated is because there are a variety of preferable legal statuses they can pursue that provide more secure working conditions. These include temporary or permanent residence permits, or citizenship, all of which give migrants the right to work on the same basis as native-born Russian citizens, without preventing the circular movement of migrants between Russia and their home country. Furthermore, beginning as early as 2012, Kazakhs and Belarussians disappeared from labour migration statistics because they were given free access to the Russian labour market within the framework of the Eurasian Customs Union (a precursor to the EEU). Data on border crossings helps to capture some of the missing labour market data by showing the volume of foreigners entering a particular country (see Table 2). These data include all foreigners crossing the border into the country for any reason (e.g. tourism, work, study, etc.). They indicate that in the years that show decreasing documented labour migration in the Customs Union, the number of border crossings increased, suggesting that labour movement in the region remained robust yet uncaptured in the official statistics.

**Table 2: Entries Recorded by Border Agencies.**

|  | 2008 | 2009 | 2010 | 2011 | 2012 | 2013 | 2014 |
|---|---|---|---|---|---|---|---|
| **To Russia** | | | | | | | |
| Total | 23,676,140 | 21,338,650 | 22,281,217 | 24,932,061 | 28,176,502 | 30,792,091 | 32,421,490 |
| CIS | 15,061,619 | 12,960,167 | 13,906,605 | 15,730,278 | 17,995,850 | 19,922,378 | 21,621,143 |
| Customs Union[9] | 2,987,261 | 2,877,183 | 3,006,549 | 3,316,639 | 4,003,284 | 4,267,106 | 4,711,160 |
| EEU | 3,998,597 | 3,663,212 | 4,018,498 | 4,459,948 | 5,327,586 | 5,913,388 | 6,230,922 |
| **To Kazakhstan** | | | | | | | |
| Total | 4,721,456 | 4,329,848 | 4,712,657 | 5,685,132 | 6,163,204 | 6,841,085 | 6,332,734 |
| CIS | 4,105,510 | 3,782,254 | 4,183,259 | 5,195,043 | 5,542,447 | 6,213,390 | 5,655,246 |
| EEU | -- | -- | -- | -- | -- | -- | -- |

Sources: (Russian State Statistical Service, 2013; Rosstat, 2011; Rosstat, 2010; Rosstat, 2015; Министерство национальной экономики Республики Казахстан Комитет по статистике, 2015; Агентство Республики Казахстан по статистике, 2013; Агентство Республики Казахстан по статистике, 2011).

---

[9] Kazakhstan and Belarus.

Once the EEU came into force, migrants from Kyrgyzstan and Armenia also began to disappear from labour migration statistics. Until August 2015, Kyrgyz citizens could not take advantage of the EEU provisions, and were thus counted according to previous procedures (i.e. patents). Once EEU procedures took over, data collection became problematic. A primary reason for this is that migrants did not know the proper procedures for registering their presence and work. For labour migrants in Russia the entry into force of the EEU was eclipsed by new patent regulations discussed above. The labour permit reform was accompanied by a major campaign by the government to create state-run migration centres that could consolidate the profits of issuing patents.[10] In the wake of these activities, the regulations for EEU migrants were virtually neglected, and so were any efforts to inform migrants of their responsibilities. Several of the government-affiliated migration centres advised EEU migrants simply that they did not need to complete procedures for getting a patent or obtain permission to work. While this is technically true, it neglects a very important aspect of the EEU provisions for the free movement of labour.

Article 96 of the EEU agreement importantly defines employment as 'activities performed under an employment contract'. This short definition has proved to be the greatest challenge both for migrants' ability to realise the benefits of the EEU common labour market, and for governments to collect data on the work of migrants within the framework of the EEU. Though the Russian migration services began to collect data on the number of contracts submitted (reflected in Table 1), this was a new procedure and therefore there are no comparative data points to date.[11] In Kazakhstan, contracts are submitted to the migration police, but there are simply no data available from this agency.

A larger problem with employment contracts is that low-skilled labour migrants (which are far greater in numbers than high skilled migrants) do not traditionally have contracts. The primacy of contracts for migrant workers is an important development because of its historical disuse marked by the small number of migrants who have labour contracts. Because of this, linking a migrant's status to a formal employment contract could put the legal status of EEU migrants in jeopardy. Reports from migrant advocates and activists in Russia indicate that many Kyrgyz workers continue to work in Russia without a contract, either because they do not believe (or know) it is necessary, or because their employers do not want to provide one. In Russia, many

---

[10] Numerous fees are involved in obtaining a patent (for a Russian language exam, medical exam, notarising and translating documents, etc.) typically totaling at least 10,000 RUB.

[11] The Eurasian Economic Commission alternatively looks at migrants registered with the national pension funds to extract data on labour migration.

employers have been reluctant to sign contracts since it would formalise the working relationship thereby obligating them to pay taxes and social insurance (Tyuryukanova 2008, Zayonchkovskaya 2007a).

A 2015 survey of Kyrgyz and Uzbek labour migrants in five regions of Kazakhstan showed that 79 per cent of Kyrgyz migrants surveyed did not have a labour contract.[12] While these survey results reflect pre-EEU procedures, it indicates significant potential problems for migrants (and employers) who are not accustomed to signing employment contracts. Furthermore, only 44 per cent of migrants reported that their employers provided residence registration (a necessary step in confirming legal status), while presumably the remainder registered themselves. This indicates that a majority of employers offer minimal support to the migrants they hire and may be unwilling to sign employment contracts if it obligates them to pay additional taxes.

A further issue is that in some cases national legislation does not yet provide the benefits promised in the EEU agreement. A case in point is the residence registration procedures for citizens of Kyrgyzstan in Kazakhstan. Despite Kyrgyzstan's entry into the EEU in August 2015, Kazakhstan did not make any legal changes in support of the free movement of labour until February 2016 when the registration period for Kyrgyz citizens coming for the purpose of work was extended from five to 30 days (citizens of Russia had prior been granted 30 days to register regardless of their purpose of stay, on the basis of a bilateral treaty). Only migrants who have declared their purpose of visit as work on their migration card are eligible for this extension.[13] Family members of migrants who will not be working (and thus have listed their purpose of visit as 'private') must register within five days.[14] This is in contravention of the EEU agreement, which states that 'Nationals of the Member States entering the territory of another Member State for employment and their family members shall be exempt from the obligation to register within 30 days from the date of entry'. The Kyrgyz consulate in Kazakhstan indicates the issue of extending a longer registration period for family members is still being negotiated between the governments, though a representative of the Ministry of Foreign Affairs in Kyrgyzstan reported this is simply an issue of Kazakhstan's compliance with its obligations and there is nothing to discuss between the two countries. Consequently, Kyrgyzstan has threatened to

---

[12] Survey deployed by the author.
[13] This information is not provided by the migration police, where registration documents must be processed, but rather is only available at the Consulates of EEU countries. The migration police do not have a website, nor are there any instructions on any Kazakhstani government website explaining registration procedures.
[14] http://tengrinews.kz/sng/kazakhstan-uprostil-registratsiyu-trudovyih-migrantov-289703/

shorten the period of stay for Kazakhstani citizens in Kyrgyzstan in retaliation for the lack of commitment to EEU norms.[15]

Both in Kazakhstan and in Russia migrants must declare their purpose of visit as 'work' on their migration card as they enter the country. Kazakhstan does not report the number of migrant cards received or the purpose of visit, and Russia only began reporting nationwide data on the category of work as purpose of visit in 2015. Various regions of Russia have published data on migrants entering with the stated purpose of work that includes several years of comparative data. Data from Moscow is informative, since it is the largest migrant recipient in Russia. Table three shows that the number of migrants arriving to Moscow with the declared purpose of work increased substantially. This is owing in part to the 1 January 2015 rule that patents could only be issued to CIS citizens with a migration card that specifies work as the purpose of visit.

Yet, it is also clear that the number of documented migrants is more than four times lower than the number of migrants who specify work as their purpose of entry on their migration card. The data in Table 3 do not include EEU migrants, since Moscow does not issue the number of work contracts received by EEU citizens, reinforcing the idea that EEU migration has been neglected in comparison with other categories of migrant workers. Yet, since Table 1 shows that across all of Russia fewer than 250,000 EEU migrants legalised their working status in 2015, even if *all* 250,000 were in Moscow and added to the 550,000 other documented workers, there would only be around 800,000 legal migrant workers in Moscow. This number is still far fewer than the 2.4 million workers arriving to Moscow with the intention to work. We can conclude from these data that because there are many more migrants entering who intend to work than are recorded as documented labour migrants, not only do data collection procedures underestimate the number of labour migrants in Russia, but bureaucratic procedures act as barriers to realising full legal status.

---

[15] https://www.zakon.kz/4797186-v-kazakhstane-sokratilis-sroki.html (Accessed 30 June 2016).

**Table 3: Labour migrants in Moscow.**

|  | 2013 | 2014 | 2015 |
|---|---|---|---|
| Work permits | 339,978 | 340,843 | 66,549 |
| Patents | 292,490 | 811,072 | 484,771 |
| Total documented labour migrants | 535,381 | 1,151,915 | 551,320 |
| Purpose of entry |  |  |  |
| --study | 72,000 | 91,500 | 115,400 |
| --tourism | 397,300 | 332,100 | 324,200 |
| --private | 673,900 | 654,700 | 479,400 |
| --work | 923,100 | 1,676,000 | 2,352,900 |
| --other | 182,200 | 169,300 | 114,600 |

Source: Moscow UFMS (Upravlenie Federal'noi Migratsionnoi Sluzhby). 2016. O migratsionnoi situatsii v gorode Moskve i osnovnykh resul'tatakh UFMS Rossii po gorodu Moskve za 12 mesiatsev 2015 goda. (О миграционной ситуации в г. Москве и основных результатах деятельности УФМС России по г. Москве за 12 месяцев 2015 года.) Moscow.

**Conclusion: Priorities vs Realities**

In practice, the Eurasian Economic Union is a political project that has a primary aim of meeting symbolic geopolitical goals rather than affecting concrete policy change. In order to meet domestic goals, while still pursuing integration, member states keep from fully implementing EEU obligations at the domestic level. As long as the economies are relatively strong, migrants continue to come to Kazakhstan and Russia. Yet, when policies are underdeveloped or bureaucratically challenging, EEU migrants are unable to take advantage of treaty provisions, remain in the informal sector and are not captured in official data.

Kazakhstan's reluctance to implement EEU obligations could indicate several things. One potential explanation is that the status quo (which includes a high proportion of informal migrants) is beneficial to employers and others who profit from migrants and their informal status, while it keeps the number of official migrants low. Because the immigrant flows to Kazakhstan are smaller than in Russia, they have not provoked a sense of crisis among the public or state officials, and therefore immigration is not high on the agenda of priority reforms.

In the Russian case, the neglect of EEU migrants can be explained by several factors. One is the relatively smaller number of migrants coming from EEU countries, and therefore less urgent attention given to developing procedures and disseminating information for these migrants. This is exacerbated by the timing of reforms, since Russia concurrently adopted dramatically different procedures for non-EEU migrants that took much of the attention away from EEU migrants. Second, the EEU labour market reforms were controversial in Russia, causing the public to fear a flood of new migrants with no control mechanisms to protect the domestic labour market. Neglecting EEU migrants serves to keep official numbers low, which is more politically palatable to the public.

In the area of migration, policy development is further impeded by the fact that there are no high-level agreements on the politics of migration. Prior to the agreement's entry into force, Kazakhstani President Nursultan Nazarbayev expressed his desire for the union to remain non-political and by his estimation this meant that certain issues such as migration and border control should not be under the purview of the EEU (Popescu 2014). In the hyper-politicised aftermath of the Ukraine crisis, migration issues (including the protection of citizens and ethnic compatriots abroad) could very well be seen as vital issues of sovereignty that states are unwilling to have decided by a supranational organisation. Because the countries of the EEU frequently draw parallels between Europe and their own experience, any lessons learned from Britain's referendum to leave the European Union, largely motivated by migration issues, could contribute to a greater reluctance on the part of EEU countries to further deregulate migration arrangements.

Insofar as the EEU affects the sovereignty of the states involved, it cannot avoid creating political conflicts within and between member states when sensitive issues are at stake. Despite Nazarbayev's hopes to limit the political content of the union, the nature of a grand-scale integration programme will necessarily raise questions that can only be answered politically. The current situation, where migration policy is vaguely defined, leaving member states to rely on national legislation and practices on the ground that do not meet EEU obligations, is one way to avoid potential conflict at the top political levels. Yet, avoiding high-level conflict will inevitably create tensions in the labour markets, as migrant workers' experience will not proceed according to the legal rights afforded them in the EEU framework. If new member states are being attracted to EEU membership with the promise of an open labour market, the realities of migrant experience on the ground is likely to be disappointing. In this context, sending states that are dependent on migrant remittances and serious about developing policies for their citizens abroad may find EEU membership less than what they bargained for.

## References

Агентство Республики Казахстан по статистике, *Казахстан в цифрах*, Astana, 2011.

Агентство Республики Казахстан по статистике, *Брошюра «Казахстан в цифрах»*, Astana, 2013.

Министерство национальной экономики Республики Казахстан Комитет по статистике. *Брошюра «Казахстан в цифрах»*. Astana, 2015.

Dreyer, I., & Popescu, N. *Do sanctions against Russia Work?* European Union Institute for Security Studies, 2014.

Fix, M., Papademetriou, D. G., Batalova, J., Terrazas, A., Lin, S. Y.-Y., & Mittelstadt, M. *Migration and the Global Recession.* Migration Policy Institute, 2009.

Hollifield, J. F., Martin, P. L. and Orrenius, P. M. "The Dilemmas of Immigration Control," in J. F. Hollifield, P. L. Martin and P. M. Orrenius, *Controlling Immigration: A Global Perspective, 3rd edition*, Stanford: Stanford University Press, 2014.

Lopez-Sala, A. "Managing Uncertainty: Immigration Policies in Spain during Economic Recession (2008-2011)," *Migraciones Internacionales 7*, no.2 (2013): 21-69.

Martin, P. "Recession and Migration: A New Era for Labor Migration?" *International Migration Review, 43*, no.3 (2009): 671–691.

Martin, P. L. "Germany," in J. F. Hollifield, P. L. Martin, & P. M. Orrenius, *Controlling Immigration: A Global Perspective, Third Edition*, Stanford: Stanford University Press, 2014: 224-250.

Massey, D. S. and Pren, K. A. "Unintended Consequences of US Immigration Policy: Explaining the Post-1965 Surge from Latin America," *Population and Development Review, 38*, no.1 (2012): 1–29.

Popescu, N. "Eurasian Union: The Real, the Imaginary and the Likely," *Chaillot Papers, No. 132*. Paris: European Union Institute for Security Studies, September 2014.

Rosstat, *Chislennost' i migratsiya naseleniya Rossiiskoi Federatsii*, 2010.

Rosstat, *Chislennost' i migratsiya naseleniya Rossiiskoi Federatsii*, 2011.

Rosstat, *Trud i Zanyatosti*, 2011.

Rosstat, *Chislennost' i migratsiya naseleniya Rossiiskoi Federatsii*, 2015.

Rosstat, *Trud i Zanyatosti*, 2015.

Russian State Statistical Service, Chislennost' i migratsiya naseleniya Rossiiskoi Federatsii v 2013 godu, 2013.

Sadovskaya, E. (n.d.). *Законная трудовая миграция в Казахстан*, Demoscope.ru, http://demoscope.ru/weekly/2014/0583/tema03.php

Sadovskaya, E. *Mezhdunarodnaya Trudovaya Migratsiya v Tsentral'noi Azii v nachale XXI veka*. Moscow: Vostochnaya Kniga, 2013.

Sadovskaya, E. *Законная трудовая миграция в Казахстан*. Demoscope. ru, 2014, http://demoscope.ru/weekly/2014/0583/tema03.php

Schenk, C. "Controlling Immigration Manually: Lessons from Moscow (Russia)," *Europe-Asia Studies, 65*, no.7 (2013): 1444-1465.

Tyuryukanova, E. "Labour migration from CIS to Russia: New Challenges and Hard Solutions," presented at *'Empires & Nations'* 3-5 July 2008 in Paris, France.

World Bank. *Russia Economic Report: The Dawn of a New Economic Era?* Moscow: Macroeconomics and Fiscal Management Practice of the Europe and Central Asia Region of the World Bank, 2015.

Ybarra, V. D., Sanchez, L. M. and Sanchez, G. R. "Anti-immigrant Anxieties in State Policy: The Great Recession and Punitive Immigration Policy in the American States, 2005–2012," *State Politics & Policy Quarterly, 16*, no.3 (2016): 313–339.

Zayonchkovskaya, Z. "*Novaya migratsionnaya politika Rossii: vpechatliayushiye resultati i novie problemi [New Immigration Policy of Russia: Impressing Results and New Problems]*" 2007, http://migrocenter.ru/science/science027.php

# 12

# Beyond Attitudes: Russian Xenophobia as a Political Legitimation Tool

MARINA A. KINGSBURY

**Introduction**

The Ukrainian conflict has had a curious effect on xenophobia in Russia, which had reached unprecedented levels in the autumn of 2013. Xenophobia in Russia was artificially stimulated by the regime in order to deflect attention from acute societal problems such as corruption, decaying democratic freedoms and the economic stagflation. The Ukrainian conflict shook up Russian society, causing the Russian State to tone down domestic xenophobic rhetoric. The attention concentrated on exploiting the threats of Ukrainian nationalism, which would be incompatible with Russian state-sanctioned xenophobia. This apparent paradox of supporting home-grown nationalism and xenophobia, but condemning Ukrainian nationalism, resembles the Soviet past, when the leaders argued for the benefits of 'good nationalism' for building the socialist state (Slezkine 1994).

Currently, the Levada Centre, a reputable Russian public opinion pollster, indicates that xenophobia has diminished somewhat, most likely due to the decrease in mass media attention to perceived societal problems caused by immigrants. Overall, in Russia xenophobia continues to be manipulated and sanctioned by the state as the regime steers popular discontent towards migrants while declaring its official intolerance to radical nationalism and racism. The current political climate is more conducive to sanctioning less aggression towards foreigners because the state deems it more in its interests. Instead, attention is focused on the threat from the West – a comfortable antagonist of Russian authoritarianism.

**Existing Theories of Xenophobia**

Xenophobia is the anti-immigrant sentiment exhibited by host societies towards immigrants from other cultural, ethnic, and religious backgrounds. One of the prevalent explanations of xenophobia in existing literature attributes hostility towards immigrants to the perceived competition for local social and economic resources. The extant literature calls it the *competition hypothesis* (Kischelt 1995; Gorodziesky, Glikman and Maskileyson 2015). Fear of immigrants is most common among groups most vulnerable to the challenges of a globalised economy. Unskilled labour and lower-middle class workers, uneducated, underemployed and unemployed individuals are expected to express more anti-immigrant sentiment. The competitive threat from the influx of a younger, cheaper immigrant labour force has been found to significantly increase anti-immigrant sentiment in European countries (Gorodziesky and Semyonov 2015; Semyonov, Raijman, and Gorodziesky 2006). Recent scholarship extends the relevance of the competition hypothesis and argues that the negative attitude towards immigrants is amplified among those who also hold conservative political views and support radical right parties (Gorodziesky and Semyonov 2015; Wilkes, Guppy and Farris 2007).

Semyonov, Gorodziesky, and Raijman (2006), using Eurobarometer survey data, found that anti-foreigner sentiment is significantly stronger in localities with higher support for radical-right parties. Their findings have been affirmed and extended by Wilkes, Guppy and Farris (2007), who argue that the strongest association between radical right party support and anti-immigrant sentiment is found for those radical right parties that promote cultural racism, which is based on the superiority of Western civilisation's culture and ways of life.

The competing *cultural theory* of anti-immigrant sentiment argues that resentment towards immigrants can be explained by the fear of losing cultural purity and the dilution of cultural homogeneity (Castles 2010; Putnam 2007; Raijman and Semyonov 2004). Recent world events add to the empirical understanding of developments across Europe by drawing our attention to the ethnic component of anti-immigrant sentiment: the increasing Islamophobia that differentiates attitudes toward immigrants based on their national and religious identity (Adida, Laitin, and Volford 2016; Givens 2007; Fredette 2014).

Much of the existing literature evaluates the merits of the competition and cultural hypotheses on the set of developed western European countries with stable national identities.

However, studies of countries that are still experiencing nation-building may offer an additional explanatory path. The statistical research of Russian anti-foreigner sentiments using the third round of the European Social Survey (2006), finds low explanatory power of either the competition or cultural hypotheses in Russia (Gorodziesky, Glikman and Maskileyson 2015). The authors ponder that low explanatory value of the existing hypotheses may be due to the different societal dynamics within Russia, stressing the aftermath of enormous societal transformation that led to a crisis of national identity.

This approach finds support among Russian scholars who place Russian anti-foreigner attitudes into a socio-historical context. Lev Gudkov (2007) argues that xenophobia can be at least partially attributed to the complex feelings of dissatisfaction and humiliation that citizens of the former world super-power may experience. This inferiority complex is akin to the Weimar syndrome. Gudkov[1] argues that xenophobia is caused by a cocktail of negative experiences, humiliation from the loss in the Cold War, and a growing instability that stems from the displacement due to the overhaul of the economic and political system following the collapse of the USSR (Gudkov 2016). Vladimir Mukomel (2015) argues that the rise of Russian xenophobia can be explained by the changing solidarities in the society, built by contemporary Russian elites on the basis of the new solidarity of traditional Russian values and order. The underlying premise of the argument is that immigration is eroding the Russian identity, Russian culture, and the Russian way of life. Together, these studies contribute an important socio-historical explanation to extant theoretical base.

**Xenophobia as an Instrument of Power Legitimation**

In addition to the existing explanations of xenophobia, I propose the political explanation. The elites manipulate popular immigrant phobias for political gain. Explanations of Russian xenophobia must include the role of the state, a tradition partially inherited from the past. Historically, the Russian Empire has been a heterogeneous state, with many ethnic and religious groups calling it home. After the Bolshevik Revolution altered the make-up of the Russian Empire, one of the tasks of the new government was the formation of the multi-ethnic state. Soviet elites played a decisive role in supporting

---

[1] 'The country, generally speaking, suffers from the strongest complex of inferiority. And is frustrated about it. A great country – but lives in wretchedness, arbitrariness, boorishness. This is a stable complex of dividedness and shame before the West' (Gudkov 2016).

tolerance in the multinational state. The USSR created a system based on multinationalism and ethnic heterogeneity (Brubaker 1994; Kellas 1998). On personal and institutional levels, the state defined and sponsored ethnic tolerance and promoted inter-personal harmony, while limitations to the freedom of movement restricted co-mingling of different ethnic and regional groups. These practices created a strong institutional barrier to the spread of explicit xenophobia.[2] At the end of the 1980s, about 20 per cent of USSR citizens had xenophobic views, while aggressive ethno-phobia was reported by six to 12 per cent of respondents. Xenophobia in Russia was significantly lower than the USSR average (Gudkov 2007, 49-50).

Upon the collapse of the USSR, the state ideology, including the support for ethnic federalism, perished as well.[3] The new Russian state opened opportunities for greater mobility of masses from within Russia as well as from abroad. In the absence of the state-enforced taboo on xenophobia and the rapidly increasing co-mingling of different peoples, attitudes towards others – immigrants from the Russian regions and abroad – started to change.

Following the wild and unpredictable 1990s, when the state held a comparatively small role in regulating societal life, the new Putin government stabilised the economy, but also launched an assault on democratic institutions, slowly working to limit political dissent, undermine the transparency of elections, and to limit the accountability of governance in Russia. Russia in the 2000s was re-classified from a partially-free state into an autocratic state by the Freedom House. Russian media has been found to be restricted, characterised by government censorship, and persecution of bloggers. Elections have become unfair and not free (Freedom House 2015). Scholars of transition classify Russia as a competitive authoritarian regime, which can be characterised by the formal existence of democratic institutions such as multi-party elections of the executive and the legislative branches, but elections are neither transparent nor fair, the freedom of media and political competition has been stifled, and the turnover of leadership as a result of fair competitive elections has not happened since 2000 (Levitsky and Way 2002).

Extant scholarship emphasises the importance of regime legitimation for authoritarian leaders. Investing in regime legitimisation allows regime leaders to ensure survival. Authoritarian leaders rely on the threat of violence and co-

---

[2] However, not consistently, as anti-Semitism was quite common (SOVA Center 2003).

[3] For a review on the establishment of Soviet policies that promoted ethnic federalism see Slezkine (1994).

optation of elites as an important source of legitimacy (Geddes 1999; Levitsky and Way 2012; Svolik 2009). Kailitz and Stockemer (2015) broaden our understanding of authoritarian legitimacy by pointing to the importance of legitimation of their authority with the masses as well as the political elites. Ulfelder (2005) finds that authoritarian leaders may increase the chances of regime survival to a greater degree when they can maintain legitimacy and thus avoid contentious collective action (riots, general strikes, or anti-government demonstrations) rather than just relying on the threat of violence and elite co-optation. Dimitrov (2009) argues that competitive authoritarian regimes do worry about popular support and try to maintain it by exploiting populist rhetoric, keeping up with social welfare spending and exploiting some form of nationalist sentiment.

I explore the argument that the Russian political establishment mounted the horse of nationalist populism in the mid-2000s to maintain popular legitimacy by taking advantage of nationalist popular moods. Authoritarian leaders often invoke anti-Western populist rhetoric to support their popularity, offering a visible, yet intangible enemy to the populace. Using the same logical framework, it can be argued that immigrants, as a form of the Other, can be portrayed as the enemy, especially if migrants are demonised as a source of evil, such as crime and terrorism. I propose that the Russian regime utilises xenophobia as a political tool to demonstrate that it is successfully addressing the threat that migrants reportedly create. This is largely an exaggerated threat, a political construction akin to the threat of the West that is used by authoritarian regimes to divert citizens' attention from internal societal problems, such as corruption, the lack of democratic freedoms, and economic stagnation. Xenophobia is utilised to maintain the regime's legitimacy in an effort to prevent contentious collective action.

**Xenophobia in Russia**

The active exploitation of social mobilisation around nationalist slogans (and the cultivation of the enemy image), as well as the growing authoritarian tendencies, created favourable conditions for the use of xenophobia as a political instrument by the end of the first decade of the 2000s. Opinion polls results indicate a rise in nationalism and transformation in the societal acceptance of others (Gudkov 2013). The old Soviet taboo on xenophobia eroded and was replaced by the increase of Russian ethnic nationalism, which can be gauged through the growing popularity of the slogan 'Russia for Russians.' Verkhovskii and Pain (2012) trace the emergence of the slogan to 2002, when the Russian ultra-nationalist movement DPNI[4] injected it into mainstream use. This slogan appealed to various radical-right, nationalist,

---

[4] Dvizenie Protiv Nezakonnoi Migratsii – Movement against Illegal Immigration.

populist movements by focusing on the visible enemy – immigrants. In 2005, Russian nationalists of various flavours organised the inaugural 'Russian March,' which became a yearly affair drawing more supporters each year.

Arguably, several factors contributed to rising migrantophobia: growing migration from ethnically-diverse Central Asian and South Caucasus countries, a rise in illegal immigration due to overly-restrictive immigration regulations, as well as acts of terrorism connected to the war in Chechnya. The change in the make-up and the growing volumes of migrant flows exacerbated the declining acceptance of migrants. If, in the early 1990s, the majority of migrants were ethnic Russians repatriating from the former Soviet Republics, at the turn of the 21st century, labour migration consisted of workers from the Central Asian republics, Southern Caucasus, Ukraine, Belarus, and Moldova. By 2007, Central Asian countries, especially Tajikistan and Uzbekistan, became the leading countries of origin of migrant labour (Florinskaya 2013).

Immigrants supplied an easy target for the growing number of nationalist groups and political factions, which had enjoyed a lack of governmental restrictions. During the 2003 parliamentary election campaign, several political parties embraced the nationalist rhetoric, including the Communist Party (KPRF) and the far-right Political Party LDPR. The Kremlin jumped on the bandwagon as well, creating the nationalist faction Rodina, which later became a stand-alone party known for its political extremism and unapologetic nationalist sentiment. In 2005 Rodina featured a xenophobic political TV ad, portraying migrants as the source of crime.[5] The party was later disqualified from participation in elections for inciting inter-ethnic hate (Grani 2005).

By 2007, public xenophobic rhetoric emanated from the powerful Russian politician, Yuri Luzhkov, the Mayor of Moscow. His reappointment was proposed by President Putin in June 2007. The same month, Luzhkov made resonating statements calling for limiting migrant quotas in Moscow.[6] The Moscow government continued the anti-immigrant rhetoric throughout the summer of 2007, calling public attention to the threats of undocumented immigration and vowing to clean Moscow of undocumented migrants (New Izvestiya 2007). The 2007 Duma election campaign took place in December

---

[5]  https://www.youtube.com/watch?v=PiBOg5jTJQs
[6]  'My dolzny obespechivat ob'em kvotirovaniya, I nam luchshe govorit o tom, chto u kogo-to voznikla nekhvatka v trudovoi sile I reshat vopros po uvelicheniju kvot, a ne zagodya dat' s izbytkom I poluchit nagruzku na meditsiny, registratsiu – i poluchit gulyaushikh migrantov' (Polit.ru 2007).

2007 without parties publically endorsing anti-immigrant rhetoric.[7] However, pro-Kremlin youth movements, such as 'Mestnye' and 'Nashi' became involved in public hunts for illegal immigrants. These 'citizens' patrols' [*druzinniki*] were often co-conducted with local police units, including raids through open-air markets and migrant dormitories (Gazeta 2007). Among the slogans used were the calls to limit migrants' presence in public transportation vocations [*ne dadim rulit migrant*] (Grani 2007). In 2008, the Kremlin-backed youth group 'Molodaya Gvardia' staged pickets of builders and FMS offices with slogans like 'our money to our workers' [*nashi dengi – nashim lyudyam*] and 'every other one – out' [*kazdyi vtoroi – domoi*] (Lenta 2008; Vzglyad 2008). This tacit approval of the 'citizens' patrols' by Kremlin-backed groups created the overall impression in society that all immigrants are undocumented and that negative attitudes towards foreign workers are common.

The mass media paid increased attention to migrant crime statistics, following press releases from the power ministries (Chudinovskikh 2009a). For example, after the Deputy Interior Minister Sukhodolskiy reported the increased incidents of crime among migrants in December 2008, several media outlets reported the news, including Interfax, Komsomolskaya Pravda, and internet portals NewsRU and RIA Novosti (Interfax 2008; Komsomolskaya Pravda 2008; NewsRU 2008; RIA 2008). In 2009, mass media focused on retranslating migrant crime statistics after a Russian Prosecutor's Office Investigative Committee official argued that crime rates rose by 134 per cent among the undocumented immigrants, who often commit the most violent offences (Infox 2009; KM 2009; Rossiyskaya Gazeta 2009). These figures were characterised as misleading by the head of the Federal Migration Office, Konstantin Romodanovsky (Vedomosti 2009). Nonetheless, the threat of heightened immigrant crime became a hot button topic publicised in Russian mass media, most of which is controlled by the state. Although crime statistics were often taken out of context, media reports resonated with the public, contributing to popular xenophobia. For instance, the media often cited data on crimes committed by migrants without comparing it to the total crime rates, creating a tendency to over-estimate crimes committed by the migrants. If taken as a proportion of total crime, migrant crime has stayed within two per cent of the total number of offenses (Chudinovskikh 2009b).

Anti-immigrant hysteria culminated in the summer of 2013 during the Moscow mayoral election which featured increased attention to the topic of

---

[7] Although, one could argue that anti-immigrant statements made by Luzhkov could be taken as such, given that Luzhkov was the vice-chairman and one of the founders of the largest pro-government party United Russia.

immigration (Abashin 2014; Kingsbury 2015). The elections were highly contested, with candidates from six Russian parties participating: the ruling United Russia, the Communist Party KPRF, the far-right LDPR, the liberal party Yabloko, centre-left Spravedlivaya Rossiya, and the new opposition party RPR-Parnas. Every candidate devoted space in their electoral programmes to discussing the ills of immigration, and the need to combat irregular movement, with several candidates openly calling for outright prohibition of migration. The campaign was dominated by the notorious interviews of Sergei Sobyanin, the acting Mayor, who opined that immigrants should not settle in Moscow, rather they should return home promptly after finishing their seasonal work[8] (RBC 2013). Several candidates from the mainstream political parties expressed their support for implementing visas for workers from the former USSR countries, who can legally cross the Russian border visa-free as per provisions of the Eurasian Economic Union. The summer of 2013 was marked by large-scale illegal migrant raids organised by the police and migration officials (Vedomosti 2013). Russian sociologists argue that such disproportionately heavy emphasis on the issues of immigration contributed to the spike of xenophobia among Russians (Volkov 2013).

The conflict in the Moscow district of Biryolovo illustrates the tactic of using xenophobia to prevent collective action against the regime. In August 2013, an undocumented immigrant from Azerbaijan attacked and killed a local man. Mass protests followed the killing. Residents took to the streets to draw attention to their grievances. According to media reports, citizens of the Biryolovo district have continuously expressed dissatisfaction with a large vegetable warehouse located in the district. As reported by local residents, the warehouse harboured illicit activity and sidestepped sanitary norms. Mass media, meanwhile, emphasised the ills of irregular immigration, claiming that it breeds crime. Riots in Biryolovo exemplified the substitution of socio-economic grievances with a xenophobic message. Citizens were frustrated that the municipal government did not address their grievance that stemmed from the perceived corruption and mismanagement in the district. The overall dissatisfaction with socio-economic problems were carried by nationalist groups, which supplied activists to turn protests into violent riots.

The mass media content during the 2013 electoral campaign could be characterised as producing a coordinated campaign to demonise labour

---

[8]  'Ya protiv togo, chtoby ety ludy prosto tak ostavalis. Esli kogo-to ostavlyat, to v pervuyu ochered russkoyazychnykh, s adekvatnoi nashim traditsiyam kulturoi. Sootechestennikov – tak my ih uslovno nazyvaem. Ludyam, kotorye plokho govoryat po-russki, u kotorykh sovershenno drugaya kultura, luchshe zit v svoei strane. Poetomy my ne privetstvyem ih adaptatshiu v Moskve' (DNI.Ru 2013).

migrants. The ills of irregular immigration became a constant theme in mass media, including reports of crime statistics taken out of context. For example, mass media reports in 2013 emphasised the increased frequency of grave crime [tiazkoe prestuplenie] such as rape or murder following the announcements by the Moscow's Prosecutor Sergei Kudeneev. He reported that migrants commit every fifth murder, every second rape, and every third robbery[9] (Lenta 2013a). However, these statistics reflects portions of solved crime, not the overall crime. When compared to the full data, there has not been a significant increase. Full crime statistics reflects small fluctuation in the levels of crime committed by migrants in Moscow; it remained at the five to seven per cent levels between 2010 and 2013, while the levels of solved crime remained between 15 and 16 per cent (Zaionchkovskaya et al. 2014).

Even the country's leadership broke their silence in 2013. The Russian state has officially positioned itself as a multi-ethnic multinational state; Russian territories are home to a sizable population of Muslims, representatives of indigenous groups, and other religious and cultural minorities. However, the official message of tolerance diverges with the practice of tacitly supporting Russian ethnic nationalism by emphasising the Russian Orthodox religion and funding nationalist youth groups (Gorodziesky et al 2015; Pain 2007; Schenk 2012). By autumn 2013, the leadership retreated from the official stance as the President made anti-immigrant public comments. In August 2013, President Putin signed into law a bill that would increase the fines for breaking migration regulations in Moscow and Saint Petersburg. Newspaper headlines reported Vladimir Putin's remarks calling on the Duma and the Administration to tighten migration regulations and especially prohibit migrants from retail occupations (Lenta 2013b). Two months later Putin argued that migrants must respect Russian culture and values and abide by Russian laws, implying that they presently respect neither.[10] Putin also stressed the necessity to stop corruption among migrants (RIA 2013). By the end of 2013, xenophobia became an outlet for public frustration with socio-economic problems, having been openly sanctioned by state officials and reinforced through the mass media.

## The Ukrainian Conflict and Mass Xenophobia in Russia

Events of the autumn of 2013 and winter of 2014 in neighbouring Ukraine,

---

[9] 'Migrantami v Moskve sovershaetsia kazdoe piatoe ubiistvo, kazdoe vtoroe iznasilovanie i kazdoe tretie – grabezi i razboi' (Lenta 2013a).

[10] 'Чтобы мы добились от мигрантов безусловного уважения наших законов, обычаев, культуры регионов, куда они приезжают' [So that we demand from migrants the unconditional respect of our laws, customs, culture of regions where they arrive] (RIA 2013).

where pro-EU demonstrations led to the escalation of conflict and the ouster of President Yanukovich, diverted public attention from the internal problems within Russia. The conflict in Ukraine has been positioned by the mass media as a conflict between the Ukrainian nationalists and the Russian-speaking Eastern Ukrainians. For the regime, justifying support for the Ukrainian separatists based on the claims of cultural discrimination appeared incongruent with using nationalist and xenophobia rhetoric inside Russia. As I showed above, throughout the first decade of the twenty-first century Russian authorities have appropriated anti-immigrant rhetoric to redirect public dissatisfaction towards immigrants. After the success of the Ukrainian Euromaidan revolution, the appeal of nationalism as a political tool lost its lustre for the Russian regime. Ukrainian nationalism was equated to fascism and blamed for Ukraine's misfortunes by mainstream mass media (Levada Centre 2014).

At home nationalist, xenophobic rhetoric became a powerful catalyst of mass protest by the end of 2013. The 2013 'Russian March' featured not only the anti-immigrant message, but also sounded out social discontent with the regime, calling for fair and transparent elections and freedom of speech (Nezavisimaya Gazeta 2013). The 'acceptable' Russian patriotic nationalism[11] utilised by the regime during the previous decade became difficult to distinguish from the 'bad' Ukrainian nationalism spearheaded by the Euromaidan movement. So the mass media xenophobic rhetoric was toned down. As reported by Levada Centre's spokesperson, federal television channels, which are the source of news to almost 94 per cent of Russians, almost eliminated xenophobic news segments about migrants (Levada Centre 2014). Instead, Russian media wrote about accepting refugees from Eastern Ukraine. The State Duma passed amendments to the Citizenship Law[12] that provided a streamlined procedure for Russian speakers [*nositeli yazyka*]. The rhetoric towards the Others – refugees, migrants, and foreigners in general, was somewhat toned down. Consequently, Russians' approval of the nationalist movements and slogans declined, as measured by the approval of the slogan 'Russia for Russians' (Levada Centre 2015). The official message became one of intolerance to radical nationalism.

This ideological shift coupled with the increased popularity of Putin following the take-over of Crimea made unnecessary diversionary tactics such as focusing on the ills of immigration. Approval ratings of the authorities and of Putin personally rose contributing to the de-escalation of protest attitudes,

---

[11] See the discussion on the Russian nationalism in Gudkov (2013) and Verkhovskii and Pain (2010).
[12] Federal Law on Citizenship of the Russian Federation [Zakon o Grazdanstve], № 62-ФЗ.

according to the Levada Centre polls.[13] The regime no longer felt the immediate threat of collective action against it. As the Ukrainian conflict developed and the EU and the US initiated sanctions to contain Russia, the regime re-focused attention towards an external enemy – the West. Media reports paid close attention to NATO enlargement in Eastern Europe and the economic and political sanctions against Russia. The woes of the Russian economy were blamed on Western sanctions and the conspiracy that the fall in oil prices was designed to suffocate the Russian economy.

Following the change in official discourse, sociologists registered the reduction in popular xenophobia. Levada Centre noted the drop in hostility towards migrants, which was immediately reported by the mass media. The Levada Centre polls reported a decreased anticipation of violent inter-ethnic conflict and reduced tensions (Levada Centre 2015). At the same time hostility towards the West has risen substantially. To gauge the frequency of mentioning the migrants in the Russian mass media, I performed a content analysis of headlines that appeared in 34 large Russian print newspapers between 2014 and 2016 (N=450). In 2014, migrants were mentioned 121 times, gasterbeiters 11 times and [Ukrainian] refugees 18 times. In 2015, migrants were mentioned 128 times, gasterbeiters 11 times and refugees [to the EU] 50 times. In the first half of the 2016, migrants were mentioned 40 times, gasterbeiters five times, while refugees [to the EU] were mentioned 13 times. This content analysis indicates that the topic of migration was not abandoned by the Russian mass media.

Rather, headlines broadened the focus on the burdensome provisions of existing migration regulations, such as the transition to the patent system, the problems of medical insurance for labour migrants, and Russian language proficiency requirements as efforts aimed at immigrant integration. Mass media wrote about the problems of access to secondary school education for migrant children. The Constitutional Court of the Russian Federation heard the case brought about by the families of migrants and refugees which contested the local residency registration requirements for school entry (Kommersant 2015). Considerable attention in 2014 was given to the accommodation of East Ukrainian refugees and to playing up the ills of radical Ukrainian nationalism: the strength of radical-right parties such as Svoboda or Right Sector in the Ukrainian parliament or ultra-nationalist marches on the streets of Ukrainian cities.

In 2015-2016, Russian media actively exploited the topic of the imminent dissolution of the European Union brought about by uncontrolled migration.

---

[13] These are the on-going polls of the authorities [organy vlasti]. The results can be found at http://www.levada.ru/indikatory/odobrenie-organov-vlasti/

The EU migration crisis, caused by the complicated security situation in the Middle East and North Africa, allowed Russian elites an additional legitimation opportunity. The unresolved migration problems within Russia have been fit into the world pattern – it no longer was the reflection of the incompetency of the Russian state, it became a universal problem with which even the EU countries cannot grapple successfully. After the Paris terrorist attacks in November 2015, Russian rhetoric intensified the theme of terrorism and the security threat that stems from uncontrolled migration.

**Conclusion**

I have argued that the Russian regime manipulated popular xenophobia to divert the attention of the masses from societal problems. By demonising migrants, the regime re-directed public dissatisfaction to the visible and often powerless migrant. These diversion tactics allowed the state to maintain legitimacy during a period in which its popularity declined. As the extant studies posit, competitive authoritarian regimes thrive and survive when they can maintain popularity. Putin's personal ratings continue at a high level, however, Russians' feelings about the regime, measured through citizens' evaluation of their lives, remain largely pessimistic, suggesting the existence of latent protest potential. The Levada Centre indices of family well-being, which reflect the subjective evaluation of families' material well-being, and indices of expectations for the future, which reflect citizens' feelings about their personal future as well as the future of the country, have remained mostly negative since 2007. The indices of family well-being and expectations for the future remain at a significantly lower level than the overall government approval rates, which combines citizens' evaluations of the President and the Administration [*index vlasti*] (Levada Centre 2016).

These measures of public opinion reveal the massive potential for the loss of popularity for the existing government which can evolve from the dissatisfaction with the poor personal well-being to the dissatisfaction with the regime. Popular xenophobia rose sharply in the fall of 2011, culminating in October 2013. At the same time, approval ratings of the government and the President fell to their lowest point in 2013, at 61 per cent. Anti-immigrant rhetoric resonated with the public, which had been pre-conditioned by the massive anti-immigrant media campaign that focused on irregular migration and crimes committed by foreigners. Immigrants were presented as a visible and common object of blame for societal ills, especially corruption, crime, public health hazard, and even road accidents. The elites promoted the negative image of an immigrant as a convenient object for public anger. Just as populist social-welfare programmes can dissipate public anger and the resolve to demand government accountability, so can shifting the blame for problems from the government to the tangible enemy – the immigrant. To avoid mass protests akin those in 2011–2012, the state must maintain the visibility of a credible threat to disperse attention from vital societal problems: degradation of the economy, the gap between the rich cities and the poor provinces, growing poverty levels, and soaring corruption.

This analysis contributes to the socio-historical explanation of Russian xenophobia, advanced by Russian scholars, by showing how complex historical, political and social events shape up patterns of xenophobia, and how xenophobia is used as a political legitimation tool in Russia. As the Russian economy suffered from economic and political sanctions invoked by the West in response to the Ukrainian conflict, immigrants were no longer the prime enemy of the state. The West became once again the source of public threat and the object of blame for socio-economic problems. The regime did not have to artificially inflate xenophobia. Anti-immigrant sentiment fell in 2014, and continued at a lower level in 2015, while animosity towards the external enemy (the US and the EU countries) was on the rise. Looking forward, the 2016 Duma elections will show whether the use of xenophobia as a political weapon is the new go-to tool in the arsenal of the regime, or if the 2013 elections were an outlier.

## References

Abashin, S. "Goryachee Leto' 2013: Vybory I Migratsiya," in *Migranty, Migrantophobii I Migratsionnaya Politika*, Moscow: Academia, 2014: 20-30.

Adida, C., Laitin, D. and Valfort, M.A. *Why Muslim Integration Fails in Christian-Heritage Societies*, Harvard University Press, 2016.

Brubaker, R. "Nationhood and the National Question in the Soviet Union and Post-Soviet Eurasia: An Institutionalist Account," *Theory and Society* 23, no.1 (1994): 47-78.

Castles, S. "Understanding Global Migration: A Social Transformation Perspective," *Journal of Ethnic and Migration Studies* 36, no.10 (2010): 1565-86.

Chudinovskikh, O. "K Voprosu O Vozmoznom Vliyanii Krizisa Na Mezdunarodnuu Migratsiu V Rossii," *Demoscope Weekly* (2009): 363-364. http://demoscope.ru/weekly/2009/0363/print.php.

Chudinovskikh, O. "Zachem Manipulirovat Tsiframi," *Rossiyskaya Migratsia* 3–4 (2009): 15–17.

Dimitrov, M. K. "Popular Autocrats," *Journal of Democracy* 20, no.1 (2009): 78–81.

DNI, "Sobyanin: Migranty Dolzny Uekhat Domoi," 2013, http://dni.ru/society/2013/5/30/253597.html

Freedom House, "Freedom on the Net," 2015, https://freedomhouse.org/sites/default/files/resources/FOTN%202015_Russia.pdf

Florinskaya, Y. F. "Labor migration in Russia," in *Migration in Russia: 2000-2013*, Moscow: Spetskniga, 2013: 164-177.

Gazeta, "Lovtsy Chelovekov.' Gazeta.Ru, 2007, www.gazeta.ru/comments/2007/09/18_e_2170198.shtml.

Geddes, B. "Authoritarian Breakdown: Empirical Test of a Game-Theoretic Argument," Paper presented at the Annual Meeting of APSA. Atlanta, GA, 1999.

Givens, T. E. "Immigrant Integration in Europe: Empirical Research," *Annual Review of Political Science* 10 (2007): 67–83.

Gorodzeisky, A. and Semyonov, M. "Not Only Competitive Threat But Also Racial Prejudice: Sources of Anti-Immigrant Attitudes in European Societies," *International Journal of Public Opinion Research* Advanced Access, 2015, doi: 10.1093/ijpor/edv024.

Gorodzeisky, A., Glikman, A. and Maskileyson, D. "The Nature of Anti-Immigrant Sentiment in Post-Socialist Russia," *Post-Soviet Affairs* 31, no.2 (2015): 115–35.

Grani, "Rodinu'Snyali s Vyborov," 2005, http://graniru.org/Politics/Russia/Election/m.98760.html

Grani, "Yarostnyi Stroiotryad," 2007, http://graniru.org/Society/m.127547.html.

Gudkov, L. "Pochemy My ne Lubim Priezhikh," Мир России 16, no.2 (2007): 48–83.

Gudkov, L. "Rossiya – Dlya Russkikh? Uze ne Stydno," Radio Svoboda, 2013, http://www.svoboda.org/content/transcript/25172654.html

Gudkov, L. "Nas Zdet Ne Neostalinism, a Koe-Chto Drugoye," 2016, http://www.fontanka.ru/2016/01/10/017/.

Kailitz, S. and Stockemer, D. "Regime Legitimation, Elite Cohesion and the Durability of Autocratic Regime Types," *International Political Science Review*, November 2015: 1-27. doi:10.1177/0192512115616830.

Komsomolskaya Pravda. "Zamministra MVD Mikhail Sukhodolskiy: 'Prestupnikov- Migrantov Stanovitsya Vse Bolshe'," 2008, http://www.spb.kp.ru/daily/24221.4/422591/.

KM "Migranty Biut Recordy Prestupnosti v Rossii," 2009, http://www.km.ru/news/migranty_byut_rekordy_prestupnos.

Infox "SKP Rossii Trebyet Daktiloskopii Priezzikh," 2009, http://www.infox.ru/authority/state/2009/06/08/SKP_Rossii_prosit_sl_print.phtml.

Interfax "MVD Preduprezdaet O Vozmoanosti Rosta Protestnykh Nastroyenii v Strane," 2008, Interfax.ru, http://www.interfax.ru/russia/53809.

Kellas, J. G. *The Politics of Nationalism and Ethnicity*, Second Edition. New York: Palgrave Macmillan, 1998.

Kingsbury, M. "Family Policy in Post-Communist Europe and the Former Soviet Union: Assessing the Impact of Xenophobia," Doctoral Dissertation, Albuquerque, NM: University of New Mexico, 2015.

Kitschelt, H. *The Radical Right in Western Europe*. Ann Arbor: The University of Michigan Press, 1995.

KM "Migranty Byut Rekordy Prestupnosti v Rossii," 2009, http://www.km.ru/news/migranty_byut_rekordy_prestupnos.

Kommersant "Prinyat Nelzya Otkazat.' Газета 'Коммерсантъ," 2015, http://kommersant.ru/doc/2786133

Lenta "Prokremlyovskoye Molodeznoye Dvizenie Potrebovalo Vyslat Gastarbaiterov is RF," 2008, https://lenta.ru/news/2008/10/31/raid/.

Lenta "Opasnyie Gosti," 2013, https://lenta.ru/articles/2013/03/09/migrant/.

Lenta "Putin Predlozil Iz'yat Migrantov iz Torgovli," 2013, https://lenta.ru/news/2013/10/03/migrants/

Levada Centre "Ukrainskii Krizis Sdelal Rossiyan Tolerantnee," 2014, https://www.levada.ru/2014/08/27/ukrainskij-krizis-sdelal-rossiyan-tolerantnee/print/

Levada Centre "Ksenophobia I Nationalism," 2015, http://www.levada.ru/old/25-08-2015/ksenofobiya-i-natsionalizm.

Levada Centre "Sotsialno-Ekonomicheskie Indikatory," 2016, http://www.levada.ru/indikatory/sotsialno-ekonomicheskie-indikatory/

Levitsky, S. R., and Way, L.A. "Beyond Patronage: Violent Struggle, Ruling Party Cohesion, and Authoritarian Durability," *Perspectives on Politics* 10, no.4 (2012): 869–889.

Levitsky, S. and Way, L. "The Rise of Competitive Authoritarianism," *Journal of.Democracy* 13, no.2 (2002): 51–65.

NewsRU "MVD Primet Mery Provit Gastarbaiterov-Prestupnikov v Moskve," 2008, http://newsmsk.com/article/26dec2008/gast_mvd.

Nezavisimaya Gazeta "Russkii Marsh: Posleslovie," 2013, http://www.ng.ru/politics/2013-11-06/3_march.html.

New Izvestiya 'Коренное Выселение,' 2007, http://www.newizv.ru/politics/2007-06-14/70911-korennoe-vyselenie.html.

Mukomel, V. "Xenophobia as a Basis of Solidarity," *Russian Social Science Review* 56 no.4 (2015): 37–51.

Pain, E.A. "Xenophobia and Ethnopolitical Extremism in Post-Soviet Russia: Dynamics and Growth Factors," *Nationalities Papers* 35, no.5 (2007): 895–911.

Polit.ru "Luzhkov Predlozil Vtroe Sokratit Kvoty Na Gastarbaiterov," 2007, http://polit.ru/news/2007/06/06/tre/.

Putnam, R.D. "E Pluribus Unum: Diversity and Community in the Twenty-First Century. The 2006 Johan Skytte Prize Lecture," *Scandinavian Political Studies* 30 (2007)

Raijman, R. and Semyonov, M. "Perceived Threat and Exclusionary Attitudes towards Foreign Workers in Israel - Ethnic and Racial Studies," *Ethnic and Racial Studies* 27, no.5 (2007): 780–99.

RBC "S.Sobyanin Ne Hochet, Chtoby Migranty Puskali Korni v Moskve," 2013, http://www.rbc.ru/society/30/05/2013/859805.shtml.

RIA "MVD RF Preduprezdaet o Vozmoznom Roste Prestuplenii Protiv Migrantov," 2008, http://ria.ru/society/20081224/157983344.html.

RIA "Migranty Dolzny Uvazat Traditsii I Kulturu Rossii, Zayavil Putin," 2013, http://ria.ru/society/20131106/975124538.html#ixzz2jtSN0QxQ.

Rossiyskaya Gazeta "Gastarbaitery Ukhodyat v Les," 2009, https://rg.ru/2009/06/09/migracia.html.

Schenk, C. "Nationalism in the Russian Media: Content Analysis of Newspaper Coverage Surrounding Conflict in Stavropol, 24 May–7 June 2007," *Nationalities Papers* 40, no.5 (2012): 783–805.

Semyonov, M., Gorodzeisky, A. and Raijman, R. "The Rise of Anti-Foreigner Sentiment in European Societies, 1988-2000," *American Sociological Review* 71, no.3 (2006): 426–49.

Semyonov, M., Raijman, R. and Gorodzeisky, A. "Foreigners' Impact on European Societies Public Views and Perceptions in a Cross-National Comparative Perspective," *International Journal of Comparative Sociology* 49, no.1 (2008): 5–29.

SOVA Centre "Vvedenie. Antiseminism v Massovom Soznanii," SOVA Centre for Information and Analysis, 2003, http://www.sova-center.ru/racismxenophobia/publications/antisemitism/political-antisemitism/2003/08/d743.

Svolik, M. "Power Sharing and Leadership Dynamics in Authoritarian Regimes," *American Journal of Political Science* 53, no.2 (2009): 477–94.

Vedomosti "FMS: Rol' Migrantov v Statistike Prestuplenii Chasto Preuvelichivayetsya," 2009, http://www.vedomosti.ru/management/news/2009/10/30/fms-rol-migrantov-v-statistike-prestuplenij-chasto-preuvelichivaetsya.

Vedomosti "V Moskve Nachinaetsya Oblava Na Migrantov-Pravonarushitelei," 2013, http://www.vedomosti.ru/politics/news/13642881/v-moskve-nachinaetsya-oblava-na.

Verkhovskii, A. and Pain, E. "Civilizational Nationalism," in Идеология «особого Пути» В России И Германии: Истоки, Содержание, Последствия, Moscow: Три Квадрата, 2010: 171-210.

Volkov, D. "Interview Na Porokhovoi Bochke," Novaya Gazeta, Levada-center, http://www.ng.ru/scenario/2013-11-26/13_interview.html.

Vzglyad "Molodaya Gvardia» Provela Piket U Zdania FMS Primorya," 2008, http://vz.ru/news/2008/12/8/236507.html?utm_campaign=vz&utm_medium=referral&utm_source=newsanons.

Wilkes, R., Guppy, N. and Farris, L. "Comment on Semyonov, Raijman, and Gorodzeisky, ASR, June 2006: Right-Wing Parties and Anti-Foreigner Sentiment in Europe," *American Sociological Review* 72, no.5 (2007): 831–40.

Zaionchkovskaya, Z., Poletaev, D., Florinskaya, Y. and Doronina, K. "Migranty i Prestupnost," *Demoscope Weekly*, no. 605–606 (2014), http://demoscope.ru/weekly/2014/0605/tema08.php.

# Conclusion

## GRETA UEHLING

Scholars of migration are well accustomed to probing the factors that prompt and inhibit human migration. The scholarship in this volume provides a thorough exploration of the motivations and directions, as well as the volume and composition of what might aptly be called 'the other European migrant crisis.' Much less often, scholars take advantage of migratory processes as a vantage point for understanding broader social, economic, and political processes. The contributions to this volume do this admirably, illuminating the migratory patterns emanating from conflict within Ukraine and shining light on how migration intersects with issues of global significance including:

- The power of migration policy to change migratory flows (Fomina, Oleinikova, Denisenko, Schenk)
- Xenophobia and the propensity to demonise migrants (Bulakh, Mukomel, Kuznetsova and Kingsbury)
- Citizenship and access to rights and resources (Fomina, Uehling, Kuznetsova, and Schenk, Ivashchenko-Stadnik)
- The role of official propaganda disseminated through news media in influencing prevailing narratives (Bulakh, Gentile, Morozov, Kuznetsova, and Kingsbury)
- Remittances as strategy of self-reliance in the absence of state support (Fomina) and economic growth (Denisenko),
- Labour migration as a driver of development (Denisenko)
- Supranationalism and integration (Schenk, Morozov, Kuznetsova)

Thus, it is possible to say the topic of migration, as treated by these authors brings together what are conventionally seen as diverse and separate areas of scholarship. In addition to generating a large number of migrants, war and conflict in Ukraine has had an impact on the way these societies see both themselves and the West in addition to (more predictably) changing migration policy and law, and affecting the economies in the region. These issues are pressing in light of the erosion of the post-Cold war order in the wider Europe.

There are three features that, particularly in combination, distinguish this volume. First, the arguments are strengthened by the authors' well-grounded use of mixed methods. In the chapters above, analyses of statistics are enhanced by ethnography, focus groups complemented by elite interviews, and financial data illuminated by first-person perspectives. Second, the volume is enriched by a decidedly international cadre of scholars, something worth noting considering the authors lacked a single disciplinary home or even conference venue in which to convene. This is to say the authors in this volume come from both Eastern and Western academic institutions, and carry out their research from the Russian Federation, Ukraine, Poland, Finland, Estonia, Turkey, Australia, the United Kingdom, and the United States. On a humorous note, the contributors have also had the good fortune not to replicate any of the geopolitical conflict that is the subject of their study! Third and perhaps most importantly, the perspectives on 'the other migrant crisis' presented here are based on primary, original and independent research. This brings authoritative insight to the topic at hand.

**New approaches**

Each of the chapters is, in its own way, theoretically and/or methodologically innovative. The volume is thus in close dialogue with contemporary social science theorising. Gentile breaks new theoretical and methodological ground by bringing human geography into close articulation with political ideology and social memory. This 'triangulation' enables Gentile to identify the mechanisms through which conflict is generated where none previously existed. This author amply demonstrates the explosive potential of fault-line cities. Ukraine is only one example how controversy over signifiers without firmly established or deeply seated meaning can be used to disrupt quotidian existence. Using this approach may prove useful for thinking about other locations where conflict is likely.

Ivashchenko-Stadnik picks up on the theme of alienation (later also explored by Bulakh). She questions the term 'civil war,' and sees the denial of external aggression as a factor that complicates resolution. She suggests (like Bulakh in the following chapter) that the treatment of IDPs as quasi-citizens does not bode well for the future. Only by providing IDPs with greater civil and political rights can social tension be avoided and human development achieved. Ivashchenko-Stadnik's methodological intervention is to disaggregate not just the migrants (typical of most migration studies) but the hosts, in this case into neighbours and friends; employers and employees; and civil society.

Bulakh brings classic anthropological theories concerned with purity and danger (Douglas 1966) successfully applied to the context of Africa's Great Lakes crisis (Malkki 1995) into Eastern Europe to analyse the aftermath of

Ukrainian migration. This theoretical approach makes vivid how the categorisation of migrants from Donbas as unpure percolates into the way they are treated, not just on the street but also by state workers and policy makers. Importantly, this work suggests that stigma may become self-perpetuating through mechanisms of bureaucratic marginalisation. Thus Ukraine's xenophobia with respect to IDPs represents not just a temporary problem to be overcome, but a considerable tear in the social fabric.

If Bulakh is concerned with the reception of IDPs, Uehling focuses more on the IDPs themselves. This chapter seeks to uncover some of the unintended positive effects of the occupation of Crimea inherent in the invention of traditions (Hobsbawm and Ranger 1983) that carry the potential to hold Ukraine together in the future. Another consequence is a growing sense of political agency that manifests itself in the myriad ways the IDPs reject the notion they are victims and insist on their ability to act and choose for themselves. Given these and other distinctions, is likely that in future studies, IDPs from Crimea will be in a separate analytic category from IDPs from the Donbas region.

This is not to say that IDPs have benefitted from their displacement. In fact, the irony is that even as the people displaced are suspected to have betrayed Ukraine, it is the Ukrainian state that has 'betrayed' displaced people first by failing to defend Crimea against Russian incursion, and second by delaying the provision of a full set of rights. The tropes of loyalty and betrayal used against the indigenous Crimean Tatars after the Great Patriotic War have been inverted with this conflict – it is now the Ukrainian state that has let down its indigenous people.

Using elite interviews, and expanding the focus further westward, Fomina maps the changes in the flow of migrants from Ukraine to Poland. This author has used official migration and banking data to identify a striking disconnect between official statements and the volume of the flows. This finding is especially significant considering how the Polish response to migrants from Ukraine is directly connected to the refugee crisis in Europe: Polish officials claim to be unable to accept Syrian refugees on the grounds that they are accepting Ukrainian ones.

Just as remittances from Russia to the three poorest Central Asian states are important, Fomina shows how remittances figure into Ukrainian migration to Poland. Fomina suggests that while it may not be highly significant macro-economically (as they are in Central Asia), impacts are felt at the level of the household. Taken together we have evidence of a true financescape (Appadurai 1991) in which capital is being redistributed (largely unofficially) from more to less wealthy countries across the region, a component of larger global flows of people and capital.

Data from in-depth interviews fills out the picture obtained from financial data and official statements to reveal that a Ukrainian-Polish civil society has been strengthened by the Ukraine crisis. Mirroring dynamics observed by Uehling (this volume) in government-controlled Ukraine, the Ukrainian émigré community in Poland has been refreshed, and Poles have had an opportunity to correct erroneous stereotypes held about Ukrainians.

While Fomina takes us westward to Poland, Oleinikova takes us south and east to Australia. Combining rich ethnographic data gathered in Australia with data from the Australian Bureau of Statistics and the State Statistics Service of Ukraine, Oleinikova analyses the structural variables influencing migration to Australia over a much longer time period than considered in any of the other chapters, beginning with dynamics around the time of the First World War. She also provides deep insight into the thoughts and feelings of different cohorts of migrants.

Oleinikova's intervention is to shows how the intersection of Australian migration policy with Ukrainian's political and economic trajectory has shaped successive waves of migrants between these two countries. The latest flow is survival oriented and not surprisingly disillusioned by the Ukrainian dream of reform. Like the migrants Fomina describes in Poland, these migrants are a symptom that exposes political and economic disarray, urgently in need of further study. In these analyses, migrants are markers that provide a barometer of public sentiment.

Just as the Russian patent system increased access to the Russian labour market (Schenk, Denisenko this volume), Australia controlled the volume and composition of migrants from Ukraine through the types of visas it made available. As seen in migration to the United States and to the European Union, migrants who do not fit the desired categories are using other channels like study, training, internships, and asylum.

In the second half of the volume, Mukomel combines media monitoring with sociological studies to explore how the response to the flow of migrants from Ukraine to Russia became polarised. Just as Bulakh demonstrated how the reception of migrants cooled within Ukraine over time, Mukomel shows how the initial enthusiasm faded as concern about jobs, an attitude of entitlement on the part of the migrants, and the inability of state structures to mediate these concerns gradually led to tension. This is particularly poignant considering the tight relationship that Russia and Ukraine once enjoyed.

Mukomel's exploration provides an important baseline for studies in the future by suggesting that if tensions between refugees and local population are not resolved, and low levels of integration continue, we can expect to see problems ahead.

Some of the more undesirable outcomes of new migration patterns are also apparent in the work of Morozov. Whereas Uehling and Fomina point to something of a silver lining in the form of stronger civil identities and societies, Morozov suggests civic identity has been in retreat in the Russian Federation. This author intervenes in the existing literature with a valuable corrective to narratives about the current crisis that prevail, especially in the mass media. From the Russian perspective of course, the West destabilised important geostrategic relationships with an irresponsible and expansionist agenda. If Morozov is correct about how the Ukrainian revolution is perceived in Russia, then the United States and Western Europe cannot distance themselves from the Russian aggression. This is crucial to understanding the crisis in its larger context – and finding diplomatic solutions.

Using the most recent statistical data (from Russian Central Bank and Federal Migration Service), Denisenko explores the size and demographic composition of migration flows to Russia. As for Fomina and Oleinikova, using multiple sources of data provides a productive starting point. However, the relative weakness of the data on migration makes disaggregating policy changes, economic trends, and geopolitical dynamics challenging. Denisenko's intervention is to track twin dynamics: with an outflow of migrants, there is a corresponding influx of remittances. Without a healthy Russian economy, however, the attraction for Central Asians is less, and remittances back to the Uzbek economy in particular are affected. This demonstrates how migration processes are not only impacted by economic changes like the price of oil, but themselves have the ability to shape subsequent economic developments. Whereas remittances from Poland to Ukraine do not comprise a large share of the Ukrainian economy, Russia is a primary source of funds for Uzbekistan, Kyrgyzstan, and Tajikistan where remittances exceed international aid.

Kuznetsova uses a discourse analysis of in-depth interviews to trace how the myth of migrants as dangerous arises. Kuznetsova's analysis provides a basis for future comparisons: that dynamics in the Russian Federation bear resemblance to migrant receiving states further West that also seek to lower crime, decrease social tension, and prevent the rise of extremism. There is another noteworthy parallel as well. The management of migrants in the Russian Federation has not just been securitised at the level of discourse: as Kuznetsova points out, the Federal Migration Service was closed in 2016 and its functions moved to the Ministry of Internal Affairs. In some respects, this mirrors the transformation of the Immigration and Naturalization Service into the Department of Homeland Security after terrorist attacks in the United States. Kuznetsova exposes the dark shadow cast on migrants by danger and risk-laden discourse, even though a positive outcome (explored by Denisenko) is that patents successfully reduced the number of irregular migrants.

Schenk's contribution to the literature is to delve more deeply into the central contention that led to the Ukrainian crisis in the first place, namely the choice to seek greater integration with Europe through the Association Agreement. This was a decisive fork in the road as Russia moved in the opposite direction with the Eurasian Economic Union (EEU). It may come as a surprise that the EEU, which is modeled on the European Union, has even more ambitious goals with regard to common labour market than the European Union. This chapter provides a source of comparison for anyone with interest in supranational governance and economic policy.

Schenk takes an approach that is replicable and could provide insight as events unfold: a gap analysis that identified the disjuncture between EEU treaty text, domestic laws and procedures with regard to migration, and migrant experiences with both. She uses government and legal texts, interviews with officials, diaspora leaders, and official immigration statistics. This is a significant accomplishment considering, as also noted by Denisenko, data on migration are missing.

The regional expression of a global phenomenon emerges here in the lack of alignment between law and practice; formal policy and actual behavior between the Russian Federation and Kazakhstan. And as elsewhere, the securitisation of migration in relation to fears leads to policies that work to encourage patterns of irregular migration.

Kingsbury takes us deeper into theories of xenophobia to elucidate a fascinating shift. The Russian state had been using xenophobia to distract attention from internal issues. With the Ukraine conflict, this was no longer a viable approach and the official rhetoric shifted away from demonising these particular migrants to blaming something else: the West. Kingsbury's intervention in the literature is to synthesise the competition hypothesis and the cultural hypothesis used to explain xenophobia. She formulates political explanation that links xenophobia to political leaders who work to construct negative attitudes that serve their purposes. This explanation resonates with chapters by Kuznetsova, Mukomel, and Morozov.

## New Questions

The chapters in this volume open up new questions that can serve as a point of reference for future studies. Here are ventured some questions for future exploration that emerge from the arguments made here.

In the first half of the volume, an empirical question is when and how, if at all, internally displaced persons will be granted the equal civil and political rights in Ukraine? Another is what will be the long term effect on Polish civil society and by extension Poland's European neighbors as a result of the incorporation of Ukrainian migrants? Third, the authors seem to concur that it would be simplistic to take the ineptitude with which the Ukraine crisis is being dealt with and ascribe it to a Soviet legacy. If this is the case, what new theoretical frameworks will help future scholars periodise the complex political and economic dynamics in the country? A methodological question this half of the volume opens up is how geography in general and borders in particular can be brought into a closer analytic relationship with the fields of social memory and political ideology.

The chapters in the second half of the volume also raise interesting questions for future explanation. While the theme of Russian propaganda is already quite prevalent in the literature today, the contribution of these authors is disaggregating propaganda effects from public opinion and official discourse without ontologising any one of them. A more wide-ranging question here concerns the European and Eastern European integration projects. When do official discourse and news media generate narratives that widen gaps (between people and countries), and exactly how much common ground is available?

## Policy Relevance

The contributions to this volume also contain insights that have considerable policy relevance. First, a theme dealt with in many of the chapters is integrating migrants. All of the entries that explore integration-gone-wrong are clear: state policies with regard to access to housing, work, and social support must be meticulously calibrated to local needs.

A second theme in the volume with policy relevance is the many ways that the economies in the region have become interdependent through labour migration and remittances. It follows that a migration policy change in, or economic sanctions on one of these countries (namely Russia) is likely to affect many other (and sometimes quite distant) countries. In other words, the effects of Western sanctions will be felt not just in Moscow, but Dushanbe,

Bishkek, and Tashkent. In light of evidence that some of the countries affected are also politically unstable, the interconnections should be of interest in policy making.

A third theme is the power of migration policy to shape human behavior. This volume is notable because it makes Eastern Europe visible to scholars of migration. Somewhat familiar will be the ways in which states manage and mold their citizenry through sorting and ranking by means of patents, permits, and migrant categories. Sorting is often legitimised by a concern for protecting national security. This is important because it is not simply a consequence of a world partitioned into territorial nation-states: these migratory flows are actively involved in making the world we know today.

A fourth theme that unites the contributions and has policy relevance is that the narratives and discourse surrounding migrants has, to a greater or lesser extent, a profound effect on how newcomers are received, whether by bureaucrats or citizens. To quote J.L. Austin (1955/1962), people 'do things' with words. Attention to the stories that are told about migrants is therefore not for scholars alone.

In closing, it is interesting to reflect for a moment on the relationship between this crisis and the West. There are many perspectives on why this 'other' migration crisis has come about. While Western analysts often demonise Russian Federation as the aggressor, this volume adds the additional perspective that from the Russian point of view, the territorial aggression on the part of Russian Federation was a reaction to what was understood, by Russia at least, as a crisis of the international system. In other words, the system had already lost its balance when the territorial incursions occurred. If there is a path to resolving the crisis, it might be found in the common ground: as Morozov points out, it is in Russia's interest, and Russians may even prefer to have good relations with Ukraine, the European Union, and the United States. It follows that even subtle policy shifts with respect to Russian Federation could yield traction for improvements that would be meaningful for the migrants described in these chapters.

# Note on Indexing

E-IR's publications do not feature indexes due to the prohibitive costs of assembling them. If you are reading this book in paperback and want to find a particular word or phrase you can do so by downloading a free PDF version of this book from the E-IR website.

View the e-book in any standard PDF reader such as Adobe Acrobat Reader (pc) or Preview (mac) and enter your search terms in the search box. You can then navigate through the search results and find what you are looking for. In practice, this method can prove much more targeted and effective than consulting an index.

If you are using apps (or devices) such as iBooks or Kindle to read our e-books, you should also find word search functionality in those.

You can find all of our e-books at: http://www.e-ir.info/publications

www.ingramcontent.com/pod-product-compliance
Lightning Source LLC
Chambersburg PA
CBHW071433080526
44587CB00014B/1825